DISCRETIONARY JUSTICE

DISCRETIONARY JUSTICE

AN INTRODUCTION TO DISCRETION
IN CRIMINAL JUSTICE

By

HOWARD ABADINSKY

Saint Xavier College
Chicago, Illinois

CHARLES   C   THOMAS   •   PUBLISHER
Springfield • Illinois • U.S.A.

Published and Distributed Throughout the World by

CHARLES C THOMAS • PUBLISHER

2600 South First Street

Springfield, Illinois 62717

© *1984 by* CHARLES C THOMAS • PUBLISHER

ISBN 0-398-05019-8

Library of Congress Catalog Card Number: 84-2478

With THOMAS BOOKS *careful attention is given to all details of manufacturing and
design. It is the Publisher's desire to present books that are satisfactory as to their physical
qualities and artistic possibilities and appropriate for their particular use.* THOMAS
BOOKS *will be true to those laws of quality that assure a good name and good will.*

Printed in the United States of America
SC-R-3

Library of Congress Cataloging in Publication Data

Abadinsky, Howard, 1941–
    Discretionary justice.

    Bibliography: p.
    Includes index.
    1. Criminal justice, Administration of — United States —
Decision making.   I. Title.
KF9223.A913   1984   364′.973′0684   84–2478
ISBN 0-398-05019–8

CONTENTS

DISCRETIONARY JUSTICE

CHAPTER 1

INTRODUCTION TO DISCRETION

This chapter will introduce general problems and principles of discretion in criminal justice. Subsequent chapters will deal with the problem of discretion in each segment of criminal justice, from police to parole.

DISCRETION: WHAT IS IT?

A dictionary refers to discretion as the ability to make decisions, freedom of choice, or having latitude. The renowned jurist Roscoe Pound wrote that "Discretion is an authority conferred by law to act in certain conditions or situations in accordance with an official's or an official agency's own considered judgment and conscience. It is an idea of morals, belonging to the twighlight zones between law and morals" (1960: 925–26). However, a civilian possesses discretion when as a witness or victim of a crime he/she must decide whether or not to notify the police. Privately-employed security personnel also possess discretion, and very little is known about how it is exercised.*

In law enforcement, discretion often refers to the use of "good common sense" or a "degree of flexibility." Instructors in criminal justice training academies, when confronted by questions about hypothetical situations that defy precise answers, tell trainees to: "Use your discretion." Unfortunately, criminal justice personnel are provided with little or no instruction on the proper use of discretionary powers.

In this book *discretion* will refer to:

> *A situation in which an employee of a criminal justice agency, within the scope of his/her duties, has the lawful authority to choose between two or more alternatives.*

DISCRETION: WHY IS IT A PROBLEM?

The Declaration of Independence states that all men are equal, and the Fourteenth Amendment to the Constitution guarantees "equal protection of the laws." Discretionary decision-making, however, results in disparate

---

*Dean Rojek (1979), for example, found private police/security personnel exercising almost unbridled discretion in the exercise of their law enforcement responsibilities.

treatment—unequal justice—and has the potential for serious abuse.

Basic to our concept of "justice" is an overriding concern with fairness. Our legal system is full of symbols indicative of this concern. We stress that "Justice is blind," and over many court buildings is a young lady carrying the scales of justice—she wears a blindfold. While the ideal is equality before the law, the reality is more complex. This complexity is compounded by officials who deny that their agency's even exercise any discretion. Herman Goldstein (1977: 93), a former police executive, notes that it was not until the early 1960s that the very existence of discretion in police work was openly recognized. I recently had a legal officer from the Chicago Police Department address my class on discretion—the speaker denied that the police exercise any discretion. In fact, the police are faced with a paradox—they are sworn to do the impossible. Statutes require the police to diligently and faithfully enforce the law—all of the law. This is often referred to as *full enforcement,* and it would require the police to investigate and arrest, among others, married couples engaging in certain consensual, but outlawed, sexual acts, or a group of friends enjoying a night of poker at home. Likewise, prosecutors are sworn to prosecute the law violators arrested by the police. The statutes do not authorize a prosecutor to annul laws by refusing to prosecute couples engaging in sodomy or friends playing cards.

DISCRETION: PROBLEMS OF GOVERNMENTAL COMPLEXITY

Government in the United States is quite fragmented. We have four levels:

1. federal
2. state
3. county
4. local (village, town, city)

Each level is further divided into branches:

1. executive
2. legislative
3. judicial

Each level of government has its own criminal justice agencies, e.g., FBI, state police, county sheriff, municipal police. The prosecutor, for example, is usually a county official, while most of the cases he/she receives are from local police agencies. Each level of government operates on its own budget and there is little joint planning on such matters as criminal justice. Thus, for example, local governments may add numerous police officers to their departments without any concern about the impact on prosecutors, county jails, court caseloads or state prison population. The impact of such actions on the use of discretion will be discussed in subsequent chapters.

The deliberate fragmenting of government was an effort to diffuse power, our Founding Fathers' way of insuring against tyranny. While a more unified administration of governmental functions, for example, a single national police force, would be more efficient, it would also carry with it the danger of totalitarianism. In simple terms, our fear of the power of government is greater than our fear of crime. To further protect the people from governmental power and its abuse, the principle of due process was made a cornerstone of justice in America.

LEVELS OF GOVERNMENT AND EXAMPLES OF CRIMINAL JUSTICE AGENCIES

FEDERAL
Supreme Court
Court of Appeals
District Courts
Attorney General
Federal Bureau of Investigation
Drug Enforcement Administration
Secret Service
Internal Revenue Service
Marshal's Service
Border Patrol
Customs

COUNTY
Sheriff/County Police
Prosecutor
County Courts
County Jail (Sheriff)

STATE
State Police/Highway Patrol
Bureau of Criminal Investigation
Attorney General
Appeals Courts
Superior Courts
Corrections/Prisons
Board of Parole
Liquor Control and Enforcement
Park Rangers

LOCAL
Police (city, town, village)
City Attorney
Local Courts/Justice of Peace

DISCRETION: THE DUE PROCESS PROBLEM

Due process of law is guaranteed in both the Fifth and Fourteenth Amendments to the Constitution. This guarantee signifies a basic distrust in the ability or willingness of government to provide justice—fairness—to the people governed. Due process places severe restraints on the ability of government to respond to criminal behavior, in the name of liberty. To protect people from the possibility of being abused by the power of government, a "price" has to be paid. That price is due process which protects the innocent *and* the guilty.

Due process requires that legal standards be applied in each instance with exacting fairness so as to minimize the risk of convicting innocent persons, while also protecting persons against the abuse of governmental power. The maximum level of due process protection is the guarantees enjoyed by every defendant in a criminal case:

(a) *The Right to Remain Silent.* The Fifth Amendment declares: "nor shall [a person] be compelled in any criminal case to be a witness against himself ... " Thus, it is the obligation of government to prove criminal charges and no person can be compelled to give evidence that may be incriminating. Furthermore, a person (suspect) must be informed of this right to silence before he/she can be questioned by the police (*Miranda v. Arizona* 384 U.S. 436, 1966).

(b) *Right to Bail.* The Eighth Amendment states: "Excessive bail shall not be required, nor excessive fines imposed, nor cruel and unusual punishment inflicted."

(c) *Right to a Jury Trial.* The Sixth Amendment guarantees that "In all criminal prosecutions, the accused shall enjoy the right to a speedy and public trial, by an impartial jury. ... "

(d) *Right to Confront Witnesses.* The Sixth Amendment provides for the defendant "to be informed of the nature and cause of the accusation; to be confronted with the witnesses against him; to have compulsory process [subpeona] for obtaining witnesses in his favor. ... " The defense can cross-examine all witnesses and attempt to impeach their testimony or credibility.

(e) *Right to Counsel.* The Sixth Amendment guarantees the accused "the assistance of Counsel for his defence." In 1963 the Supreme Court ruled that states must provide counsel for all indigent defendants in felony cases (*Gideon v. Wainwright* 372 U.S. 335). In 1972 this was extended to misdemeanors where imprisonment might result (*Argersinger v. Hamlin* 407 U.S. 525).

(f) *Double Jeopardy Prohibited.* The Fifth Amendment states: "nor shall any person be subject for the same offence to be twice put in jeopardy of life or limb." Thus, a person found "not guilty" cannot be tried again for the same crime.

In addition, each defendant in a criminal case is protected by the *exclusionary rule,* a legal principle that generally prohibits evidence obtained illegally by the government from being used in a trial. Thus, even evidence which unquestionably proves a defendant's guilt "beyond a reasonable doubt," cannot be used to secure a conviction if that evidence was not secured in a legally proper manner.

These due process guarantees are substantial, and they constitute a major reason for the use of discretion in the prosecutorial segment of criminal justice. This will be discussed in subsequent chapters.

Herbert Packer (1968) refers to "Two Models of the Criminal Justice Process," and he provides an important vantage point from which to view due process and its opposite, *crime control.* In later chapters we will be referring to these models and the role they play in fostering discretionary justice. The *Crime Control Model* stresses the need to repress criminal activity. In this model the criminal justice system has the high purpose of protecting the law-abiding citizen from criminal acts. To accomplish this task the Crime Control Model "requires that primary attention be paid to the efficiency with which the criminal justice process operates to screen suspects, determine guilt, and secure appropriate dispositions of persons convicted of a crime" (1968: 158). Efficiency requires that government have the ability to apprehend, try, convict and sentence a high proportion of criminal offenders. For the model to operate successfully, it must produce a high rate of apprehensions and convictions. This requires *speed* in dealing with a large number of cases, and speed requires informality and uniformity—limits to the amount of challenges to the system (for example, claims that evidence was secured improperly).

> The presumption of guilt is what makes it possible for the system to deal efficiently with large numbers, as the Crime Control Model demands. The supposition is that the screening process operated by the police and prosecutors are reliable indicators of probable guilt. Once a man has been arrested and investigated without being found to be probably innocent, or to put it differently, once a determination has been made that there is enough evidence of guilt to permit holding him for further action, then all subsequent activity is directed toward him based on the view that he is probably guilty (1968: 160).

The Crime Control Model operates with a great deal of confidence in persons employed by the criminal justice system and allows them to provide a process that is akin to an assembly line—speed and efficiency. This approach runs into the *Due Process Model* which, Packer notes (1968: 163), "looks very much like an obstacle course."

The *Due Process Model* stresses limits placed on the ability of government to investigate and convict persons suspected of committing crimes—privacy, individual security and liberty are not to be sacrificed for efficiency. The Due Process Model also stresses the possibility of error. Thus, while the Crime Control Model relies on the abilities of investigative and prosecutorial personnel to present a reasonably accurate account of what actually took place in an alleged criminal event, the Due Process Model stresses the possibility of error:

> People are notoriously poor observers of disturbing events—the more emotion-arousing the context, the greater the possibility that recollection will be incorrect; confessions and admissions by persons in police custody may be induced by physical or psychological coercion so that the police end up hearing what the suspect thinks they want to hear rather than the truth; witnesses may be animated by a bias or interest that no one would trouble to discover except one specifically charged with protecting the interests of the accused (as the police are not) (1968: 163).

CRIME CONTROL	DUE PROCESS
efficiency	liberty

The distance between crime control and due process can be conceived of as a zero sum continuum. Any action, e.g., legislation or court decisions, that moves in a single direction does so at the expense of its opposite. For example, legislation that would undo the exclusionary rule would increase police efficiency. However, it would also lessen the ability of the courts to control police misconduct—the courts would have to accept evidence seized in an unlawful manner.

DISCRETION: BASIC PRINCIPLES

Throughout this book we will be making reference to some basic principles concerning the use of discretion in criminal justice. To make these principles meaningful, we must understand the many purposes of law. Some laws are merely *symbolic;* that is, they were enacted as an expression of society's concern with certain behavior. For example, in Illinois, and many other states, adultery is a crime, albeit a misdemeanor. The law is clearly not meant to be enforced as evidenced by a total lack of any enforcement efforts by the police or prosecutors. Law, viewed from a functional perspective, is the process of compelling individuals to act in accordance with rules so that all may live, if not in harmony, at least with a minimum of discord. The criminal law is a device by which society ensures that at least a minimum standard of behavior is observed. It was never intended by legislating authorities that all laws should be enforced with the same degree of rigidity. While most laws do not provide alternatives, society expects the enforcers of its laws to exercise some degree of judgment—

discretion—in deciding when to invoke the criminal process.

This exercise of discretion must meet the "test" of fairness. The *fairness test* is a basic principle of law enforcement that demands discretionary decisions be related to the objective of the particular law, the goals of the enforcement agency, and how these objectives and goals relate to the situation within a particular community. If the exercise of discretion is related to the personality of the offender, his/her political views, his/her race or religion, or economic status, it fails the fairness test and is, thus, an abuse of discretion.

Another basic principle with respect to the exercise of discretion is: *The more serious the offense, the less leeway for judgment* (Task Force on Policing in Ontario, 1967: 15–16; edited):

> This principle suggests a greater latitude for judgment for offenses which, in the contemporary view, are more regulatory than seriously criminal in nature. It suggests very little, if any, latitude for serious crime. A concept which emphasizes this elastic relationship with the law is essential for providing law enforcement officers with the ability to judge how the law should be applied in any particular situation. Latitude in the use of judgment is both appropriate and necessary for those offenses which society in its contemporary mood regards with some tolerance. This is especially true where a broader community purpose may be enhanced in so doing. Offenses which the community regards as serious or grave, however, permit less judgment and require the letter of the law to be enforced.

This principle is easy to recognize when we consider the crimes of murder and disorderly conduct. We expect that in the case of murder, if sufficient evidence and the suspect is available, that an arrest and prosecution will result—no discretion. In the case of disorderly conduct or other similar misdemeanors, reprimands and warnings would be considered possible alternatives to an arrest. There are many cases that fall somewhere in-between, cases in which the officer, in his/her discretion, determines "seriousness," as in the following account (adapted from Task Force on the Police, 1967: 15–16):

> The officers received instructions from the dispatcher to handle a fight in an alley. Upon arrival they found a group of young men surrounded by their parents, wives and children. One of the young men, *A*, had a couple of knives in his hand. While the knives were within legal limits, Officer Berg took them (and later disposed of them in a refuse container). Another young man, *B*, stood by his mother. The third, *C*, stood by *A*.

> The mother of *B* had called the police, she was the complainant. She claimed that *C* had attacked her son with a knife and she demanded that *C* be arrested and jailed. *C* readily admitted he had been fighting with *B*, but he claimed that he had just tried to protect *A*. *C* had obviously been drinking and was

very belligerent. He indicated a readiness to take on anyone and everyone, including the police. He kept shouting and antagonizing the officers.

A attempted to explain the situation. He stated that he had been the one originally fighting with *B* and that *C* had merely come to his aid. *B* concurred in this account. though he did not reflect much concern as the supposed victim of the attack. *A*'s mother-in-law interrupted to claim that *A* was innocent; that the fight was *B*'s fault. *B*'s mother now entered the fray and accused *A*.

The confusion spread and, in the meantime, other police officers arrived at the scene and the number of observers had grown. Berg and Reilly decided to take the participants to the police station where conditions would make it possible to make a more orderly inquiry.

At the station the families and participants were separated and talked with individually. The mother of *B* insisted on signing a complaint against *C* and *A*, but finally relented when *A* promised not to allow *C* to come to his apartment. *C* was then formally arrested and charged with disorderly conduct. *A* and *B* were sent home with their wives and mothers. By charging *C* with disorderly conduct rather than a more serious crime, the officers observed that they were saving themselves some paperwork. They felt that their action in letting the mother of *B* sign a complaint against the loudmouthed *C* had served to pacify her.

CONTROL OF DISCRETION

Discretion in criminal justice cannot be eliminated. Indeed, as we shall see in later chapters, attempts to eliminate discretion merely displace it into another part of the system. There are ways, however, to control discretion and prevent the abuse of discretionary justice. Three general methods will be applied in each of the parts of the criminal justice system under discussion in subsequent chapters:

1. *Statutes/Laws* that set limits or parameters on discretion (e.g., minimum and maximum sentences beyond which a judge cannot reach).

2. *Administrative Rules* that are promulgated by criminal justice agencies to limit the discretion of their employees (e.g., rules governing the use of firearms by the police).

3. *Supervisory Controls/Review* whereby superiors review the activities of lower ranking personnel to ensure uniformity and thus limit or control discretion (e.g., requiring an assistant prosecutor to check with his/her supervisor before agreeing to a plea bargain arrangement).

The judicial branch of government can also act to limit discretion. The role of the courts, however, is passive and judges cannot seek out areas of discretion in order to apply controls. Thus, judicial action with respect to controlling discretion is unplanned and haphazard.

The opinion of peers or colleagues is an *unofficial,* yet potentially powerful, control limiting discretion. A police officer can be constrained in the exercise of discretionary powers by what s/he believes will be the opinion or reaction of fellow officers. In other words, even when it appears that the officer has discretion, the officer may feel that s/he has no choice at all. A prosecutor will routinely consult with colleagues and their opinions will, likewise, limit his/her choice of action.

Tradition or *precedent* is another powerful restraint on discretionary powers. For example, in most jurisdictions the police do not enforce laws against gambling when the violation is "social" in nature (as opposed to commercial). However, they usually feel compelled to enforce the law even in cases of social gambling (e.g., among friends in a private residence) when a complaint is received (e.g., from an angry wife or neighbor). If it is an established precedent in the district/circuit, judges may feel compelled to grant probation to certain first-offenders.

An important issue (to be discussed in later chapters) concerning precedent/tradition relates to their being published. Should the police, prosecutors, judges be required to spell out their operating rules? What if some of these operating rules are contrary to law, e.g., not enforcing gambling laws when the violation is non-commercial?

As the jurist Charles D. Breitel has noted (1960: 427): "The question then is not how to eliminate or reduce discretion, but how to control it so as to avoid the unequal, the arbitrary, the discriminatory, and the oppressive."

REVIEW QUESTIONS FOR CHAPTER 1

1. What is discretion?
2. Why is discretion a problem?
3. What is meant by full enforcement?
4. Why is government in the United States fragmented into four levels and three branches?
5. Why doesn't the United States have a national police force?
6. What are the due process rights of the accused in a criminal case?
7. What is meant by the crime control model of criminal justice?
8. What is meant by the due process model of criminal justice?
9. What is the exclusionary rule?
10. What is the relationship between the seriousness of an offense and discretion?
11. What is meant by laws that are symbolic?
12. What are the unofficial ways that discretion is controlled?
13. What are the official ways of controlling discretion?

CHAPTER 2

DISCRETION AND THE POLICE

HISTORICAL OVERVIEW

Policing in America is accomplished by approximately 20,000 state and local law enforcement agencies and several thousand private firms. There are about 13,500 "general-purpose" police forces providing police protection within incorporated municipal and township areas: enforcing the law, preserving the public peace, maintaining traffic safety and apprehending accused violators of the law (U.S. Bureau of Justice Statistics, 1980: 5). Policing in the United States is by tradition a local responsibility, and one county may have dozens of separate police agencies. In Cook County, Illinois, for example, which includes the City of Chicago, there are 125 local police departments, in addition to the State Police, Secretary of State Police, Sheriff's Police, and Park Preserve Police. While there is no national police force in this country (such as the Royal Canadian Mounted Police), there are federal agencies that perform a police function, e.g., Federal Bureau of Investigation, Drug Enforcement Administration, Internal Revenue Service, Customs, Border Patrol, Secret Service. The focus of this chapter, however, will be local (municipal) policing, although a great deal of the discussion can be applied to law enforcement agencies other than the *police*. There are about 400,000 full-time sworn police officers in the United States.

Throughout its history the United States has shown great ambivalence over the police—a "necessary evil" would not be too strong a characterization. "Modern" policing can be traced back to 1844 when the New York State Legislature established a unified (day and night), paid police force for New York City. Within the next two decades most large urban areas established similar departments. However, as in New York City, these police departments were often an adjunct of, and completely subservient to, the corrupt political "machines" that dominated many cities. In New York, the Society of Tammany, known as Tammany Hall, dominated the political scene, except for occasional reformist successes, well into the twentieth century. The stalwarts of Tammany were often saloon-keepers who, with the help of street gangs and the connivance of the police, controlled the electoral process in New York City. Jonathan Rubinstein (1973: 372), in his classic study of city police in Philadelphia, notes:

Many police captains were actually little more than gambling and liquor commissioners whose primary responsibility was to enforce the illegal licenses which the political machines granted to favored operators. The police did not organize protection, but carried out the orders established by the elected leaders of their city or state. Policemen were frequently employed as steerers, bouncers, and doormen for gambling houses and speakeasies.

In Minneapolis the police were placed in charge of crime; that is, in a supervisory capacity. Lincoln Steffens (1957: 47) reported that in 1901 the mayor organized professional criminals and had them work "under police direction for the profit of his administration." As if to compound these "inadequacies," the conduct of the police was often brutal and this brutality was directed against those too powerless to effectively complain. Steffins, in his autobiography (1958: 207)), recalled that during the 1890s in New York City he

... stood and saw the police bring in and kick out their bandaged, bloody prisoners, not only strikers and foreigners, but thieves too, and others of the miserable, friendless, troublesome poor.

In some areas of the industrial north, local police and sheriffs were reluctant to exert the type of force against strikers—many of whom were friends and relatives or voting constituents—demanded by employers. As a result, state police forces, beginning in Pennsylvania in 1905, began to develop. In those states with little or no union activity, there developed an alternative statewide agency referred to as the "Highway Patrol," whose activities were limited mainly to matters involving vehicular traffic.

Recurring problems of corruption and brutality have plagued police agencies. At the same time demands are often made on the police to "get tough," to "crack down," to do something—anything—to deal with the problem of crime. But, even otherwise law-abiding persons enjoy gambling and other "vices," while the proliferation of radar detectors reveals a great deal about American notions of "law and order."

It is against this background that we will examine the issue of police discretion.

POLICING: REACTIVE AND PROACTIVE

There are two basic approaches to law enforcement. The *reactive* is a response to citizen complaints. Most detective bureaus contain reactive units that receive complaints about such offenses as robbery, burglary and rape which they investigate in order to develop enough information to identify and apprehend the offender. A citizen can easily mobilize a reactive police response with a telephone call about a "crime in progress."

The *proactive* approach requires law enforcement officers to actively "look for trouble," to seek out violations of the laws and those who violate them. Certain offenses do not have what are conventionally conceived of as "victims." These so-called "victimless crimes," gambling, prostitution, drugs, require proactive policing. The problems of discretionary justice in such an approach to law enforcement will be discussed later in this chapter.

The largest part of a police budget is allocated for motorized patrol, which includes both reactive and proactive aspects. The police cruiser moves in search of parking, traffic, and more serious offenses, while being available to respond to citizen requests for service. The high visibility of police uniforms and vehicles is also designed to serve as a deterrent to law-breaking. It also makes it easier to observe, and thus control, police behavior. A police officer in uniform and a "marked" police vehicle can easily be observed by both the public and supervisory police officials. Control over police behavior is a continuing problem.

The officer involved in proactive law enforcement is quite difficult to supervise (read: control). As is the norm in drug enforcement, he or she often acts the part of a criminal. James Q. Wilson (1978: 22) refers to such persons as *instigators:*

> a legally neutral term referring to a law enforcement officer who, by assuming the role of a criminal, provides an opportunity to commit a consensual crime [e.g., selling drugs] for a person who is ready, willing and seeking an opportunity to do so.

Since in these situations there is no victim-complainant, the only information that an officer's superiors will receive about his/her activities is information the officer him/herself provides.

Patrol officers are organized on a military model: uniforms, military-type ranks with a strict chain of command organized hierarchically (from top to bottom), assembly/roll call, etc. However, in practice, police patrol is quite different from military service; in particular is the lack of direct supervision. In the military an infantryman is usually in direct visual and/or verbal contact with a superior, a corporal, sergeant, or lieutenant. The basic unit in a police department is the patrol officer in a vehicle or (infrequently) on foot. After roll call and the order to "fall out," the patrol officer breaks off contact with his/her supervisor. William Walsh (1983: 26) points out:

> While law, policy, and procedures attempt to regulate the discretionary power of police officers, autonomy is an integral part of their operational milieu. In fact, it is not unusual for the average operational supervisor to have visual contact with a patrol officer only three or four times a shift, lasting from five to 10 minutes per contact. In those agencies that are

responsible for miles of public highway and vast rural areas, the autonomy of officers is even greater.

Almost all of the discretion exercised by a patrol officer is without the constraint of direct supervisory control. Chief Justice Warren Burger (quoted in Carlton, 1978: 26–27) has noted:

> In the broad terms of public administration, I think it would be a safe assumption that the scope of discretion enlarges as we look upward in the hierarchy of government. In other words, the higher the rank, the greater the discretion. But this is not true in police work. The policeman on the beat, or in the patrol car, makes more decisions and exercises broader discretion affecting the daily lives of people, every day and to a greater extent, in many respects, than a judge will ordinarily exercise in a week . . . and no law book, no lawyer, no judge, can really tell the policeman on the beat how to exercise this discretion perfectly in every one of the thousands of different situations that can arise in the hour to hour work of the policeman.

The Chief Justice advises (Carlton, 1978: 27) "guidance by way of basic concepts that will assist the officer in these circumstances. . . . "

POLICE OBJECTIVES AND GOALS

The police mediate between the community and the legal system. They are the major representative of the legal system in their transactions with the public and they are the most visible symbol of governmental authority. They are responsible for enforcing all criminal laws, regardless of the willingness of the citizenry to be policed. Given their small numbers relative to the magnitude of their task, the police regard themselves as the "thin blue line" maintaining law and order in the community* (Reiss, 1972: 1).

The police have four primary goals:

I The control of crime. *Keep acceptable level*
II The protection of life and property.
III The maintenance of peace and order.
IV The safeguarding of Constitutional rights (e.g., to assemble to demonstrate or for religious worship).

The American Bar Association (1973: 2) points out that these goals represent "The highest duties of government. . . . "

The four goals of the police are operationalized through ten objectives:

---

*"Since they see the public as hostile to the police and feel that their work tends to aggravate this hostility, they separate themselves from the public, develop strong in-group attitudes, and control one another's conduct, making it conform to the interests of the group" (Westley, 1972: 110).

1. Prevent crime.
2. Investigate criminal activity, identify offenders and, when appropriate, effect arrests and participate in court proceedings.
3. Promote and preserve peace and order.
4. Protect Constitutional guarantees.
5. Ensure and facilitate the safe movement of persons and vehicles.
6. Aid persons who are in danger of physical harm, e.g., trapped in a vehicle, in a building with a gas leak.
7. Aid to persons in need of care, e.g., accident victims, children, the mentally ill.
8. Resolve conflict between persons that has the potential for disturbing the peace or resulting in violence.
9. Provide a feeling of security in the community.
10. Provide information and help educate the public about the law and criminal activity, and establish and maintain a positive community attitude toward the police.

DISCRETION AND THE POLICE CHIEF EXECUTIVE

A "typical" police chief executive will have between two (in smaller communities) and four (in large cities) sworn officers for every 1000 persons in his/her jurisdiction, with an organization whose manpower allocations approximate the following:

—*Staff and Inspections:* internal investigations; personnel; training; research and planning; public information; community relations = 6 percent.

—*Patrol* = 60 percent.

—*Traffic* = 10 percent.

—*Investigation* = 13 percent.

—*Juvenile* = 3 percent.

—*Auxiliary Services:* records; communications; criminalistics; detention; property = 8 percent.

The police agency will operate on the basis of a 168-hour week. Wayne LaFave (1965: 102) points out:

> The police and other enforcement agencies are given the general responsibility for maintaining law and order under a body of criminal law defining the various kinds of conduct against which they may properly proceed. They are then furnished with enforcement resources less than adequate to accomplish the entire task.

Using his/her discretion, the police chief must decide how to allocate scarce resources, how to deploy his/her officers. The chief renders decisions about the priority levels of the various police activities such as routine patrol, traffic and parking enforcement, vice (prostitution and gambling) enforcement and juvenile services. In most instances the police chief has the total authority to allocate personnel in a manner he/she believes will aid in attaining police objectives. The chief is advised "to assess accurately the communities' police needs and to formulate methods of meeting these needs" (Police Chief Executive Committee, 1976: 86). However, the police chief operates in a difficult environment. His/her resources are inelastic. Attention (resource allocation) given any single activity, e.g., patrolling mass transit facilities, reduces attention that can be given other activities, e.g., assigning officers to educational institutions. Increasing the number of plainclothes officers to deal with vice activity reduces the number of uniformed officers available for patrol or traffic duties, and vice-versa. The *service* function of the police (see objectives 6, 7, and 8 listed earlier in this chapter) may detract from *crime control,* and either may detract from the *order maintenance* function of the police.

Wilson ((1976: 99) argues that while a police chief can, in his own discretion, significantly effect the level of vice in the community, "the chief's policies are also constrained by community characteristics":

> The social composition of the city is one determinant both of the potential market for illicit services and of the degree to which public opinion will tolerate activities that serve that market. In almost all cities with a substantial lower class and in almost all large cities whatever their class composition, there will be a demand for vice and gambling that will be served by those residents who find such enterprises profitable. In small, upper-status communities, on the other hand, whatever demand exists will be served, if at all, only with great difficulty.

Wilson (1976: 99) also points out that vice enforcement is dependent on other agencies: "Prosecutors must prosecute, judges must convict, and sentences must be imposed that are severe enough to raise the cost of doing business above what the market for such services will support."

The police chief has no control over other actors in criminal justice, prosecutors, judges, parole boards, whose activities affect crime control, nor does he/she influence in any significant way welfare agencies and hospitals which affect the service function. Albert Reiss (1971: 115) points out that each critical juncture in the criminal justice system exercises control over other segments from police to parole:

> The system of criminal justice is organized as an input-output system. Although each organization in the hierarchy is granted jurisdiction over particular decisions, each also has considerable discretion over what to create or accept as inputs and whether or not to send these inputs on to the next level as outputs. This exercise of discretion critically affects the

system of justice, by substantially reducing the amount of output in the movement from one level of the hierarchy to the next.

Even with a substantial increase in resources, the police cannot hope to impact on a variety of crimes, from shoplifting to murder, which usually occur in areas not routinely subjected to police patrol. In addition, legislative bodies may pass laws or ordinances that give substantial enforcement responsibilities to the police without providing sufficient resources to accomplish the task. The Police Chief Executive Committee notes (1976: 84):

> When that happens, police chief executives must determine the priority of the new task, and then, based on that priority and the extensiveness of the task, assign responsibility and personnel to do the job. Whether the new task is to register security and private police, enforce a new law prohibiting the sale of merchandise by sidewalk venders, or inspect alarms, it dilutes the efforts of the police if adequate funds do not accompany the new responsibility.

In setting priorities the chief operates with a handicap: he actually has very little information about how well the force is preventing crime, apprehending criminals and maintaining order (Wilson, 1976: 57): "The police share with most other public agencies—the schools, foreign ministries, antipoverty organizations—an inability to assess accurately the effectiveness of their operations." The police chief cannot rely on crime statistics since they are deficient and too easily manipulated.

CRIME STATISTICS

The basic mechanism for compiling crime statistics in the UCR: *Uniform Crime Report* published by the FBI. The UCR divides offenses into two major categories. Part I offenses are those most likely to be reported (by victims or witnesses) which occur frequently and which are serious by nature or frequency of occurrence. They are:

1. Criminal homocide
   (a) Murder and non-negligent manslaughter
   (b) Manslaughter by negligence
2. Forcible rape
   (a) Rape by force
   (b) Attempted forcible rape
3. Robbery
   (a) Using a firearm
   (b) Using a knife or cutting instrument
   (c) Using other dangerous instrument
   (d) Strongarm robbery

4. Aggravated assault
   (a) Using a firearm
   (b) Using a knife or cutting instrument
   (c) Using other dangerous weapon
   (d) Using hands, fist, feet, etc., causing aggravated injury.
5. Burglary
   (a) Forcible entry
   (b) Unlawful entry (no force)
   (c) Attempted forcible entry
6. Larceny-Theft
7. Motor vehicle theft
   (a) Automobiles
   (b) Trucks and buses
   (c) Other motor vehicles
8. Arson

Part II offenses are those that do not meet the test of frequency or seriousness, and some are "victimless" insofar as they do not usually have a victim-complainant: prostitution, drugs, gambling. Other Part II offenses include: simple assault, forgery, fraud, embezzlement, receiving stolen property, weapons possession, driving under the influence. Corporate crimes (e.g., pricefixing, criminal negligence) would not appear in the UCR at all. Data for Part II offenses are based on arrests rather than frequency of occurrence.

The eight categories in Part I (referred to as *Index Crimes*) depend on the police, that is they are crimes reported to or known to the police which are then submitted to the FBI. Complaints to the police which are determined (by the police) to be false or baseless are counted as "unfounded complaints." The number of unfounded complaints is subtracted from the number of offenses known and the latter form the basis for the UCR reports. The "unfounding" of crimes is problematic. In Chicago, for example, there is a long tradition of "killing crime" by unfounding many reports of crime. This has the effect of reducing the (statistical) crime rate and presents a better (but obviously false) image of the city. There are additional problems with the UCR.

The UCR contains frequency of occurrence statistics for (index) crimes which are reported to the police, or which become known to them (by their own efforts); it does not reveal the actual rate of crime. A police department that adds more officers is also likely to increase the number of crimes known to the police and, ironically, it will cause the (statistical) crime rate to go up. Likewise, more efficient and responsive police management may increase crimes known to the police and encourage more victims and witnesses to report crimes. This will have the effect of increasing the rate of (statistical) crime (and can serve as a source of embarrassment for an otherwise excellent police chief). On the other hand, an inefficient (perhaps corrupt) department with a poor public image will cause citizens to be reluctant to report crimes and, thus, the (statistical) crime rate will be correspondingly low.

In order to correct some of these obvious deficiencies, since 1975 crime victimization surveys have been conducted for the U.S. Department of Justice by the U.S. Bureau of the Census. These National Crime Panel (NCP) or "Victimization Studies/Reports" are the result of interviews with randomly selected households and business establishments in an effort to gauge the extent of (actual) crime in the U.S. The NCP has consistantly found that the number of crimes recalled by victims is significantly higher than those known to the police (as reported in the UCR). Most victims of (even serious) crime do not report it to the police. There is one exception: auto theft. Most motor vehicles are insured against theft and the insurance company will not honor a claim unless a report has been filed with the police. The UCR statistic for criminal homocide is also more reliable. Every death requires a death certificate indicating the cause of death certified by a physician. Suspected homocides must be reported to the police and/or medical examiner or coroner.*

TRAFFIC ENFORCEMENT

Traffic is one aspect of policing which can easily be subjected to measurement and over which the police chief can exert a great deal of control. It is within the chief's discretion to create a specialized traffic enforcement unit or to set "norms" or some other euphemism for ticket quotas. The chief may do both: for example, establish a special traffic enforcement unit whose officers are to write one ticket per hour, while expecting other patrol officers to write at least two per shift. Officers whose ticket record fails to meet the standard are counselled by their sergeant, who is monitered by others in the police hierarchy ensuring that the quota is maintained. However, while traffic law violations are the single most frequent reason for contact between police officers and citizens, they are a source of citizen irritation and traffic stops appear to have little or no effect on accident rates or subsequent driving practices (Lundman, 1979: 161).

---

*This is not to say that there are no problems with statistics on homocide. Investigations of medical examiner's offices revealed numerous mistakes, e.g., in one recent New York City case "it was discovered by accident that the severed head of an unidentified woman believed to have drowned actually contained a bullet. . . ." A three-year federal study revealed that 70 percent of the 240 crime laboratories operated by government (federal, state, county, local) "failed to perform even a simple blood test correctly" (Grunson, 1983: 6E). Of course the bodies of some murder victims, e.g., Jimmy Hoffa, are never found.

HARASSMENT

The police may respond to the problem of inadequate resources and due process protections that interfere with crime control, by the systematic use of harassment. This practice refers to an arrest being made that is *not intended* to result in the prosecution of the defendant; it is illegal. "These arrests serve what the police perceive to be deterrent, rehabilitative, or punative functions" (LaFave, 1965: 437). Joseph Goldstein (1960) states that harassment occurs when a law enforcement officer uses his/her powers of arrest under circumstances that will not permit a successful prosecution, or where no prosecution is intended. In Chicago, for example, during the early 1980s, it was the policy of the Bureau of Field Tactical Services (police street gang unit) to arrest known gang members whenever they congregated for "disorderly conduct." The arresting officers had no intention of even appearing in court for the purpose of prosecution and the defendants were always set free—after a night in a police lock-up.

Harassment is often used to deal with prostitution and gambling because of a combination of two factors (LaFave, 1965: 483):

> (a) the difficulty of detecting the offenses by methods which will produce evidence which will be both admissible in court and not offensive to the trial judge; and (b) the fact that conviction in the case of the offenders of these types typically results in the imposition of a small fine or other sentence which seems not particularly effective in rehabilitating the offender, deterring others, or achieving any objective beyond those served by the arrest and release practice.

In other words, police cynicism may cause officers to disregard the time-consuming practices necessary to arrest and successfully prosecute persons for prostitution and gambling, in favor of quick, easy, "instant justice."— harassment.

A police chief executive may, explicitly, but more likely implicitly, encourage harassment. The chief who fails to allocate adequate resources for dealing with prostitution and gambling, while demanding a high level of effectiveness, invites the use of this tactic. Prostitutes will be subjected to mass arrests without sufficient evidence to justify an arrest: "To get them off the streets." The tactic may be used repetitively until the offenders are forced to leave the area. The tactic can be quite effective which, despite its illegality, can explain its popularity. Commercial gambling (as opposed to social gambling) can also be subjected to harassment. In such cases, extra-legal police conduct may include the destruction of gambling records and/or gambling paraphernalia and the confiscation of gambling proceeds, money, without any arrest being made.

In addition to the obvious problem of a police chief countenancing extra-legal police conduct, looms the specter of corruption. Since the non-arrest harassment of gamblers will not be recorded, it cannot be subjected to any real control or oversight. The seizure of money will provide an incentive for officers to continue the practice even after a chief orders a halt to the "crackdown." From confiscating money to accepting money for not harassing is often a small gap bridged by too many officers. Vice enforcement has traditionally been a focal point of corruption in most large cities.

Harassment is sometimes the product of overzealous officers reacting to an "order" (from a mayor or police chief) to "crack down on...." It is sometimes a reaction to the shooting of a police officer or other crime that outrages sensivities. When harassment is the result of official "proclamation," the problem can have serious long-term consequences for the police agency. Once freed from legal constraints and departmental regulations, it becomes difficult, if not impossible, for a police agency to bring its officers back under control—the "license" to engage in extra-legal conduct is difficult to "revoke." A police hierarchy that permits, perhaps encourages, such conduct cannot easily discipline officers for rule-violative behavior.

DISCRETION AND "STYLES" OF POLICING

The police chief executive sets the policy and tone for his/her agency, and the resulting "style" affects discretion. Before turning to specific items of police officer discretion, we will examine the issue of "style."

James Q. Wilson (1976) in his classic work (*Varieties of Police Behavior*) delineated three styles of policing. These refer to the predominant strategy of the department with respect to responding to less serious violations of the law and the order maintenance function. In each, serious violations of the law are dealt with in a serious manner.

1. *The Watchman.* The primary concern is order maintenance and the police are allowed/encouraged to ignore common minor violations involving traffic and juvenile offenses and, to a lesser extent, vice. The seriousness of an offense is judged not by what the law says, but by the immediate circumstances, the persons or groups involved: teenagers, blacks, families, prostitutes.

2. *The Legalistic.* The patrol officer is expected to be a strict enforcer of the law—all of the law. Differences between between neighborhoods and community groups do not impact on enforcement and there is a high rate of arrests and traffic ticket issuance. This style fits well into a view of police *professionalism* to be discussed shortly.

3. *The Service.* In this type of department the police take all requests for

service seriously, be it for law enforcement or order maintenance. While interventions by the police are frequent, as would be expected with a *Legalistic Style,* arrests are not. It is a type of approach often found in middle class communities where the public expects their officers to look neat and be courteous, and where arrests for minor infractions are avoided whenever possible.

In his study of three California police departments, Michael K. Brown (1981) did not find evidence for the departmental styles presented by Wilson (1976). The decisions of patrol officers, he argues, are not significantly affected by the chief. Brown notes that the size of the community, and hence the size of the department, has an impact on discretion (1981: 128): "In a small department there are more constraints on a patrolman's discretion." The police officer's style and use of discretion, Brown reports, was affected by the officer's learning process (1981: 128).

Herman Goldstein, former Executive Assistant to the Police Superintendent of Chicago, notes (1977: 101):

> What typically happens is that officers discover, upon graduating from their recruit training and taking their first assignments, that they are constantly being called upon to make decisions; that relatively little of what they were taught seems to apply to the situation they confront; and that they are often without guidance in deciding what to do in a given situation. They gradually learn, from their association with more experienced personnel and their supervisors, that there is a mass of "know-how" upon which they must draw. Practices they find, vary a great deal. Some seem so well established that they take on the quality of a standard department operating procedure utilized uniformly by all personnel.... [While] other informal practices are common only to the personnel working within a single area or under a particular supervisor.
>
> ...[As a result] officers assigned to routine patrol activities—especially if they work alone—usually develop distinctive styles that reflect a blend of practices learned from their associates and supervisors that are modified by their own values, the kinds of incidents they handle, and the individuals to whom they must relate.

Elizabeth Reuss-Ianni (1983: 8) states that this process serves to limit discretion by defining a set of rules to which the officer is socialized:

> These rules are then internalized as part of the street cop culture that guides decision making and places limits on discretion and performance.

Brown (1981: 101) argues that discretion and its control are better understood by the relationship between patrol officers and field supervisors/ sergeants. The chief, he notes, is preoccupied with the department's relationship to outside groups and institutions such as the city council, news media, Chamber of Commerce, community organizations:

The chief, through his actions, policies, and official pronouncements, may set the tone for the department, but the responsibility for enforcing rules, investigating citizen complaints, motivating patrolmen, and often deciding what constitutes an abuse of police power lies with field supervisors, the sergeants and watch commanders. It is their interpretation of department rules and the chief's policies that determine how stringent discipline will be, and whether or how departmental controls influence the choices of patrolmen.

However, the supervisor's authority in a police organization has important limitations. The sergeant does not resemble his/her military counterpart. S/he is, as Jonathan Rubinstein (1973: 56) notes, "a foreman whose men are scattered over many city blocks. His men rarely work in his direct sight and he needs their goodwill just as they need his protection and advice to get the job done properly." Rubinstein points out (1973: 449):

> The sergeant does not lead his men into their work, he supervises them. He needs their active cooperation or he will be a failure. Every sergeant understands this. If his men dislike him or feel that he is not competent, there is no way he can force them to do the work in a way that will satisfy the captain and the inspector. If the men are working well and doing the things that keeps the captain and the lieutenant happy, he will let them get away with many things which he personally disapproves but does not consider worthwhile fighting over.

PROFESSIONALISM

Using a dictionary definition, a professional has an occupation (profession) "requiring training in the liberal arts or the sciences and advanced study in a specialized field" (*American Heritage Dictionary,* 1981). A compilation of the attributes of a profession include (Niederhoffer, 1967: 19):

1. High standards of admission
2. A special body of knowledge and theory
3. Altruism and dedication to the service ideal
4. A lengthy period of training for candidates
5. A code of ethics
6. Licensing of members
7. Autonomous control
8. Pride of the members in their profession
9. Publicly recognized status and prestige

In policing, however, professionalism often refers to upgrading the police by requiring a college education, extensive pre-service and in-service training (in a police academy); in addition, the use of modern managerial techniques and sophisticated communication and information storage and retrieval equipment (computers). Professionalization becomes confused with modernization.

Ianni (1983: 212) notes the existence of "two cultures" in large, modern police departments: *management cops* represent a form of police professionalism which contrasts with *street cops.*

> Now there are two cultures which confront each other in the department: a street cop culture of the good old days, working class in origin and temperament, whose members see themselves as career cops; opposed to this is a management cop culture, more middle class, whose members' education and mobility have made them eligible for jobs totally outside of policing, which makes them less dependent on, and less loyal to, the street cop culture.

The management cop criticizes the "old ways" and is opposed to the informal fashion of management that characterizes the street cop culture.

Police professionalism has meant separating the department from political influences originating from the outside. The move to "professionalize" has caused the police to be more independent of the political process. This independence has also freed the police from having their use of discretion subjected to outside scrutiny. This has implications for controlling police discretion which will be discussed later in this chapter.

A vital element of a profession, *autonomy,* such as that enjoyed by a doctor or lawyer, actually runs counter to many decades of police reform. A decentralized—more autonomous—police force often meant control by corrupt ward bosses in the areas where they were dominant. Efforts at reform resulted in greater centralization of the law enforcement function, particularly with respect to gambling, commercial sex, liquor and drug violations. Specialized plainclothes units were placed under headquarters command. Civil service reforms resulted in centalized control over the hiring of police officers. Reform meant greater bureaucratic control over police officers and a profession is judged, in part, on the degree of freedom from bureaucratic control. Jerry Wilson (1975: 167), former Chief of Police for Washington, D.C., states:

> It may very well be that all this emphasis on professionalization and on education of police officers will ultimately be beneficial to police service. The day may come when only college graduates will be permitted to serve as police officers. It is more likely, however, that such a goal will never be achieved; the police service would be far better served by recognition of what it actually is: a dignified occupation which can be adequately performed by many high school graduates, a craft. . . .

One aspect of a profession which has often been incorporated into the working model of police professionalism—*detachment*—has important im-

lications for the issue of discretion. Detachment can mean avoiding personal
involvement, refusing to allow personal feelings or prejudices to influence
decisions or actions, and a restrained, yet concerned, approach when carrying out official responsibilities. In policing it can also mean an inflexible
approach to law enforcement and order maintenance, carrying out a uniform,
and usually high, level of intervention and enforcement. Instead of exercising discretion, there is an insistence on a single standard of behavior for all
civilians in all neighborhoods. The law and powers of citation and arrest are
applied to insure conformity to middle class standards of behavior.

If the department provides police services to neighborhoods with significant non-middle class populations, this aspect of professionalism can be a
source of citizen irritation, anger or outright hostility. For example, in many
working class areas there is greater tolerance of noise and a greater accep-
tance of boisterous behavior than in middle class areas. There is a tendency
for large numbers of people to congregate on the street, particularly during
the summer, and outdoor recreation may include card playing, or other
types of gambling, beer and wine drinking, and the use of streets for
ball-playing. While such activities would not be tolerated in middle class
neighborhoods, attempts to impose a middle class standard of order maintenance in diverse neighborhoods can be problematic. In such circumstances
the patrol officer may be well-advised to exercise some discretion. The
President's Commission on Law Enforcement and Administration of Justice
notes (1968: 267):

> Some people ordinarily conduct their social lives on the street, particularly
> if they live in neighborhoods where the housing is dilapidated and over-
> crowded and where there are few parks or other recreational facilities. Break-
> ing up such groups, rather than contributing to public order, is likely to have
> the reverse effect.

Herman Goldstein (1963: 147) adds:

> Police officials too often fail to recognize that there are many in the communi-
> ties which they serve who have an inherent distaste for authority—and
> especially police authority. Joining with others of the same view and those
> whose beliefs are more firmly grounded in a support for our democratic
> processes, these people closely guard against the improper use of authority
> by the police. It behooves law enforcement officials to refrain from unneces-
> sarily creating a situation which annoys such individuals. Such situations can
> often be avoided through the exercise of proper discretion.

William Westley (1972: 49) points out:

> In spite of his [the police officer] ostensible function as protector, he usually
> meets only those he is protecting them [the public] from, and for him *they*
> have no love. The fight in the bar, the driver in a hurry, the bickering mates,

the overtime parker, the cutters of edges and the finders of angles; the underworld—bitter, sarcastic, afraid; none of these find the policeman a pleasant sight. To them he is the law, the interfering one, dangerous and a source of fear. He is the disciplinarian, a symbol in brass and blue, irritating, a personal challenge, an imminent defeat and punishment.

DISCRETION AND PATROL OFFICERS

Patrol is usually accomplished by uniformed officers assigned to marked vehicles. In some departments this may include two-wheeled vehicles and even foot patrol in heavily populated and business areas. William Gay, et al. (1977:2) notes:

> The primary emphasis of uniform patrol has been to establish a high sense of police visibility and presence in the community as a means of deterring and preventing crime, responding quickly to calls for service in order to apprehend suspects, and providing timely responses to non-crime service demands.

An analysis of the workload of patrol officers reveals four basic functional categories (Gay, et al., 1977: 3–6):

1. *Calls for service* account for about 25 percent of the officer's time and usually provide police chief executives with the basis for making decisions about the number of patrol officers deployed in each geographic subunit (e.g., district, precinct).
Calls for service include "crime in progress" as well as mundane non-crime requests.

2. *Preventive patrol* accounts for about 40 percent of the patrol officer's time although "it is frequently fragmented into small segments of time separated by service calls and the performance of administrative duties" (Gay, et al., 1977: 5). During this time the officer moves randomly through his/her beat with almost total discretion about how to use patrol time with little direction from supervisors. Sergeants will sometimes identify specific items for patrol officers to be aware of, for example, an increase in purse snatchings by teenagers, or information that "wanted" persons (for whom warrants have been issued) have been seen in a certain vicinity.

3. *Administrative tasks* account for about 20–25 percent of a patrol officers workload. This includes preparing the patrol vehicle, transporting prisoners and papers, writing reports, running departmental errands, and appearing in court. It may also include personal business.

4. *Officer-initiated activities* account for about 10–15 percent of an officer's patrol time. In some cases this activity is the result of observing something suspicious or the commission of a crime which can lead to an arrest.

Other officer-initiated activities include traffic and pedestrian stops and interrogations.

Discretionary decisions related to the patrol function include (Gay, et al., 1977: 22):

(a) How many watches/shifts should there be and what should be their time spans, e.g., 12–8, 8–4, 4–12; special high crime hours: 6 P.M.–2 A.M.?

(b) How many officers and vehicles should be assigned to each watch/shift?

(c) How should beat boundaries be constructed within geographic subunits (districts, precincts, areas), and should they reflect daily or weekly fluctuations in the workload, e.g., calls for service?

There have been a variety of programatic responses designed to improve the effectiveness of patrol. For example, "Directed Patrol" which focuses on specific types of crime, burglary or perhaps street robberies, and deploys officers, often in a variety of disguises or street clothing, in areas with numerous reported incidents. Calls for service can be prioritized: those needing an immediate response, e.g., "crime in progress;" those that can be handled by a delayed response or even an appointment, e.g., burglary incident; those that can be handled over the telephone or by having the caller walk-in, e.g., auto theft. It is beyond the scope of this book to review these programs.

The officer is trained and directed to look for violations of law in the course of his/her patrol activities (proactive policing). If a violation occurs, in order to lawfully effect an arrest the officer must have *probable cause,* which according to the United States Supreme Court (in *Draper v. United States* 358 U.S. 307, 1959) exists

> "where the facts and circumstances within their [arresting officers'] knowledge and of which they had reasonable trustworthy information are sufficient in themselves to warrant a man of reasonable caution in the belief that an offense has been or is being committed. . . . "

The Texas Criminal Justice Council (1974: 161) defines probable cause as:

> That set of facts or circumstances based on reliable information or personal knowledge or observation by an officer which reasonably show and would warrant an ordinary prudent man in believing that a particular person has been guilty of, is threatening, or is about to commit some offense against the law.

Every patrol officer—as a *sworn officer*—has taken an oath to enforce the law; *all* of the law, and to do so all s/he requires is probable cause. But, does the existence of probable cause *require* an arrest? Or, can the officer use discretion and decline to arrest, the existence of probable cause not withstanding? LaFave (1965: 68) notes that: "There has been no express legislative delegation of discretion to the police." However, Kenneth Culp Davis (1963: 87) points out:

Legislative bodies have long acquiesced in the assumption of power by the police, legislation has long been written in reliance on the expectation that law enforcement officers will correct its excesses through administration, the legislation often reflects unrealistically high aspirations of the community and hence compels the law enforcers to temper the ideals with realism, and the system we have is the product of natural evolution through responses to the multiplicity of community needs.

LaFave (1965: 70) adds:

Poor draftmanship and a failure to revise the criminal law to eliminate obsolete provisions have contributed to existing ambiguities. However, even where care has been taken, it has not been possible to draft substantive provisions which are entirely free from ambiguity. This is a result not only of limitations upon the effectiveness of language but also of the ability of a legislature to envisage all of the day-to-day law enforcement problems which may arise.

LaFave (1965: 95) notes that certain lawmaking may only be intended to serve an educational purpose, "to guide the individual conscience, but is not intended to be used to coerce compliance." We may refer to such statutes as *symbolic;* they permit elected officials to go on record in opposition to behavior widely considered immoral, such as statutes against adultery (a Class A misdemeanor in Illinois, for example).

More practical concerns that explain the existence of discretion were discussed earlier—the conservation of scarce police resources. A police officer who arrests someone for a minor offense will be "out of service" for a length of time during which the officer will not be available to respond to other duties that may have a higher priority. The nature of legislative enactments, legislative intent, and the scarcity of police resources help to to explain the existence of discretion.

Wilson (1976: 85–139) provides a way of categorizing discretion along the dimensions of law enforcement or order maintenance, police-invoked or citizen-invoked action:

1. *Police-Invoked Law Enforcement.* The police officer acts on his/her own authority, if not initiative. This is usually the case with gambling, prostitution and even traffic enforcement, although it can be in response to a general public concern.

2. *Citizen-Invoked Law Enforcement.* In such cases the civilian is exercising his/her discretion to mobilize the police (Reiss, 1971: 114). Studies reveal that many, if not most, crimes are not reported to the police. Unless the suspect is still on the scene, the officer serves principally as a report-taker.

3. *Police-Invoked Order Maintenance.* On their own authority, if not initiative,

the police intervene in situations of actual or potential disorder.

4. *Citizen-Invoked Order Maintenance.* A civilian mobilizes the police to deal with a public or private disorder.

Wilson (1976: 89) argues that cases one and four offer the officer situations with the greatest amount of discretion. In case two, the police officer has the least amount of discretion except when the suspects are juveniles. Case three is in the intermediate range of discretion subject to the possibility of departmental policy and control. In each case Wilson focuses primarily on the nature of the community and the style of the police department.

Donald Black (1980) argues that the social standing of the victim/complainant and the offender is the key to understanding the exercise of police discretion. The police will consider it more serious when a middle class person complains about a person of lower status, than when the complaint is made in the opposite direction. In other words, if a white businessman complains about a black teenager, we would expect a greater amount of police activity than if a black teenager complained about a white businessman (all other things being equal). Black (1980: 5) states:

> police work will vary with its location and direction in social space. This means, for example, that how the police handle a particular case will depend upon the social characteristics of the alleged offender and of the complainant or victim, and with the nature of the relationship between the parties.

Thus, the police will respond differently to middle class persons in a middle class environment, than they would to lower class persons in a ghetto. They will treat an assault by a lower class black on a middle class white more seriously than vice-versa, or when the same crime involves both a black victim and a black perpetrator.

This prejudicial response to crime between minority persons has been criticized by other observers such as LaFave (1965: 114): "The obvious dilemma is that the Negro continues to be judged by a different standard because it is assumed that he has a greater tolerance for certain kinds of antisocial conduct. . . ." Sanford Kadish (1962) refers to calculated non-enforcement in certain neighborhoods as being based on a presumed lesser standard of morality among blacks or other minorities. Thus, the rape of a black woman by a black male will be treated less seriously than the rape of a white woman, and assault laws may not even be enforced when victim and perpetrator are black.

Police discretion is also affected by the *attitude test.* A civilian who does not show proper deference when confronted by the police "fails the attitude test." The attitude of a person subjected to police scrutiny or questioning, for example a motorist stopped for a defective taillight, is often a determining variable with respect to the action taken by the police. A motorist who is courteous and expresses respect for the police and their authority (and perhaps acknowledges his "wrongdoing") is more likely to escape a citation than the motorist who asks: "Don't you guys have anything better to do?" Since police discretion is related to the seriousness of the offense, the deciding factor in less serious instances will often be deference. In such circumstances an arrest for disorderly conduct may result when the *real* "crime" was a failure to show proper respect for police authority.

The relative differences between the social status of the police and civilians involved in a particular incident can affect the exercise of discretion. Thus, a well-dressed, middleaged male will be treated differently than a black teenager in jeans and sneakers. When an officer discovers that the person he has stopped for a traffic infraction is a police officer, he may decide not to cite, usually referred to as a "professional courtesy." Female offenders, if they display traditional role expectations, may also receive lenient treatment by the police (see Visher, 1983). Police officers may be higher, lower or equal in status to persons in any enforcement situation, and this will affect their discretionary decisions (Black, 1980: 5).

A police officer on patrol is confronted with the reality of rarely being on the scene of any incident from its inception. Like the movie patron who enters a theater when the film is already running, the police officer must attempt to reconstruct events based on what s/he now confronts. This requires the exercise of discretion based on supposition—an uncomfortable situation. It can be even more serious when violence and/or weapons are in evidence. A colleague related just such an incident. As a patrolman he came upon the following scene:

Three adolescent black males were assaulting a white male, apparently a taxi driver (his cab was nearby with the driver's door open). It was in the early evening in an area where a predominantly white neighborhood ended and a predominantly black neighborhood began. Two of the black males were struggling with the driver while a third held what appeared to be a piece of lead pipe.

Assault on a cab driver with robbery as the probable motive, flashed through the officer's head. He exited from the patrol car, revolver in hand: "Freeze!" The driver continued to struggle and the the third black male turned and began to approach the officer, pipe in hand. "Freeze or you're dead;" the officer shouted, "drop the pipe and you three on your bellies!" The three protested but slowly went prone on the street. The officer backed up a few steps and, without taking his eyes off of the three, reached into the patrol car and called for additional units.

Two patrol units responded and a crowd began to gather. The three young blacks were handcuffed and told to "Shut up." The cab driver stood by his taxi. Two middle-aged whites, a man and a woman, approached the officer:

"Officer," one said, "you've arrested the wrong persons. The officer responded with a puzzled look. "That cabbie is a menace. He rounded the corner and almost ran those boys down. When they yelled at him, he stopped the cab and attacked them with a lead pipe. He oughta be in jail!" Several other persons came over to support their neighbor's observations.

DISCRETION AND CALLS FOR SERVICE

As mentioned earlier, calls for service account for about one-quarter of a police officer's patrol time. These service calls originate with a police (civilian or sworn) operator who receives an incoming telephone call from a civilian via the police emergency number, 911. (Requests for service, particularly in emergency situations, may be conveyed via the telephone company operator). The operator interprets the request, reduces it to writing on a small card, and it is referred to a dispatcher. The dispatcher (civilian or sworn) usually has a lighted panel in front of him/her with the numbers of the vehicles assigned to his/her sector, and a detailed sector map. The card is timepunched and a patrol unit is dispatched; that unit's light on the panel is switched off. When the assignment is completed and the unit reports "back in service," the panel light is turned on again and the time is punched on the dispatch card.

In some departments personnel alternate between functioning as operators and dispatchers. In small departments the same person may receive calls and dispatch patrol officers. Eric Scott and Stephen Percy (1983: 128) refer to operators as *gatekeepers* who

> mediate initial agency interactions with citizens demanding service and assess caller eligibility and the exact nature of the service request. Dispatchers are response coordinators, determining the specifics of police response and communicating relevant information to patrol officers.

The dispatcher exercises discretion over how much information to convey to a police officer (Rubinstein, 1973: 88):

> What the dispatcher tells a man when he gives him an assignment is all the patrolman knows about what he will find until he actually arrives. The dispatcher must tell him everything relevant to the job in the most economical way to avoid wasting air time. He must also try to get the entire message across in one attempt, since repetitions slow the patrolman's response time and ties up the radio channel.

Many police departments use radio codes to keep conversations confidential from those who might monitor the radio frequency with a scanner, e.g., tow-truck operators, lawyers/"ambulance chasers," police buffs, criminals.

After a period of time, however, "scanners" usually are able to comprehend the code and a new one is needed, e.g., once every three years. This means that officers must learn a new code and will totally confuse other law enforcement agencies who may share the same frequency, e.g., sheriffs or state police. There are those who advocate using "plain talk" over the radio, and some departments have been using visual computerized dispatching systems.

A computer-assisted dispatch system generally operates in the following manner:

(a) A complaint is received by the operator who uses a typewriter keyboard to enter it onto a visual display terminal.

(b) The computer checks the address to ascertain if it is within the agency's jurisdiction, while the complainant is still on the telephone line. The computer can check not only street addresses, but also street intersections, parks, public buildings and other sites likely to be referred to by name instead of address.

(c) The computer checks to see if the complaint has already been received/reported by another person.

(d) After the complaint has been recorded by the operator it is transmitted to the dispatcher and displayed on the dispatcher's visual display screen.

(e) The computer checks the location of the complaint against vehicles in service and displays the best units for the assignment. The dispatcher enters his/her choice on the keyboard and the assignment is displayed on the video terminal in the patrol car.

(f) The computer moniters each step of the dispatch process and records the times reported and maintains an update on the status of all patrol units. The status of any complaint can be displayed by entering the appropriate code on the keyboard. Computer-assisted or not, the elements of discretion remain essentially the same.

Scott and Percy (1983: 130–41) divide up the tasks of operators and dispatchers:

1. *Determination of Eligibility.* Does the caller fall within the geographic boundaries of the agency's jurisdiction? This is a "yes" or "no" question without discretion. For requests deemed an emergency, there is little discretion present. However, the request for service may actually be a need for information, and here the operator has a great deal of discretion over the quantity and quality of the information provided. There may also be alternatives to dispatching a patrol unit, e.g., making a referral to another agency or to a police report-taker; again, a question of discretion.

2. *Interpreting and Coding Service Requests.* The operator must make sense

of the request and callers may be excited and incoherent. After sufficient information is secured the request is coded into police agency-relevant terminology for the dispatcher. Because the information is frequently ambiguous, the operator has a great deal of uncertainty and, thus, must use discretion in determining how to code any request for service. The dispatcher must prioritize requests based on seriousness and urgency — a discretionary call.

If the volume of calls exceeds the ability of the police to respond adequately, service queues form and discretion is exercised by the dispatcher over the priority ordering of (even urgent/emergency) requests for service. The dispatcher must decide which unit to send, usually the closest, but sometimes specialists or a patrol supervisor. The dispatcher determines the number (if any) of backup units to be dispatched.

REQUESTS FOR SERVICE: DOMESTIC DISTURBANCE CALLS

The nature of policing results in a basic role conflict for the police officer. As a *peace officer* his/her role emphasizes qualities of courage and physical prowess. As a *public servant,* his/her role emphasizes qualities of sympathy, humanity, patience and care. The Task Force on Policing in Ontario (1974: 12) noted that the role of the police officer is often based on a less than accurate assessment of what it is that the police actually do:

> There is much popular confusion about the nature of a police officer's job. Television, movies and the novel portray the police officer, gun in hand, leading a perpetual war against crime. Personal danger is an ever-present reality. Armed robberies do occur, and the individual officer is sometimes required to meet lethal force with lethal force. Routine situations can blossom into violence.

> The domestic disturbance is regarded as the most dangerous of all police situations. Most officers never have occasion to use their service revolvers. Routine traffic enforcement is more likely to turn up a stranded motorist than a criminal suspect. A radio dispatch holds more promise of a cat in a tree than of a homocide.

> Police officers spend relatively little of their time involved with crime or criminal activity. Estimates vary, but perhaps as much as 80% of an officer's duty is taken up with assisting citizens, maintaining order, ensuring the smooth flow of traffic and pedestrians, and routine patrol.

> This confusion in role is evident in the professional police literature as well. A conventional school of thought focuses police attention on a sharply defined, if less sharply identified, "criminal element" and urges the application of the most powerful modern technology toward its eradication. A

second school of thought casts the modern police officer in more of a social worker role. . . . *

It is in this role as a social worker that the police officer must often respond to the domestic disturbance, traditionally considered by police officers to be undesirable or "garbage calls" (Bard and Zacher, 1976: 11): "These situations receive low departmental priority, training for them is minimal, and the goal of officers on the scene is to leave as soon as possible. Police service in disturbances earns few rewards from the department; those doing the job do not consider it 'real' police work." Because of these realities, the police response to a domestic disturbance is filled with a great deal of discretion.†

There is no set definition of a "domestic disturbance"; it is a general category referring to (Levens and Dutton, 1980: 15):

> any request for service (both requests for police presence and advice/ information) arising out of conflicts occurring in, broadly defined, domestic situations including arguments or fights between husband and wife, partners in common law relationship, man and woman; parent-child/teenager problems; verbal or physical disputes between relatives or unrelated persons occupying the same household or dwelling; disturbances caused by landlord-tenant disputes; neighbour arguments; interpersonal struggles over child custody; violation of separation orders; non-compliance with eviction orders; and "keep the peace" requests for police to attend and stand by in case domestic disputes arose or became violent.

Morton Bard and Joseph Zacker (1976: 10–12) distinguish between three general approaches that may be taken by police officers (using their discretion) when responding to a domestic disturbance:

---

* . . . many officers like the excitement of chases, the danger-filled episode, the life-threatening intervention at a crime scene. The danger and unpredictability allows for a degree of satisfaction and is not a 'negative' feature of the work in the eyes of its practitioners. It may be that without the expectation and realization of exciting episodes, many officers would leave for other, better paid, work. It may be just such a promise that keeps officers awake on long, monotonous, boring nights and keeps them with the force for twenty to twenty-five years. The police possess what might be called a 'threat-danger-hero' notion of their everyday lives.

"The formal structure of rewards within police departments also perpetuates this ideology. Violent or dramatic public action—either in solving or preventing a crime, shooting a man, or aggressively patrolling traffic—is considered to be a source of promotion, leads to commendations and medals, and is much admired by police colleagues. . . . The highly unpredictable but potentially dangerous scene is a possible, although not highly probable, feature of police patrol" (Manning, 1977: 302).

†"Not only is the interpersonal conflict situation a difficult one to handle from the standpoint of the intensity, intimacy, and complexity of the social relationship; frequently the difficulty is compounded by the police themselves, who, through the use of traditional methods of intervention become the catalytic element that escalates a verbal battle into a physically abusive fracas; and too often redirects the intramarital violence towards the intervening officer" (Levens and Dutton, 1980: 69).

1. *Authority.* In this response the officer takes charge, defines the situation, and, without seeking anyone's suggestions, imposes a (usually temporary) resolution. Bard and Zacher (1976: 53–55) offer some examples:

THE AUTHORITY APPROACH

Case Number One

The police were summoned to the scene of a dispute between two men, one of whom was described by the radio dispatcher as having a weapon. The dispute occurred in the public area of a housing project, and several people had gathered at the scene before the police arrived. Upon arrival, investigating Officer A ordered the crowd to disperse under threat of arrest. Officer A then located one party, Mr. B, who was being berated by a woman not involved in the initial dispute. Mr. B said that a Mr. C had attacked him and had a weapon; he asked Officer A to go with him to Mr. C's apartment. The officer ordered Mr. B to remain in his own apartment while the officer went to visit Mr. C.

The officer searched Mr. C for a weapon as soon as he entered Mr. C's apartment. When he found no weapon he interviewed Mr. C. During the interview, a friend of Mr. C's arrived and was ordered to leave. Upon detecting inconsistencies between the stories of Mr. C and Mr. B, Officer A told Mr. C to stay in his apartment (with an assisting officer) while he went back to Mr. B.

Returning to Mr. B's apartment, the officer said that he had found no weapon and that the stories conflicted. Mr. B then admitted that he had started the dispute, as well as the assault, insisting, however, that Mr. C had a weapon. The officer told Mr. B that Mr. C did not want to press charges, and Mr. B said that he did not want to do so either. Officer A returned to Mr. C, informed him of Mr. B's decision, and left the scene.

Explanation. In this case, the officer imposed his authority throughout the intervention, even during the interviews. He ordered people to leave when he arrived at the scene; he ordered Mr. C's friend to leave the apartment; and he ordered Mr. B to remain in his apartment. At one point the officer used the relayer-mediation approach by transmitting information from Mr. C to Mr. B. Also, at another point he obtained Mr. B's "agreement" (see mediation approaches) not to press charges. However, these points of similarity to other approaches were relatively minor elements compared to the officer's consistent use of authority.

Case Number Two

A tenant called the police because the landlord had boarded up his apartment, in spite of the fact that he had paid his rent. When the officer arrived, he interviewed the complainant outside the house, asking questions to determine exactly what had happened. The tenant showed his rent receipts and a letter from the landlord's lawyer proving that he had the right to remain in his apartment.

The officer then entered the house to speak to the landlord. There was much confusion inside, because several members of the landlord's family were present and no one spoke much English. The officer attempted to communicate through one man who spoke some English, but the man was very excited. A woman then told the officer the name of the person who owned the house, and the officer told the excited man not to interfere. Then, communicating through the woman who had spoken up, the officer tried to obtain the landlord's story. The excited man continued to interfere, and was arrested when he refused to calm down.

After further confusion, the landlord, his wife, and the officer went to an interpreter, who explained the story to the officer. The officer telephoned the landlord's lawyer. The officer informed the landlord (with the lawyer's consent) that he had no right to nail the tenant's door shut, that he could go to court if he wanted to evict the tenant, and that they would all go back to remove the boards from the tenant's apartment. After the boards were removed, the officer ordered everyone to go into the house and left the scene.

Case Number Three

A woman called the police because her estranged husband had taken their infant child after accusing her of having an affair with another man. The officer arrived at the woman's house, asked her for her story, and drove her to find the husband. After finding the man, the officer obtained his story and told him that the wife had a right to the child, and that he could be arrested for taking the infant. The officer then left with the wife and child.

Explanation. This is a case of using authority because immediately after interviewing the parties the officer imposed a solution ("Your wife will leave with this child").

2. *Negotiation.* The officer encourages the parties to reach an agreement by focusing on the issues in dispute. Without stressing authority, the officer makes suggestions or offers advice. S/he may act in a more passive capacity, allowing the disputants to negotiate a settlement, stepping in only to act as a referee: "Don't shout," "No fighting." The officer may assist one or both parties in communicating with each other, especially in cases where the officer has had to physically separate the persons. Bard and Zacker (1976: 55–56) provide some examples:

THE NEGOTIATION APPROACH

Case Number One

This dispute occurred between a brother and sister, Bill and Ethel. Ethel was having a big family party. During the party, Bill, who was drunk, urinated on the floor. Ethel became upset and took away his car keys. Bill then called the police.

By the time the officers arrived, Bill had disappeared. The officers finally found him in a local bar, and took him back to Ethel's house. After hearing both sides of the story, one officer suggested that Bill go home. Bill agreed to do so if he got the car keys back. The officer suggested to Ethel that she return the keys to Bill the next day if he agreed to go home immediately. Ethel agreed. The officer went back to Bill and told him that Ethel would return the keys on the following day. Bill agreed to this solution and the officers drove him home.

Case Number Two

A woman called the police because her neighbors were making too much noise.

The officer knew the woman to be oversensitive to noise, but he also noted that the upstairs tenants were playing their music very loudly. He went to the complainant's home to ask her what the problem was. He explained that people had a right to make noise in their own homes, that she should leave them alone, but that he would ask them to be a little quieter. He then went upstairs and informed the neighbors of the complaint. They complained about the woman downstairs. The officer sympathized but said they were being a bit too loud. He told them that the woman might be less bothersome if they did turn down the music. They agreed to do this, and the officer left.

3. *Counseling.* In this response the officer treats all disputants as persons who have an underlying problem about which they are unaware. S/he attempts to elicit information to help disputants gain a better understanding of the problem. The goal is to get them to handle the problem with better judgment. The officer may give advice and/or remind the parties of their responsibilities. Bard and Zacher (1976: 56–58) provide examples:

THE COUNSELING APPROACH

Case Number One

A mother felt that her common-law husband was too intoxicated to take their young daughter out for the evening. She called the police and asked them to remove her husband from the apartment, which was in her name.

The officer, having had previous contact with the parties, greeted them and the child in a friendly manner. He pointed out to the parents the unfairness of subjecting their daughter to a scene with police intervention. He told the parents that it was their obligation to the child to assume parental responsibilities and to manage their disagreements in ways so that police intervention would be unnecessary. The officer said that if they were unable to do so, they should consider separation. He brought to their attention the troubled history of their relationship and the necessity of taking constructive steps, either to strengthen their relationship or to terminate it. As a short-term solution, the officer persuaded the father to leave for the evening.

Explanation. In this case, the officer focused consistently upon the familial relationship. He attempted to increase the parents' ability to recognize the impact of police intervention on their child, and reminded them that it was their responsibility to prevent such intervention. He exhorted them to use their judgment to review and take constructive steps regarding their relationship.

Case Number Two

The conflict involved a middle-aged man and his wife. They had been married only a short while and were planning to separate. The wife had apparently been drinking. This upset her husband and he threatened to cut her throat. The wife called the police.

When the officers arrived, the husband seemed surprised that his wife had called the police, but he politely invited them in. He called his wife, who explained her story to the police. The husband then told his side of the story.

The officer suggested that since they were going to separate shortly anyway, perhaps it would be best if they could end their time together peacefully. He said that since their arguments seemed to lead to violence, they should try to stay away from one another if they felt the situation was getting tense—perhaps one of them could leave the house for a while, or they could stay in separate rooms.

At the officers' suggestion, the couple agreed to sleep in separate rooms. By this time, they were talking calmly to each other. The officers left.

Case Number Three

A married couple argued over the husband's drinking. When the wife told the officer that her husband was drunk, the officer replied that he was not, and that the officer would not remove him from the house. The wife left, and the officer asked to hear what the husband had to say. The man said the real problem was their sex life. The man said that he was working so hard to make money that he couldn't satisfy his wife in other ways. The officer suggested that the best thing would be to talk to each other to try to save their relationship.

Case Number Four

A woman called the police after her husband had been drinking and had accused her of having another man.

The officer introduced himself and, leaving the assisting officer with the husband, asked the wife to calm down, sit down, and tell him what had happened. He then called the husband into the room and asked them both how long they had been married, if they had been happy during that time, and why they could not communicate with each other. Then he brought in their three-year-old son and reminded them how important he was and how bad it was to have him see the police in their home. The officer reminded them of how different it must have been when they first met, how in love they were then, and how they never argued. He asked if the husband thought he needed Alcoholics Anonymous, to which both replied that he did not really have a drinking problem. The officer then explained that their problems were not serious enough to be fighting over. The couple apologized to each other, and the officer left after giving the child a piece of candy.

Case Number Five

A married couple had an argument resulting in the wife's nose being broken by her husband.

The officer asked the wife for her story, if she wanted her husband arrested, if she loved her husband, and where he could find the husband. After locating the husband, the officer informed him that his wife was in pain, and asked him if he loved his wife and what had happened. He then brought the two together and asked them to talk and apologize to each other. He reminded them that their child would never forget incidents like the present one, and suggested that if one spouse began to argue the other should remember her or his responsibilities and leave. He said that if they both acted like children there would be no one to govern their child. Reminding them that they were lucky this time—the husband had had no charges brought against him; the wife had only a broken nose—the officer left.

There are many observers who would be troubled by the exercise of police discretion in the last incident. A woman had been assaulted and her nose broken. The officer had knowledge of a violation of the law resulting in serious bodily injury, and he located the offender; there was probable cause for a lawful arrest. (In cases involving misdemeanor assaults, only 16 jurisdictions permit an officer to make an arrest when s/he did not witness the attack. McLeod, 1983: 398). But, the victim did not insist on an arrest, although she did call the police. Joseph Goldstein (1960) argues that to place the decision to arrest in the hands of the victim undermines the deterrent effect of the law and may also encourage private revenge. A study by the Police Foundation (Sherman and Berk, n.d. [1983?] questions the wisdom of the non-arrest approach to domestic violence.

Throughout the 1960s and early 1970s an ever-increasing number of police departments were training their officers in family crisis intervention. Some departments provide officers with a list of social agencies and direct them to leave referral information with the disputants (Hanewicz, et al., 1982).* In more elaborate programatic responses, the officer makes the referral and the police department, in conjunction with social workers, conducts a follow-up. By the mid-1970s, however, feminists began to argue against this police emphasis on "social work" and in favor of the enforcement of laws against *battery* even in domestic situations.†

The Police Foundation (Sherman and Berk, n.d.) was interested in testing the police practice of avoiding arrests in cases of domestic violence. With the cooperation of the Minneapolis Police Department, calls for service involving domestic violence (limited to cases of simple/misdemeanor assault) were systematically assigned a response:

(a) arrest (43% of those arrested were released within one day; another 43% were released within one week);
(b) advice/counseling;
(c) mediation and order the suspect to leave for eight hours.

Sherman and Berk report (n.d.: 2):

The behavior of the suspect was tracked for six months after the police intervention, with a variety of measures. Preliminary analysis of the official recidivism measures suggests that the arrested suspects manifested significantly less violence than those who were ordered to leave, and less violence than those who were advised but not separated.

---

*Goldstein (1979: 251) cautions against using this approach, fearing that the referral will become an end in itself, and "the police and others advocating the use of such a system will not concern themselves adequately with the consequences of referral. If referral does not lead to reducing the citizens' problem, nothing will have been gained by this ... It may even cause harm: Expectations that are raised and not fulfilled may lead to further frustration; the original problem may, as a consequence, be compounded; and the resulting bitterness about government services may feed the tensions that develop in urban areas."

†The New York City Police Department, in an experimental program, trained police officers in the use of mediation. However, Goldstein notes (1979: 246–47), the department failed to distinguish sufficiently those cases in which wives were repeatedly subjected to physical abuse. As a result, a lawsuit was instituted in which it was argued that the police are *mandated* to enforce the law when *any* violation comes to their attention. While the latter is a questionable legal assertion, the police department agreed that its personnel would no longer try to reconcile the parties or to mediate when a felony was committed.

POLICE DISCRETION: "STOP AND FRISK"

It is a common practice, usually empowered by statute, for the police to stop persons whose behavior is suspicious and to detain them briefly (e.g., not more than twenty minutes) for questioning and identification. The *Illinois Criminal Law and Procedure* (38: 107–14), for example, provides for "Temporary Questioning without Arrest":

> A peace officer, after having identified himself as a peace officer, may stop any person in a public place for a reasonable period of time when the officer reasonably infers from the circumstances that the person is committing, is about to commit or has committed an offense as defined in . . . this Code, and may demand the name and address of the person and an explanation of his actions.

This stop is based on "suspicion," not probable cause, and, thus, does not legally amount to an arrest. Furthermore, the Illinois code, supported by the U.S. Supreme Court in *Terry v. Ohio* (394 U.S. 1, 1968), provides for a "Search During Temporary Questioning" (38: 108–1.01): "When a peace officer has stopped a person for temporary questioning . . . and reasonably suspects that he or another is in danger of attack, he may search the person for weapons"—a frisk.

The police authority to "stop and frisk" is filled with discretion. "Who" becomes defined as "suspicious" is a matter of the police officer's judgment. It is usually a decision of low-visibility that will not come to the attention of anyone beyond the officer and the person stopped (unless it leads to an arrest). It is not difficult to imagine that certain persons are more likely to be subjected to police intrusion, regardless of their actions. A 1983 case that reached the U.S. Supreme Court provides an example.*

Edward Lawson, a young black male with unconventional hair (long braids) and clothes (white flowing robe) was stopped by the police in California at least fifteen times during a thirty-month period. He was also convicted of "disorderly conduct" for being in violation of a California statute that made it a crime "to loiter or wander upon the streets or from place to place without apparent reason or business," and for a person to refuse to "identify himself and to account for his presence when requested" by the police. The suspicious behavior on the part of Lawson was walking in mostly white neighborhoods at night or early in the morning. The California law was

---

*Kolender u Lawson, 103 S.Ct. 1855, 33 CrL 3063 (May 2, 1983). In a 7-2 decision, the Court struck down that part of a California statute that required a person "to identify himself and account for his presence" because it "vests virtually complete discretion in the hands of the police to determine whether the subject has satisfied the statute."

declared unconstitutional, but the issue of "stop and frisk" discretion remains.*

DISCRETION AND SPECIAL CASES: JUVENILES AND MENTALLY ILL

The police deal with a great many non-criminal tasks, and some involve the problems of persons with a special status. Juveniles (usually persons under 16 or 17), by virtue of their age, and the mentally ill, by virtue of their incompetence, present the police with special problems of discretion. Juveniles may be taken into custody by the police if they are found on the street or in a public place in need of medical or other type of treatment or care. This does not constitute an arrest and, thus, does not require probable cause. Juveniles can be taken into custody for behavior that does not constitute a violation of the criminal law; for being

   (a) beyond the control of parents or guardians;
   (b) habitually truant from school;
   (c) addicted to drugs;
   (d) neglected or abused.

The police respond to the behavior of juveniles, criminal or otherwise, differentially; that is, in some instances they may arrest, or take into custody and refer to parents or a social agency, or reprimand and warn, or totally disregard the behavior: "kid stuff." The response of an officer will depend on how he/she perceives the behavior and the particular youngster, and the policy of the police department. There is often a special juvenile unit and Aaron Cicourel notes (1976: 190):

> Many juvenile activities that might go unnoticed or regarded as "minor" pranks will not be so viewed by the juvenile officers ... because ... [the juvenile may fit] their conception of the potential delinquent, and they will seek him out whenever there is reported "trouble" in his neighborhood. Routine juvenile activities, therefore, can be turned into serious "delinquent acts."

---

*The police may use a variety of techniques to avoid the appearance of a "stop" and interrogation. Christopher Gaffney (1981: 173–74) reports that his patrol partner spotted someone who appeared "suspicious." The officer pulled the squad car over to the curb and asked: "Did you hear anything that sounded like a traffic accident around here?

"The man replies he has not, and Jerry asks if he would mind giving us his name and address so we can list it in our report. He would be helping us document that we were in the area and found nothing. The young man is glad to find us being friendly and seems happy to be in a position where he can do us a favor. He gives us the information, and Jerry draws him into further conversation about what a nice evening it is. Before long, the man volunteers his reason for being out and about at this hour."

Edwin Schur (1973: 120) cautions against an overreaction to juvenile
misconduct, lest we set in motion a complex process "of response and
counter-response beginning with an initial act of rule violation and developing into elaborated deliquent selfconceptions and a full-fledged delinquent
career." Items such as "attitude" or the "middle-classness" of the youngster
and the officer's perception of the parents and the home environment will
impact on the exercise of discretion, usually in all but the most serious
felony cases. (The juvenile justice system is discussed in Chapter 6).

The *mentally ill* have become an increasingly difficult police problem.
Changes in mental health theory resulted in the release of large numbers of
patients from fortress-type state hospitals to community-based treatment
programs. In theory, psychotropic drugs and a variety of public and private
support systems in the community would provide better service and at a
lower cost. In practice, many patients were "dumped" into a community
where helping resources are scarce or inadequate, amidst a public that is
frightened by "crazy" persons. Budgetary problems experienced by state and
local governments have reduced the level of mental health funding, increasing the police problem. The police are often the only emergency service
ready and available to deal with mentally ill persons. How the police
respond is a matter of state law, available resources, and the amount of
training and skill of individual officers.

While there are a very small number of mentally ill persons who present
a danger to others, many are so passive and withdrawn that they cannot care
for themselves adequately. They may become a source of public nuisance or
embarassment. When their need for care is mixed with a violation of the law,
anything from disorderly conduct to battery, the officer must decide—a
discretionary decision—to arrest or detain for treatment. A decision in favor
of treatment means the officer must find a mental health facility available
and willing to accept the offender as patient. This can be a time-consuming,
if not frustrating, experience.* When the officer is successful, the patient
may be confined for only a short time and returned to the streets as part of
continuing police problem. Two police departments, San Francisco and Los
Angeles, have special police support units for cases of mental illness, while

---

*Egon Bittner points out that "officers complain that taking someone to the psychiatric service of the
hospital is a tedious, cumbersome, and uncertain procedure. They must often wait a long time in the
admitting office and are occasionally obliged to answer questions of the admitting psychiatrist that appear
to place their own judgment in doubt. They must also reckon with the possibility of being turned down by
the psychiatrist, in which case they are left with an aggravated problem on their hands. The complaints
about the hospital must be understood in the light of a strong and widely respected rule of police
procedure. The rule demands that an officer bring all cases assigned to him to some sort of closure within
reasonable limits of time and effort. The ability to take care of things in a way that avoids protracted and
complicated entanglements and does not cause reprecussions is, in fact, a sign of accomplished craftmanship
in police work that runs a close second to the ability to make important arrests" (1967: 164–65).

other departments have responded by increasing training and arranging for better liason with mental health agencies (Taft, 1980).

There is another case of special status that can be confusing and troublesome to police departments whose jurisdiction contains persons with *diplomatic immunity*. These are representatives of foreign governments that have total or limited immunity from arrest detention, or prosecution for any criminal offense. There are about 48,000 such persons in the United States. They may be:

(a) United Nations Secretariat Officers and their families who must be extended full criminal immunity.
(b) United Nations Mission Officers who are entitled to immunity only when acting in their official capacity.
(c) Diplomats and their families who must be extended full criminal immunity.
(d) Service staff of the U.N. Secretariat or Missions or Counselor Officers who have limited immunity.

Discretionary judgments can occur when, for example, a diplomat is stopped for driving under the influence of drugs or alcohol. For information about diplomatic immunity, contact the United States Department of State, Office of Protocol, Washington, D.C. 20520; telephone (202) 632-7984.

OTHER SPECIAL CASES: GAMBLING AND INTOXICATED DRIVING

There are cases in which a violation of the criminal law occurs, but the violators are not routinely perceived (by police and public) as *criminals*. Noncommercial *gambling* does not usually result in police attention, although it violates the law in most states. A dice or card game in a private residence will be routinely ignored by the police unless there is evidence of a "house cut," something which transforms the nature of the game from "social" to "commercial." The police may experience some difficulty distinguishing between social and commercial gambling and, on such occasions, may take each member of the group aside and ask them to identify all of the other players (LaFave, 1965: 90). Although state law usually does not distinguish between the two types of gambling, police discretion in such cases may be implicit. As Davis notes (1963: 87): "legislation has long been written in reliance on the expectation that law enforcement officers will correct its excesses. . . ."

"Intoxicated Driving" (ID) or "Driving Under the Influence" (DUI) or "Driving While Intoxicated" (DWI) are some of the ways in which statutes refer to the prohibition against operating a motor vehicle while impaired by alcohol or other intoxicating substance. "Impaired" usually refers to a blood

alcohol level of at least .10 as measured by a "breathalyzer" or blood test.*
The impaired driver accounts for a substantial number of fatal accidents and
there has been increasing concern over this "crime" problem. There are
some indications, however, that increasing the penalties for this offense
reduces the inclination of the police, prosecutors and judges to fully impose
the law. Thus, increasing sanctions may also increase the use of discretionary powers which undermines the legislative intent.

The important elements of police discretion in cases of impaired driving
are contained in a *New York Times* story (Margolick, 1983: 13) It concerned
the actions of two police officers in the small Massachusetts town of Ware,
population 9,500 (details not contained in the story were added by the writer
and are fiction).

At 1:50 A.M., on Sunday, May 14, 1978, two Ware police officers observed
a vehicle driving erratically on a lonely country road and they pulled the
vehicle over. The driver, Donald Fuller, stated that he had just left the Cue
and Cushion Lounge and was on his way home. He admitted to "a couple of
beers" and was polite to the officers. The officers considered several options:

(a) Detain Mr. Fuller for a roadside sobriety test and possible breathalyzer
examination at the county headquarters of the state police. The Ware police
force had only four officers in two patrol units on duty. The arrest of Mr. Fuller
would pull half of the force out of service, probably for the rest of the tour.

(b) Require Mr. Fuller to leave his vehicle and drive him home or to a
telephone to call for a cab or a friend to drive him home. The officers would
take away his car keys to insure that he did not try to drive home again.
Fuller had only a short distance to drive and the officers received a service
call from the police dispatcher.

"Go home and drive carefully," the officers told him. At 2:10 A.M., Mark
and Debbie Irwin, their three-year-old son Steven and 20-month-old daughter Jane, were driving on Route 32 when an automobile careened around a
curve and rammed into their car. When Mrs. Irwin regained consciousness,
she had four broken ribs, a fractured left arm and a punctured lung. Steven
had a fractured skull. Mark and Jane were dead, as was Mr. Fuller. A blood
test revealed Mr. Fuller's blood alcohol level to be twice the amount necessary to make him legally intoxicated.

When and how should police discretion be controlled? In the case before
us hindsight makes it easier to evaluate the actions of the officers. What if
Mr. Fuller returned home safely? In policing, limitations on discretion must
be implemented in advance of police activity. The actions of police officers
and the limitations placed on their discretionary judgments must enhance
the goals and objectives of policing discussed in the first chapter.

---

*This means that it is usually illegal to drive if the alcohol level in the driver's blood reaches one-tenth of
1 percent, the equivalent of about three martinis.

DISCRETION AND CRIMINAL INVESTIGATION

"Traditionally, prevention of crime is assumed to be the primary function of the general service police department, and patrol is assumed to be the fundamental unit for obtaining that objective. Most departments will, therefore, establish a patrol division as the basic and principal line unit of the department, containing most of its manpower. The other nearly indispensible line unit of the department will be the criminal investigation or detective division" (J. Wilson, 1975: 136). Jerry Wilson (1975: 137) points out that the line of responsibility between patrol and investigation, between patrol officers and detectives, often is overlapping. In general, however, patrol has first response responsibility and detectives conduct any follow-up investigation that may be required, particularly when the crime is serious, e.g., burglary, robbery, rape, murder.

Arthur Niederhoffer (1969: 82) notes that the public accords great respect and prestige to the detective, far more than it grants to the uniformed beat patrolman. Goldstein questions the basis for this phenomenon, seeing it as part of the myth and fantasy that surround detectives and criminal investigations (1977: 56): "a considerable amount of detective work is actually undertaken on a hit-or-miss basis; and that the capacity of detectives to solve crimes is greatly exaggerated."

Investigative (detective or "plainclothes") units may be organized on a decentralized basis, with each detective a generalist responsible for investigations in a specific geographic area. Or, investigative units may operate out of a central headquarters. Some departments have both decentralized and centralized units, the latter usually being specialized units such as homocide, sex crimes, burglary, robbery, auto theft, property crimes and vice or organized crime units specializing in gambling, prostitution and drugs. Vice units are involved, almost exclusively, in proactive policing using undercover techniques and informers. The use of informers will be discussed later.

The Investigative Process (Greenberg and Wasserman, 1979: 17–20). The process begins when a patrol officer responds to the scene of a crime. S/he is responsible for assisting the victim(s), conducting a preliminary investigation, and determining the location of any witnesses. The patrol officer must secure the crime scene and decide if evidence technicians are required. Because the patrol officer is expected to return to patrol ("back in service") as quickly as possible, the preliminary investigation usually involves only basic information: the crime scene, the victim(s), suspects and witnesses, if any. This information is turned over to the investigative division.

As noted above, the patrol officer exercises discretion over the need for evidence technicians. In addition, the manner in which s/he writes up the preliminary investigation can influence the investigator's response to the case. For example, a patrol officer responding to a complaint of a rape reports the incident as a "possible rape," thereby putting the complainant under a cloud of suspicion (Sanders, 1977: 86). The patrol officer responding to a complaint of kidnap and robbery writes in the preliminary investigation report that the complainant's story is an unlikely one.

The preliminary report or incident report is screened and distributed to the appropriate investigative unit. Within each unit a case is assigned on the basis of geography, or current caseload, or the investigator's area of specialization. After the assignment is made, a major area of discretion unfolds. Investigators evaluate each case: "Every morning when I got to the office, the detectives would be going through the morning's batch of reports. They sat around reading and commenting on them trying to decide which ones should be worked and which ones shouldn't" (Sanders, 1977: 77). The case must be *real:* phony cases are rejected as when a married woman claimed rape to cover a marriage infidelity. The investigator will determine the *worth* of a case. In doing this s/he will reach beyond the penal code violations indicated in the report. For example, an "attempted murder" may be logged as a "disturbing the peace" when it involves a husband and wife quarrel—"nothing but a glorified domestic" (Sanders, 1977: 84).

Donald Cawley (Greenberg and Wasserman, 1979: 18) notes that each detective informally sorts his/her cases into two categories: "(1) those which are worth pursuing because information and leads are alive and likely to lead to solution and (2) those which will never be solved on the basis of information available (and on the basis of experience gained in attempting to track down similar cases in the past)."

During the follow-up investigation phase, the investigator is likely to exercise discretion by classifying each of his/her cases into one of three priorities:

(1) Suspect has been identified, witnesses remain to be interviewed, or there are strong leads (e.g., a license plate number of perpetrator's car).

(2) Case is serious enough to warrant attention even in the absence of concrete leads. The victim may be re-interviewed, or the crime scene may be searched again for evidence, and new witnesses sought.

(3) Case is routine and there are no obvious leads. It may be checked against other cases in the files, but little action will be taken unless new evidence is discovered.

When the suspect is in custody (as a result of patrol response or the investigator identifies, locates and arrests him/her), the investigator will interview him/her and may arrange for lineups in cases where the suspect may have been seen by the victim and/or witnesses. The investigator will also testify in court if the case goes to trial.

In Inglewood, California "criminal cases which came to the investigative division were read by an investigative supervisor who then assigned these cases throughout the section by crime (such as burglary, robbery, forgery, auto theft, and so forth)" (Powell, et al., 1980: 54). This system has deficiencies as noted by Craig Powell Powell, Bruce Hoberg, and Lyle Knowles (1980: 55):

> These practices often led to particular investigators carrying a very high caseload, frequently including numerous unsolvable cases. This unevenly distributed workload continually created morale problems. After cases were assigned, detectives were given little, if any, direct supervision, unless they were dealing with matters of extreme departmental or community concern. All decisions made about procedures and time periods regarding investigations were left to the discretion of the individual investigator.

There are other deficiencies. Bernard Greenberg (et al., 1977: xx) notes that "a large number of [serious felony] cases essentially 'solve themselves.' " James Q. Wilson (1978: 17) reports:

> A substantial body of evidence gathered in many different cities strongly suggests that investigators actually account for only a small portion of the arrests of even the most serious criminals and that even these few are caught not because of the detectives' skill at logical inference, scientific inquiry, or investigative techniques, but because a victim or witness has already supplied a positive identification of the suspect.

Greenberg (et al., 1977: xx) adds: "unless relevant information had been attained at the crime scene by the responding [patrol] officer, if the offender had not been apprehended, the chances of the case being solved at the detective level were minimal."

In response to these deficiencies the Inglewood Police Department, and many other departments, instituted the MCI program.

MANAGING CRIMINAL INVESTIGATIONS (MCI)

In 1975 the Rand Corporation published a report (Greenwood, Chaiken, and Petersilla, 1975) which stated that the patrol officer is the key figure in solving crimes. The report noted that more than half of all serious crimes reported to the police receive no more than superficial attention from investigators. The report stated that investigators spend more time on paperwork than on identifying perpetrators. It recommended an increased role for the patrol officer and the use of a managerial system that graded cases according to their "solvability." Cases with a low grade would be inactivated immediately, conserving investigative resources for cases that are more likely to be solved.

Under this system it is the responsibility of the patrol officer to:

(a) locate and interview the victim and witnesses;
(b) detect physical evidence, e.g., fingerprints, toolmarks; and
(c) prepare an initial investigative report "that will guide the initial investigators and provide sufficient documentation of effort to determine whether a case should be assigned for continuation or immediately suspended for lack of evidence" (Greenberg and Wasserman, 1979: 21). In some programs the patrol officer may also make a recommendation that the case be closed or continued.

The case screening process (which determines if a case is to be continued or closed) involves "solvability factors." These are given numerical weights whose total determines what will happen to a case. In one city a score above 6 is required and each investigative item is scored from 0–4:

Event Report

						Points
N	P	F	G	E*	Is there a witness?	4
N	P	F	G	E	Is a suspect named?	0
N	P	F	G	E	Is a suspect known?	0
N	P	F	G	E	Is a suspect described?	2
N	P	F	G	E	Can a suspect be identified?	0
N	P	F	G	E	Can a suspect vehicle be identified?	0
N	P	F	G	E	Is there a distinguishable M.O.?	0
N	P	F	G	E	Is a pattern present?	0
N	P	F	G	E	Is stolen property traceable?	0
N	P	F	G	E	Is physical evidence present?	0
					Total	6

Screening Decision: *No Follow-Up*

*Code: N–None P–Poor F–Fair G–Good E–Excellent

Greenberg, et al. (1977: xxv) present the scoring in cases of robbery:

Information Element	Weighting Factor
Suspect named	10*
Suspect known	10*
Suspect previously seen	10*
Evidence technician used	10
Places suspect frequented named	10*
Physical evidence	
Each item matched	6.1

Vehicle registration
   Query information available   1.5
   Vehicle stolen   3.0
   Useful information returned   4.5
   Vehicle registered to suspect   6.0
Offender movement description
   On foot   0
   Vehicle (not car)   0.6
   Car   1.2
   Car color given   1.8
   Car description given   2.4
   Car license given   3.0
   Weapon used   1.6

INSTRUCTIONS
(1) Circle the weighting factor for each information element that is present in the incident report.
(2) Total the circled factors.
(3) If the sum is less than 10, suspend the case; otherwise, follow up the case.
(4) Weighting factors do not accumulate; i.e., if both the auto license and color are given, the total is 3.0 not 4.8.

*These values as calculated actually exceed the threshold of 10. The values provided here are conceptually simpler and make no difference in the classification of groups.

CRIMINAL INFORMANTS

There are many in and out of law enforcement who believe that most investigators are as good as their informants. The "snitch" or "stoolie" can make a detective "who could never have passed an I.Q. test, could hardly write an intelligible report, and whose techniques of investigation constantly violated every recommended principle of scientific investigation" appear brilliant (Niederhoffer, 1969: 84).

The criminal informant (as opposed to the civic-minded citizen informant) must be active in the criminal "underworld" or subculture if he/she is to be effective. This activity is problematic, since in return for cooperation the informant often receives immunity from arrest (LaFave, 1965: 134). LaFave (1965: 135) states that this immunity extends only to crimes with willing "victims," drug addicts, prostitutes: "For this reason burglars or similar offenders are not granted immunity." Jerome Skolnick (1967: 129) states: "In general, *burglary detectives permit informants to commit narcotics offenses,* while narcotics detectives allow informants to steal" (italics in the original). This does not, however, necessarily constitute immunity, since, according to Skolnick, detectives merely overlook crimes committed by their informants when the crime occurs in another detective's organizational jurisdiction/ specialty. The detective, in return for informant cooperation, is in a position to withhold an arrest of the informant when he/she has committed a crime, bring about a reduction of charges or make a recommendation for a lighter sentence (Skolnick, 1967: 137).

Robert Misner and John Clough are critical of the relationship between police officers and their informants as an abuse of discretion (1977: 715):

> Unhampered police discretion is said to be vital to the successful use of informants in law enforcement, but the practice has received too little judicial scrutiny, perhaps because of the underlying assumption that the decision to defer prosecution of informants is only the other side of the decision to prosecute and therefore is within the scope of prosecutorial and police discretion. Evidence persists, however, that little or no systematic check is made on the official's exercise of discretion to divert the arrestee, and informants are often "recruited" in situations suggesting abuse of discretion and coercion.

The authors argue (1977) that the usual relationship between police officers and criminal informants is a violation of the Thirteenth Amendment's prohibition against "involuntary servitude," *peonage,* a status or condition of compulsory service based on the (legal) indebtedness of the informant (peon) to the detective (master).

Skolnick (1967) notes that the detective may also pay his/her informant money which he/she realizes will be used to purchase narcotics. In cases with which the writer is familiar, detectives also paid informants with contraband heroin. Misner and Clough (1977: 745) argue:

> Diversion practices that allow an arrestee to avoid prosecution by becoming an informant are only superficially beneficial to the arrestee and society. The arrestee temporarily avoids confinement through conviction, but as an undercover informant in the narcotics area he is often subjected to serious physical danger and further exposure to drugs that may lead to conviction on new charges.

Joseph Goldstein (1960) argues that statutes do not empower the police to grant partial or total immunity in exchange for information or cooperation; it is a power they have assumed. He questions whether this assumption of discretionary powers is consistant with legislative intent. If the intention of legislative bodies in passing these laws is to prevent the use of controlled substances because they are harmful to their users, the narcotic informant system clearly violates this intent. Indeed, the cooperation of addict-informers is often based on an attempt to prosecute non-addict drug traffickers. Drug addict informants are allowed, often abetted, to continue their abuse of controlled substances in order to help in actions against those who (sell but) do not use drugs. Unfortunately, as most drug enforcement investigators are quick to point out, this system is the only one that they are able to use with any degree of success.

CONTROL OF DISCRETION

The police chief executive exercises discretion by setting priorities for a department whose jurisdiction usually contains diverse elements (Garmire, 1977: 27):

> The political process within each community obviously varies with local priorities and needs. Even in the smallest communities, economic and social variables produce varying service expectations. . . .

> Municipalities, communities, and even neighborhoods do not agree on what police priorities should be. Just as many communities have experienced major disagreements about school location, school curricula, provision of welfare benefits, or protection of housing patterns, so there have been major disagreements about what the police should be doing and how it should be done.

Bernard Garmire (1977: 28) notes that decreasing governmental resources have accompanied increased demands for police services, but "Few police agencies have established a mechanism for assigning priorities to the various aspects of their function. And those agencies which have considered priorities have rarely seen priority setting as being a matter for public discussion." Garmire argues that the wide discretionary powers of the police chief should be mediated by public involvement and input into the setting of priorities, and joint discussions with the mayor or city manager.

Garmire (1977: 29) notes:

> The detrimental influence of partisan politics exerted historically on many police agencies, and also the development of the "professional" model of an independent police, have caused many chief municipal executives to maintain a stance of noninvolvement in police matters.

Attempts by a mayor to deal with concerns expressed about police operations may be viewed as "interference" by a police chief. Garmire cautions against a police chief confusing proper executive accountability with political interference. Only a municipal chief executive (in some jurisdictions in conjunction with a police board/commission) can provide meaningful control over the exercise of discretion by a police chief executive. (Many of the police chief's discretionary powers may be limited by police unions and labor agreements. Promotions may be limited by a civil service or merit board outside of the chief's control, and even minimum training requirements may be mandated by state law or a state police training council/board).

In the first chapter we noted that discretion can be subjected to some control by:

1. statutes
2. administrative policy/rules
3. supervisory controls

Statutes, however, can only limit, not actually control, police discretion. For example, by decriminalizing certain activities heretofore illegal, e.g., possession of small amounts of marijuana for personal use, the police are removed from involvement in this matter. A statute can prohibit the police from using deadly force (a firearm) against certain fleeing criminal suspects, limiting discretionary powers. Davis (1969) advocates tailoring criminal statutes along practical lines, making them enforceable. He also wants legislative bodies to clarify those powers enjoyed by the police and those that are withheld from them, for example, with respect to informants.

The American Bar Association Advisory Committee on the Police Function (ABA) argues (1973: 125):

> If the exercise of governmental authority is to be subjected to appropriate controls and if the citizenry, local governments, and even police administrators are to have an opportunity to influence police practices, it is clear that a much greater degree of structure and control must be introduced into the whole area of discretionary decision-making on the part of police personnel.

The ABA committee advises (1973: 125):

> Police discretion can best be structured and controlled through the process of administrative rule-making by police agencies. Police administrators should, therefore, give the highest priority to the formulation of administrative rules governing the exercise of discretion, particularly in the areas of selective enforcement, investigative techniques, and enforcement methods.

Davis (1969; 1974) emphasizes the need for administrative rule-making in whose absence many legal practices are apt to be created by personnel with limited education at the bottom of the organization hierarchy. He is supported by Joseph Goldstein (1963) and the President's Commission on Law Enforcement and Administration of Justice (1968: 267):

> Police departments should develop and enunciate policies that give police personnel specific guidance for the common situations requiring the exercise of police discretion. Policies should cover such matters, among others, as the issuance of orders to citizens regarding their movements or activities, the handling of minor disputes, the safeguarding of the rights of free speech and free assembly, the selection and use of investigative methods, and the decision whether or not to arrest in specific situations involving specific crimes.

Fred A. Wileman (1976: 50) points out that the development of comprehensive police policy will shift the focus of "incidents" to questions of policy rather than individual acts of police officers. Was there a violation of policy: "yes," "no." If "no," meaning the officer conformed to policy, then the debate moves from the totally emotional arena surrounding the incident toward a consistant approach in a continuing dialogue on what the agency *ought* to be doing as a matter of policy. He notes that comprehensive policy development will also result in greater consistancy of officer supervision: "The focus of supervision can be on policy and conformance to it, rather than on isolated acts or monthly arrest totals." This also permits the agency to change policies and methods in a logical and orderly fashion. Instead of an often chaotic approach, amending existing policy that has been developed in a comprehensive manner, can be accomplished in a way that is reasoned and organized.

Perhaps the most compelling argument for comprehensive policy development is that it promotes consistency and allows policy to be effectively transferred to new officers (Wileman, 1976: 51):

> No longer would an agency have to depend solely upon veterans telling recruits "how we do it out here"; instead, the veteran can show the recruit policy in action. If comprehensive policy is made a major part of the recruit training curriculum, what is learned in the academy will began to be much more consistent with what is happening in the field.

The Texas Criminal Justice Council (1974: 176) in conjunction with the International Association of Chiefs of Police developed a set of *Model Rules for Law Enforcement Officers* which candidly states: "An officer is not obliged to make an arrest in every instance," notwithstanding the existence of probable cause. The model rules (1974: 178) are explicit about non-enforcement policies, but include stringent requirements for such policy: "Where it has been determined that certain criminal laws shall not be enforced, the officer shall not arrest for those offenses. This determination should be made only through an established administrative rule-making procedure which provides for citizen participation and judicial review." The rules require that an officer (1974: 177) "be able to articulate the reason(s) for his failure to arrest a particular offender." Albert Reiss does not consider this sufficient (1971: 205): "Police officers should be required to make an official record of *any* contact with a citizen when the encounter is terminated, whether or not an arrest is made." Reiss suggests that this could be accomplished in the form of "warning citation," similar to a traffic ticket, giving one copy to the civilian and a copy to the department. LaFave (1965: 154) notes, however, that officers are loath to file any report unless an arrest is made even in departments where a record is made of all complaints to which an officer has been dispatched. He states (1965: 155): "There is even less probability of a report being made when the officer observes the offense and decides not to make an arrest." Rules requiring a report in such non-arrest cases are often ineffective (LaFave, 1965) or may be dependent on supervisory controls.

Davis (1969: 143) believes that the most important control over discretionary actions is probably supervision by superior officers; "sufficient supervision can be a good protection against arbitrary exercise of discretion." The knowledge that one's behavior will be observed by others exerts a form of control over that behavior. When the possible observer or (after the fact) reviewer is a superior officer, the control exerted will be enhanced. Rubinstein notes (1973: 33): "Although his badge has the city's name embossed on it, the patrolman's real employers are his sergeant and lieutenant." However, Rubinstein (1973: 450) points out that there are real limitations on the ability of superior officers to exert control over patrol officers: "Perhaps supervisors would like to have the authority people attribute to their rank, but they do not."

There is a natural reluctance on the part of police departments to develop comprehensive policy and the accompanying rules. Some police practices are at variance with statutory law, such as granting immunity to informants or not enforcing gambling laws in the absence of commercial aspects. Other police practices such as the arrest of prostitutes and "undesirables" for disorderly conduct may amount to harassment, an illegal practice. Police policy governing selective enforcement can also provide an offender with a ready legal defense in the event of an arrest that is contrary to police (stated) policy. This can have the effect of nullifying legislative enactments and are, thus, a source of potential embarrassment.

REVIEW QUESTIONS FOR CHAPTER 2

1. Why can much of the earlier history of policing in America be characterized as "unsavory?"
2. What led to the development of state police forces?
3. What is the difference between reactive and proactive policing?
4. What types/classes of crime require proactive policing?
5. What is the essential difference between the way a police force is organized and its personnel operate and the military?
6. What is the most important discretionary power of a police chief executive?
7. What are the four (4) primary goals of the police?
8. Why are the police severely limited in their ability to reach their goals?
9. Why are the crime statistics provided by the FBI in their Uniform Crime Reports (UCR) of limited use in evaluating a police department?
10. What is the advantage of a police chief stressing traffic enforcement?

11. What is meant by police harassment?
12. What are the three (3) styles of policing referred to by James Q. Wilson?
13. What are the three basic approaches the police may use in responding to domestic disturbance calls/situations?
14. What is the problem with the common police practice of not making an arrest in cases of domestic violence?
15. What is the level of evidence required for a peace officer to "stop and frisk?"
16. What are the special problems inherent in dealing with special status cases such as juveniles or the mentally ill?
17. What is the danger of the police overreacting to juvenile misconduct?
18. What discretion can be exercised in "social" gambling and intoxicated driving cases?
19. What are the elements of discretion for a patrol officer's involvement in criminal investigation?
20. What are the elements of discretion for a criminal investigator/detective?
21. What is the MCI (Managing Criminal Investigations) program?
22. What are the problems of discretion inherent in the use of criminal informants?
23. How can the relationship between a criminal informant and a police officer be considered "peonage?"
24. What is the most effective way of controlling police discretion? Why?
25. Why would a police chief be reluctant to publish comprehensive policy and rules governing his/her department?

CHAPTER 3

LAWS, LAWYERS, AND DISCRETION

HISTORICAL OVERVIEW

In this segment of criminal justice lawyers are central to all of the important tasks that are accomplished. Before looking at the role of defense counsel, prosecutor and judge, we will review legal education and the practice of law in the United States.

Prior to the twentieth century a law degree only required an (undergraduate) education of three years. In 1850 there were only 15 law schools in the United States. This increased to 31 by 1870 and 61 by 1890. However, most lawyers did not graduate from law school (e.g., Abraham Lincoln) and admission to the practice of law had few requirements into the twentieth century (Mayer, 1969). In 1870, Christopher Columbus Langdell was appointed professor and then dean of the law school at Harvard University. Langdell revolutionized legal education by introducing the "case method."

By reading and analyzing appellate-court opinions the law student learns how to spot similar issues in factually different situations and gains an understanding of judicial thinking (Margolick, 1983: 22):

> [Langdell] argued that the law was a science that could be reduced to a finite number of principles embedded in court decisions. Speculation into jurisprudence and other, loftier disciplines [e.g., sociology, political science] was banished from Dean Langdell's world. Cases, he maintained, were the lawyers' specimens, and law libraries were for them what 'laboratories ... are to the chemists and physicists, the museum of natural history to the zoologists, the botanical garden to the botanists.'

Martin Mayer (1969: 86) refers to this as the Socratic method: "By presenting several cases with substantially different facts all resolved by judges on the basis of a similar *ratio decidendi* (reason for the decision), Langdell would force the aspiring to see what was and was not legally relevant."

By 1910 there were 124 law schools using the Langdell method. Under Langdell's leadership at Harvard, legal education now required a(n undergraduate) college degree before entry into law school. The case method and higher requirements for a legal education raised the status of the legal profession and coincided with the rise of bar associations. The lawyer as scientist was set apart from lay persons and there was now justification for a monopoly on the practice of law which the bar associations were successful in bringing about. Admission standards to the practice of law were raised and the cost of "justice" increased accordingly. For the vast numbers of poor persons securing legal services was made difficult if not impossible. On the other hand, the lawyer scientist in the early decades of the twentieth century received substantial fees by advising and representing corporate clients.

Waves of immigrants flocked to American shores in the first two decades of the twentieth century. The need for legal services amongst the urban masses and the desire among the ambitious sons of immigrants for a legal education resulted in the growth of "local" law schools, including many night law schools for working students. Instead of the case method, these schools tended to focus on the practical aspects of law and prepared their students to pass the state bar exam. (The "national" law schools did not prepare students for the state bar; their students came from many different states).

These factors resulted in a stratified legal profession. Stratum one lav jers are the top graduates of such national law schools as Harvard, Yale, Columbia, Stanford, New York University, the Universities of Michigan, Chicago, Virginia, Pennsylvania and California at Berkeley (Margolick, 1983: 21) who go on to work for elite law firms whose clients are the nation's leading corporations.* These students have an entry level salary of between 40 and 50 thousand dollars. Stratum two lawyers are graduates of top law schools, or top graduates of less prestigious law schools, who work as employees of leading corporations—corporate attorneys. They are sometimes persons recruited away from elite law firms. Such persons are also found holding important government posts, usually at the federal level. Stratum three lawyers are divided into a number of subcategories.

The stratum three attorney (who occasionally can have an income greater than stratum one and stratum two attorneys when he/she is an outstanding trial lawyer) is part of a small law firm, a government employee, or a solo practitioner. In this category is found the "criminal lawyer."

CRIMINAL LAWYERS

According to *U.S. News and World Report* (December 19, 1983: 59) there were 650,000 licensed lawyers in the U.S. in 1983, and Barbara Curran (1983: 1) estimates that "by the close of 1987, there will be three-quarters of a million licensed lawyers."

---

*These corporations are usually found on the *Fortune* (Magazine) "500" list: e.g., Levi Strauss (represented by Baker and McKenzie of Chicago, the largest law firm in the United States with 622 attorneys); Exxon, the richest corporation in the U.S. (represented by Baker and Botts of Houston with 244 attorneys); Eastman Kodak (represented by Sullivan and Cromwell of New York with 242 attorneys); General Motors (represented by Well, Gotshal and Manges of New York with 259 lawyers).

Eighty percent of all practitioners have their offices in a metropolitan area and about half of all lawyers are in solo practice. Together, solo practitioners and lawyers practicing in 2- or 3-lawyer firms constitute almost two-thirds of all practicing lawyers. Lawyers in firms of 4 to 10 lawyers account for an additional 17% of practicing lawyers and lawyers in firms of 11 or more account for the remaining 20% of private practitioners (Curran, 1983: 4).

Ten percent of the total lawyer population work in private industry, one-quarter of whom were employed by "*Fortune* 500" companies (stratum two: corporate attorneys). About nine percent of all attorneys work for government, two-thirds at the state and local level, 39% of whom are prosecuting attorneys (Curran, 1983: 6–7). There are roughly about 30,000 attorneys who handle criminal cases more than just occasionally, and a substantial number of them work for government as public defenders or prosecutors. Few private attorneys handle only criminal cases (based on Wice, 1978: 29). Attorneys in private practice encounter many difficulties with criminal cases. Except for those who regularly represent persons involved in organized crime or wholesale drug trafficking, criminal lawyers have a problem getting paid. This problem is so significant that lawyers usually demand a retainer—"upfront money"—before they will accept a case, and this is often the only money they will receive from a client. ("Boy Scouts" usually don't require the services of a criminal lawyer).

A preoccupation with securing and getting paid by clients are factors keeping most lawyers away from criminal practice. There is also the negative public image of such practice and what Paul Wice (1978: 90–91) refers to as "guilt by association." Because most criminals are poor (at least those who are arrested and prosecuted in state courts), the criminal lawyer must aim for "quantity over quality": attempting to handle many cases for a (relatively) little money as opposed to a few cases for large fees. This requires a great deal of activity, travelling from court to court and constantly being in a courtroom, and this is physically debilitating for most lawyers. Wice notes that there are few "older" criminal lawyers because the profession "burns out" its talent by middle age.

THE PUBLIC DEFENDER

A criminal defendant who can be subjected to a term of imprisonment is entitled to be represented by counsel. Since most criminal defendants are poor, many cannot afford to hire a private attorney. Such persons qualify for legal aid, usually in the form of the Public Defender, a public official who serves as a counterpart to the prosecutor. Sometimes an indigent defendant may be assigned private counsel by the judge, a lawyer in private practice who is paid by the state on a case-by-case basis.

The Public Defender is a form of "legal welfare" which many recipients are reluctant to accept. Such defendants may express a version of the folk wisdom which declares: "He who pays the piper calls the tune." Jonathan Casper states (1972: 110) the defendant's view of the Public Defender:

> any two or more persons receiving money from a common source must have common interests. In the context of defendant-public defender relations, it urges that since both the prosecutor and the public defender are employed by "the state," they *cannot* fight one another. He who pays the piper calls the tune in this world, and if the same source is paying the public defender and the prosecutor, the reasonable expectation is that they will work together.

Defense counsel, privately retained, court assigned or public defender, has a singular role: advocate. Whether a defendant is believed to be guilty or innocent, whether he/she has paid for counsel or not, in the adversary system of American criminal justice the role of a defense counsel is clear: to achieve the best possible outcome for his/her client. To do less constitutes a breach of the canons of the legal profession whose "Code of Professional Responsibility" requires that "A Lawyer Should Represent a Client Zealously Within the Bounds of the Law."

While most prosecutors are elected,* the Public Defender is usually appointed, often by the judges of the county/circuit. New York City does not have a Public Defender, but finances the Criminal Division of the Legal Aid Society, a private, non-profit organization with a 47-member board of directors, to represent indigent defendants (except those accused of homocide who receive the services of court-assigned counsel).

THE PROSECUTOR

The prosecutor, sometimes called a District Attorney, County Attorney, State's Attorney, County Solicitor, etc., is an elected official in 46 states. On the federal level, the U.S. Attorney General, appointed by the President, appoints United States Attorneys who are responsible for prosecuting violations of federal law. The prosecutor receives a great deal of media attention and many prosecutors use the office as a vehicle for higher office. Most prosecutor's offices suffer from a high rate of turnover as assistants with a few years of trial experience leave for more lucrative opportunities in private practice.

The prosecutor has two basic roles:

1. to enforce the law on behalf of the people in the name of the state; and

---

*In Alaska, Connecticut, Delaware, and Rhode Island prosectors are not elected.

2. to ensure that justice is accomplished by not prosecuting those for whom evidence is lacking or whose guilt is in serious doubt.*

The prosecutor is the most powerful person in criminal justice. His/her office determines who will be prosecuted and for what charges/violations of law. Henry Glick (1983: 158) states:

> Following arrest, *prosecutors generally have the greatest influence in criminal cases.* In some cities, police have the authority to prosecute defendants accused of minor crimes. They also bring other cases before judges in the preliminary stages of the judicial process. However, in most cities, and generally in most serious crimes, prosecuting attorneys make all decisions concerning prosecution. Prosecutors also are permitted to change the charges suggested by the police and may decide to drop cases altogether even though they have gone through various additional judicial steps.

These decisions made by the prosecutor's office are not the subject of any regular official scrutiny and, in the absence of malfeasance, the discretion of a prosecutor's office is virtually unlimited. John Lundquist (1971: 489) states:

> Courts throughout the country have interpreted statutes so as to permit substantial and rather unrestrained discretion in the decision of whether or not to prosecute, and generally, hold that the prosecutor is "vested" with broad discretion to protect the public from crime both by statute and by the authority existing at common law.
>
> ... The courts consistently have held that the disposition of all criminal action rests solely in the honest discretion of the prosecutor; if he prosecutes or refuses to prosecute based on corrupt motives, the only remedy is a collateral proceeding to remove him from office or to bring criminal charges against him.

The American prosecutor has far more power than that enjoyed by any of his/her Western European counterparts. Jack Kress (1976: 109) points out that this is the result of the evolution of the public office of prosecutor from what was historically a common law concept of private prosecution. A crime was originally concieved of, not as an act against the state but, as a private offense, a wrong inflicted on the victim. In such a system the (private) person prosecuting a case would obviously have the right to discontinue prosecution, negotiate a settlement, or insist on a trial. However, whereas in England the

---

*"The state's attorney in his official capacity is a representative of all the people, including the defendant, and it is as much his duty to safeguard the constitutional rights of the defendant as those of any other citizen. His duty is not only to secure convictions but to see that justice is done. His desire to win the case should be subordinated to his duty to do justice, for it is as much the duty of a prosecuting attorney to see that a person on trial is not deprived of his statutory or legal rights as it is to prosecute him for the crime with which he may be charged. It is the duty of a prosecutor holding a quasi-judicial position not only to prosecute the guilty but also to protect the innocent" (Lundquist, 1971: 498).

Attorney had the power to end a private prosecution, the American prosecutor inherited the power of private prosecution, in addition to the "power to
moniter and mitigate their own decisions, thereby making their discretion
almost total—well nigh unreviewable in theory and even less reviewable in
practice."

While the police, from whom the prosecutor receives most of his/her
cases, are usually local in jurisdiction, the prosecutor is usually a county
official. Thus, a single prosecutor's office will be working with dozens of
local police agencies, each with a varying degree of competence. We will
later examine police-prosecutor relations.

THE JUDGE

There are two basic types of judge: trial judges and appellate judges. We
are interested in the trial judge who may sit in a lower court or a superior
court. The lower court (in some states such as Illinois, the misdemeanor part
of the superior court) hears cases for which the penalty usually does not
exceed one year of imprisonment. This includes misdemeanors, traffic and
perhaps juvenile cases. The superior court hears felony cases (crimes punishable by more than one year of imprisonment). The lower court is known
as a court of "limited jurisdiction;" the superior court is known as a court of
"general jurisdiction."

Judges may be appointed or elected, or sometimes a combination of the
two: appointed for a brief "trial" term, and then subjected to election on a
"retention ballot." The electoral process may be partisan (by party) or
non-partisan. In the federal system all judges are appointed by the President
for life terms. The terms of state trial judges vary, with the average being
from six to eight years, although most judges are routinely reappointed or
re-elected if their service has not been unsatisfactory.

The basic role of a trial judge is that of referee. He/she ensures that the
rules of law and proper judicial process are adhered to by defense and
prosecution. In cases where there is a jury trial, the judge determines issues
of law while the jury is to determine "facts." When a defendant waives the
right to a jury trial and requests a "bench trial" instead, the judge will
determine facts as well as guilt or innocence.

THE CRIMINAL JUSTICE PROCESS

The main components of criminal justice are on different levels of
government: police (local), prosecutor (county), prisons (state). Each level of
government determines its own needs, prepares its own budget, and raises its
own revenues. There is little, if any, coordination between local, county and

state government and this results in a misallocation of total criminal justice resources. Because of their high visibility and the public's perceived need for safety, about 54 percent of the money spent on criminal justice is allocated for policing. The remaining 46 percent is shared by the rest of the system: public defenders, prosecutors, judges, probation officers, court security and clerical support staff, jails, prisons and parole services.

The result of this misallocation is a large number of police officers who, by exercising their powers of arrest, bring more cases into the judicial system than the judicial system can adequately handle. In addition, in order to affect an arrest the police require only probable cause. The prosecutor, however, requires a much higher level of evidence to justify a full prosecution since he/she may have to convince a jury of the defendant's guilt "beyond a reasonable doubt": probable cause requires that there are reasonable grounds to believe a specific crime has been committed by a specific person; beyond a reasonable doubt means that the evidence is complete and conclusive—reasonable doubt about the defendant's guilt are removed from the juror's mind. The plea bargaining that results from these two problems will be discussed shortly.

After an arrest is made, if the charges constitute a felony or serious misdemeanor, the subject will be photographed and fingerprinted. The fingerprints are submitted to a central computerized clearinghouse for a search of any previous fingerprint record. The printout that results is referred to as a "rap sheet." The police fill out an arrest report and a complaint is drawn up by the police (usually by a detective) or an assistant prosecutor. In some jurisdictions permission from the prosecutor's office may be required to file a felony complaint. In some states a judge may be required to issue a felony warrant before any felony charges will be considered by the court.

Depending on what time of the day the arrest occured and whether it happened on a weekday, Sunday or holiday, the subject may have to spend 24 hours or longer in detention before appearing in court. At the first appearance the primary question is one of bail. The first appearance may actually be a "bond hearing" at which bail is the only question considered. It is also a matter with considerable discretion.

BAIL

Bail is a monetary (or other valuable) security which is put up by, or on behalf of, a criminal defendant to insure his/her return to court to stand trial. If the defendant fails to appear, the bail is forfeited. While the Eighth Amendment prohibits "excessive" bail, the Supreme Court (*Mastrian v. Hedman,* 1964) declared: "Neither the Eighth Amendment nor the Fourteenth Amendment requires that everyone charged with a State offense must be given his liberty on bail pending trial." Indeed, in most murder cases defendants are routinely held without bail being set. The issue of bail being "excessive," however, is quite relative. A bail of $25 can be "excessive" to a defendant with no resources.

In some states a bail bondsman, a privately licensed entrepreneur, will put up a defendant's bail bond in exchange for a fee, usually ten percent of the bail bond. For example, a bail of $10,000 would require a fee of $1000 for which the bail bondsman deposits with the court the cash bail ($10,000) or its equivalent to gain the defendant's release pending trial. The use of a bail bondsman tends to undermine the basic intent of bail—to insure the defendant's return to court. In this case, the bail bondsman's money, not the defendant's, would be forfeited in the event of a failure to return to court ("bail jumping"). Bail bondsmen often employ "skip tracers" to pursue bail jumpers In some states, e.g., Illinois, the defendant can deposit ten percent of his/her cash bail to secure release. When the trial is over, the defendant, if he/she has returned to court as directed by the judge, receives 90 percent of this amount back. For a bail of $10,000 the defendant would have to put up $1000, of which $900 would be returned at the completion of the case. Defendants may also be released without any bail: "Release-on-Recognizance" (ROR).

What are the bases for a bail decision? Different judges have different philosophies concerning bail. Some may only consider the likelihood of the defendant returning to court. Others may, in addition, consider the likelihood of the defendant committing criminal acts while free on bail. Bail in such cases can be viewed as a form of "preventive detention."* In any event, the judge will review the defendant's "rap sheet." He/she will consider the seriousness of the present allegation(s), and any past criminal behavior. The record will be checked to determine if the defendant is on probation or parole which may preclude the defendant from making bail. The judge will consider the defendant's past history of returning to court or bail jumping. Other items that will interest a judge include: employment status, marital status, children, amount of time living in the community and at current residence, history of drug addiction. Some of this information may not be readily available at the time bail is to be set. Some courts will use probation personnel to make inquiries and to verify information from the defendant. Judges can also be influenced by the prosecutor, defense counsel, or the police.

There is evidence to suggest that the police may exert a considerable influence on the setting of bail. They may do this by the manner in which

---

* ... preventive detention does not violate the Constitution because bail is considered to be a privilege, subject to judicial discretion" (Dow, 1981: 66).

they describe a defendant, e.g., "friendly and cooperative," or "abusive and threatening." The police may be concerned that the defendant, if free on bail, will present a threat to, or otherwise interfere with, witnesses. Through the prosecutor, the police may argue for high bail in order to pressure a defendant into being "cooperative"—becoming an informant. The prosecutor may try for a high bail in order to keep the defendant incarcerated—a means of "softening him/her up," making the defendant more amenable to a plea of guilty. Traditionally, county jails, where defendants who cannot make bail are held in detention, are miserable institutions providing little or no recreation. (Most defendants prefer a state prison to a county jail.) Remaining in jail has other serious disadvantages for a defendant. If employed, he/she is liable to lose the job; he/she is also away from family and friends and cannot assist in the preparation of his/her legal defense. The research of Peter Greenwood and his colleagues (1975: xxiii–xxiv) revealed

> that defendants who remain in jail have a much lower chance of being either dismissed or acquitted and a greater chance of receiving a felony sentence if convicted. Several hypotheses can be constructed to explain this finding. First, the system may tend to prejudge defendants, often granting release to those who have weaker cases against them. Second, defendants who are not able to secure bail or ROR may be less competent or less motivated to avoid being found guilty. Finally, the characteristics that make a defendant unacceptable for release (no funds, no community ties) may also lead to higher conviction rates and harsher sentencing rates by the court. None of these explanations sounds particularly just.

Suzann Buckle and Leonard Buckle (1977: 78) found that "85 percent of defendants in jail before trial pleaded guilty, while only 46 percent of those on personal recognizance did so. Moreover, whether or not they pleaded guilty, they were convicted more often and given more severe penalties upon conviction." In addition to the disadvantages already noted, the Buckles (1977: 79) state that

> the physical presence of the defendant in jail imposes practical limitations on the defense's ability to bargain strongly. A defender whose client is incarcerated has less chance to "stall out" prosecuting witnesses, to negotiate a solid client-attorney relationship, or to bargain with other court officials with the same assurance that the defendant can hold out for a good settlement. Dispositional bargaining based on the client's success with a treatment program, of course, depends on the availability of the defendant to begin treatment before trial and hence his freedom from jail.

> Finally, the appearance of the defendant in the dock at trial has an effect on the conduct of the defense. The attorney is less able to confer with his client during the trial or hearings; his client's appearance after being in jail makes it more difficult for him to create a favorable image and the attorney must

cope with the impression made by the fact that is client is plainly labeled by the court as unworthy of trust to appear at trial.

PLEA BARGAINING

The prosecutor has little control over intake: s/he is dependant on the police for cases entering the system and for this the police only require probable cause. William McDonald, et al, (1982: 25) report:

> In all jurisdictions for most crimes the investigation and arrest decisions are controlled entirely by the police. Except for the comparatively rare investigation originating in the prosecutor's office, the prosecutor plays virtually no direct role in the initial stage of the process.

The stage at which the prosecutor first becomes involved varies. In some jurisdictions it occurs within 24 hours of the arrest and before the initial filing of charges. In other jurisdictions it occurs after initial filing and within a few days of the arrest. (In some jurisdictions it may take considerably longer). Prosecutorial review of a case enables the office to screen out very weak or unimportant cases. An early review can save a considerable amount of working time for the system (and a lot of aggravation for the defendant). However, at the early stage certain information needed to properly assess a case may not be available, e.g., line-ups, forensic reports, evaluation of witness credibility.

In any event, the defendant will make an initial appearance or arraignment at which time the official charges will be read, the need for appointed counsel considered, and bail may be set or reviewed (if already set at a bond hearing). Typically, these hearings last only a few minutes. If the case is a misdemeanor it may be adjudicated at this time, often by a plea of guilty or dismissal of the charges. The lower courts where this activity usually takes place often routinely overlook the rights of a defendant in order to speed up the disposition process: "rough justice." Since penalties are usually minimal, most defendants do not protest. There is an *Alice in Wonderland* quality to this setting. A defendant who has been unable to make bail and is willing to plead guilty to a misdemeanor charge often receives "time served," a sentence equivalent to that which he/she has already served: "Sentence first— verdict afterwards," in the words of the mad queen of "Wonderland." The defendant who pleads guilty leaves the court a convicted but free person. On the other hand, a defendant who insists on his/her innocence and demands a trial will be returned to jail to await a turn at due process. That this type of plea bargaining may encourage the legally innocent to plead guilty is obvious.

If the charge(s) constitute a felony the case is referred to a superior court (or the felony part of a unified court system). Here a preliminary hearing is held to determine probable cause. This "probable cause hearing" is actually a short, mini-trial during which witnesses are called by the prosecution and the defense attorney may cross-examine and call his/her own witnesses. The judge must determine if the accused is to stand trial or if the case is to be dismissed for lack of evidence—no *prima facie case*. The judge may also determine that there is insufficient evidence to support a felony charge, but there exists probable cause for a misdemeanor proceeding.

In some states the prosecutor may avoid a preliminary hearing by presenting his/her evidence directly to a grand jury. This enables the prosection to avoid disclosing important aspects of the case so early in the process. Grand juries consist of 23 citizens who hear charges presented by the prosecution. The proceedings are non-adversarial—the defendant is not represented— and secret, neither the public nor the news media may be present at a grand jury session. Grand juries, because they usually "rubber stamp" the wishes of the prosecutor, almost always return a "true bill," indicting the defendant. This has the effect of bringing the defendant to trial for a felony. A finding of "no true bill" causes the defendant to be released from custody or if free on bail to have the bail money returned.

In states that do not routinely use the grand jury, the prosecutor files an *information:* a concise statement charging the defendant with a felony crime(s). Unless deemed deficient by a judge, the information serves to bring a defendant to trial.

Few cases entering the criminal justice system result in a jury trial, and 85–95 percent of all criminal convictions are the result of plea bargaining. This widely practiced method of disposing of cases is often condemned in the popular media as an abuse of discretion resulting in lenient sentences for serious offenders. On the other hand, it is attacked for being unfair to defendants who must choose between waiving their constitutional right to a jury trial or running the risk of a substantially higher sentence if found guilty after a jury trial. (See Uhlman and Walker, "He Takes Some of My Time; I Take Some of His," 1980, for an example of the effect of a jury trial on sentencing dedecisions). Despite this criticism, some observers see plea bargaining as a natural, and not harmful, outgrowth of our legal system. Thus, two positions can be delineated with respect to views on plea bargaining.

1. *Closed System.* Plea bargaining is the result of a distortion of the goals of criminal justice resulting in a system that is pathological.

2. *Open System.* Plea bargaining has evolved as a rational approach to problems in criminal justice that balances law enforcement, efficiency, and due process.

We will examine each position.

PLEA BARGAINING: A CLOSED SYSTEM

Earlier in this chapter it was pointed out that a disproportionate amount of resources go into policing compared to other components of the criminal justice system. Indeed, it is obvious that criminal justice is a system that is not *systematic.* The term systematic implies orderly planning and a coordination of parts that simply does not occur in criminal justice. Instead, each agency presses for its own needs without regard for the system as a whole. This creates a situation that can be depicted in the form of a funnel: police agencies bringing an enormous amount of cases into a system which must process them in spite of insufficient resources. The result is a bottleneck leading to high rates of dismissal, plea bargaining, any mechanism for relieving the congestion.

The regular "players" in the court system, those who spend a great deal of time in courtrooms, private attorneys, public defenders, prosecutors, judges, and support staff (clerks, bailiffs) have a stake in maintaining the system on an operating basis. Furthermore, each player has an interest in reducing the amount of time and energy expended while maximizing returns (benefits). The requirements for maintaining an overburdened court system conflict with the ideals for which the system was created—*justice.* Justice is a goal that requires a deliberately slow and exacting concern for due process. The fundamental method for ensuring due process is the *adversarial model:* two, more or less equal legal combatants, defense counsel and prosecutor, meeting on the field of justice before a referee and a jury of peers. Abraham Blumberg (1967: 18) argues that the Supreme Court in its landmark decisions (*Gideon* and *Miranda*) reflects a concern for the ideals of justice that do not reflect the realities of the judicial process:

> ...the Supreme Court reiterates the traditional legal conceptions of a defense lawyer based on the ideological perception of a criminal case as an *adversary, combative* proceeding, in which counsel for the defense assiduously musters all the admittedly limited resources at his command to *defend* the accused.

This *Perry Mason* version of justice conflicts with reality.

The justice ideal is operationalized through the adversarial process. The requirements of the system, however, cause the ideal of justice to be abandoned in favor of goals that benefit the system (Blumberg, 1967: 19–20):

> Organizational goals and discipline impose a set of demands and conditions of practice on the respective professions in the criminal court, to which they respond by abandoning their ideological and professional commitments to the accused client, in the service of these higher claims of the court organization.

All court personnel, including the accused's own lawyer, tend to be coopted to become agent-mediators who help the accused redefine his situation and restructure his perceptions concomitant with a plea of guilty.*

Blumberg is implying, nay accusing, defense lawyers of being "con men" whose singular purpose is to convince clients to plead guilty. William Alschular (1975: 1179), taking a similar but more adequately-researched position, states:

> . . . the presence of counsel does not provide a significant safeguard of fairness in guilty-plea negotiation.
>
> . . . This system subjects defense attorneys to serious temptations to disregard their clients' interests—temptations so strong that the invocation of professional ideals cannot begin to answer the problems that emerge. Today's guilty-plea system leads even able, conscientious, and highly motivated attorneys to make decisions that are not really in their clients' interests.

The question is "Why?" Let us review the practice of criminal law by attorneys in private practice.

The typical private attorney who handles criminal cases is in solo practice or one he/she shares with a partner or two. (There are also a small number of lawyers whose entire practice consists of traffic or minor offense cases. They are unwilling or unable to deal with cases that require more than one or two brief court appearances, and spend most of their time in the corridors of lower courts seeking clients. They may operate out of a briefcase—no office, no overhead—with only a business card and perhaps an answering machine). His/her clients have very limited resources and tend to be unreliable with respect to paying for legal services. For this reason the attorney usually demands an advance payment, and this amount may be all that the attorney ever receives no matter how many hours of work the case requires. Thus, the private attorney must be concerned with the possibility of a case going to trial, particularly a time-consuming jury trial.†

---

*"Both P.D. [Public Defender] and D.A. [District Attorney] are concerned to obtain a guilty plea whenever possible and thereby avoid a trial. At the same time, each part is concerned that the defendant 'receive his due.' The reduction of offense X to Y must be of such a character that the new sentence will depart from the anticipated sentence for the original charge to such a degree that the defendant is likely to plead guilty to the new charge and, at the same time, not so great that the defendant does not 'get his due'" (Sudnow, 1965: 262)

†Research by Peter Greenwood and his colleagues (1975: xxiv) revealed that "clients of private attorneys are much more likely to make bail, *more likely to plead guilty, less likely to demand a jury trial,* and more likely to receive a felony sentence upon conviction than clients of public-defenders and court-appointed attorneys" (emphasis added). Research by Gerald and Carol Wheeler (1980) revealed that in Houston, Texas court-appointed attorneys and private counsel appeared to be equally successful in obtaining nonconvictions for their clients.

Most attorneys who specialize in criminal cases depend on a high turnover of clients who can afford only modest fees. Without high volume and the investment of a modest amount of time in each case, many a private defense counsel would go broke. Yet private counsel must maintain a reputation for vigorous defense in order to attract new clients. Public defender organizations charged with representing all indigent defendants prefer a quick disposition because their manpower barely suffices to handle their case load. But they seek to establish a reputation for effective representation of defendants (Eisenstein and Jacob, 1977: 26).

Private defense counsel and public defenders share a great deal in common with prosecutors and judges: a similar educational background, and professional, economic and intellectual ties that bind them to the system rather than to the client. "In short, the court is a closed community" (Blumberg, 1967: 21).

The defense lawyer, private counsel and public defender, is socialized into this closed system. He/she learns that a price must be paid for failing to understand and/or abide by system rules: "In the process of handling their cases, new defense attorneys learn that the reality of the court differs from what they had expected; through rewards and sanctions, they are taught to proceed in a certain fashion" (Heumann, 1978: 57). He/she learns to avoid legal challenges that may be seen as frivolous to prosecutors and judges and gain the emnity of both (Heumann, 1978: 62):

The hostility of prosecutors and judges to these time-consuming motions is communicated to the new attorney. First, the prosecutor or judge may simply call the defense attorney into his office and explain that the motions are needless formalities. If this advice is insufficient to dissuade the newcomer, sanctions such as "hassling" the attorney by dragging the case out over a long period of time, closing all files to the attorney, and even threatening to go to trial on the case, ensue.

The prosecutor and the judge can keep a defense attorney on the run, forcing him/her to return to court many times on a single case for his/her small fee. Most private attorneys "overbook." They have more than one case scheduled for the same day, since the odds dictate against both cases being ready for adjudication. (It is a tricky bureaucratic task to assemble all of the actors and paperwork/documents necessary for a criminal case to procede on schedule: complainants/witnesses are sick or unable to take off from work *again;* police officers are injured or busy with a case in another court; the jail fails to produce the defendant on time; court papers have been misfiled, etc.)* However, at times both cases may be ready and the lawyer will have to request a continuance for one or the other. If the prosecutor agrees, a continuance will be routinely granted. If the prosecutor objects and the judge is also opposed, the attorney will be in an untenable situation.

For the defense attorney being "disagreeable" involves serious risks, as Alschuler notes (1968: 68):

> A defense attorney must enjoy good personal relations with the prosecutor's staff if he hopes to remain effective as a plea bargainer. Prosecutor's offices, by contrast, can allow themselves the luxury of refusing to enter plea agreements with individual attorneys. A defense attorney therefore knows, first, that he needs the prosecutor's office and, second, that the prosecutor's office does not need him.†

The prosecutor's office assists the defense attorney in the task of controlling his/her client by instilling fear. A client fearful of a long term of incarceration is more easily manipulated into a guilty plea. Michael Cox argues (1975: 34):

> Prosecutors have great leverage; they draft the charges and generally make recommendations on sentencing. These prosecutorial prerogatives put the defendant at a disadvantage. A prosecutor may "overcharge," either horizontally (e.g., in a bad check case charge uttering, obtaining by false pretenses, and forgery, even though they may overlap and be multiplicious for sentencing), or vertically (e.g., always charge homocides as first degree murder). Through overcharging, an accused is immediately put on the defensive. If the case is tried on the merits, a jury will often react by thinking (even if only subconsciously), "There are so many charges and they are so serious; the

---

*This problem has been chronic in New York City where only one of every three detained defendants was delivered to court on time: "Failure to deliver such defendants when they are due in court causes delays and adjournments that worsen the already serious backlogs plaguing the local justice system" (Fried, 1983: 31). While significant improvements have been reported, cases in New York City are apparently still being dismissed because of nonappearances due to a failure to produce jailed defendants in court.

An investigation in Cook County (Chicago), Illinois revealed that 40 to 50 court files turn up missing every day and knowledgeable insiders believe that most are stolen by lawyers and law clerks hoping to delay cases in court. Although such action is a felony, no one has ever been prosecuted for theft of a file from the court clerk's office (Frantz and Mount, 1983: 1).

†Alan Dershowtiz (1983: 355), Harvard law professor and prominent defense attorney, notes:

> The prosecuting attorney wields enormous power in the day-to-day life of a defense attorney and can exert considerable influence on the fate of his clients. Since plea bargaining is the dominant mode of resolving criminal cases, the defense lawyer must always look for a deal; and it is the prosecuting attorney who must agree to it. In some jurisdictions the prosecuting attorney also makes sentencing recommendations that often carry considerable weight with the judge.
> . . . the prosecutor can make the defense attorney's life pleasant or miserable in countless small, but important, ways: by agreeing to or opposing continuances; by opening or closing files for discovery; by waiving or insisting on technical requirements; by recommending or denigrating the attorney to prospective clients; by being generally agreeable or disagreeable.

defendant must be guilty of something." The number of charges/specifications and the "degree" are at the heart of plea negotiations. As an added incentive to deal, a prosecutor may threaten to recommend a high sentence if conviction is obtained after a trial on the merits.

A defendant is, thus, placed in an untenable position. If he does not deal and the prosecutor has overcharged, the accused faces a jury that may believe him guilty of something. If the defendant is convicted, the prosecutor, to retain credibility, must follow through and recommend a stiff sentence.

Alschuler notes (1968: 95):

> . . . overcharging and subsequent charge reduction are often the components of an elaborate sham, staged for the benefit of defense attorneys. The process commonly has little or no effect on the defendant's sentence, and prosecutors may simply wish to give defense attorneys a "selling point" in their efforts to induce defendants to plead guilty.

While privately-retained counsel is under pressure to resolve cases quickly, a public defender also experiences pressure, from trial judges (Alschuler, 1975: 237):

> The process may begin with a judge's suggestion that a certain plea agreement would be fair, and if a defender accepts this suggestion, the matter is at an end. Defenders who resist judicial suggestions too often, however, are frequently forced to endure abusive remarks from the bench:
>
> > You're a quasi-public agency. You should be interested in *justice*.
> > Haven't you got any client control?
> > You spend too much time on hardened criminals.
> > No private attorney would take this case to trial. You must be awfully eager for experience.
> > When will you bend to reality?
> > You guys believe your clients too much.
> > You're acting like a private lawyer.

His/her position as a court "employee" adds to the defendant's negative view of the Public Defender (Casper, 1978: 4):

> . . . what attracts defendants to private lawyers is, for a large number of them at least, the notion that, because of the financial exchange between lawyer and client, the lawyer will be more committed to the defendant's interests. It is money that provides a sense of control, the leverage to insure that lawyers will listen to their clients, take instructions from their clients, and generally exert themselves on their client's behalf. Moreover, not only does the client fail to pay, and thus lack this leverage over public defenders, but someone else does. And that someone else is "the state"—the very institution that is proceeding against the defendant. Thus, public defenders suffer not only from the fact that they are imposed upon defendants rather than being

selected, and from the absence of financial exchange, but they are employed by the enemy.

As Arthur Rosett and Donald Cressey (1976: 40) note: "there is a real risk that the courthouse will lose all sense of purpose and will become totally preoccupied with itself and the institutional and professional interests of those who run it." According to the proponents of the *closed system* view, this has already happened.

PLEA BARGAINING: AN OPEN SYSTEM

Lundquist (1971: 517) presents an oft-repeated reason for the existence and persistence of plea bargaining: an overburdened court system:

> The purpose and goal of liberal prosecutorial discretion, has been subverted and perhaps irreversibly altered to meet the exigencies of the moment. Where the courts, at an earlier time and under less compelling circumstances, upheld prosecutorial discretion because it allowed the prosecutor the opportunity to "see that justice is done" without going to court, the courts today uphold the same discretion, because without it, there can be no justice at all—the system would collapse.

This view is contested by Milton Heumann (1978: 157) who notes that guilty pleas have been the outcome of most criminal cases for almost a century, even when the courts are not overburdened: "The trial is not—and has not been—the central means of case resolution." This is because "prosecutors, defense attorneys, and judges share the basic belief that plea bargaining is the appropriate means of disposing of many, if not most, criminal cases" (1978: 156).

> Court personnel simply recognize the factual culpability of many defendants, and the fruitlessness, at least in terms of case outcome, of going to trial. From these perceptions flows the notion that if the obviously guilty defendant cops a plea, he will receive some award. Whether the defendant believes this results from his show of contrition, or, more prosaically, from saving the state time and money, is not of concern here; the fact that he perceives that he receives a reward is the key point. Similarly, prosecutors and judges do not believe that they accord this reward simply to "move the business." They feel that by giving consideration to the defendant who pleads guilty, they are furthering their own professional goals (sorting serious from nonserious cases, obtaining certain time in serious cases, and so on) ... it is not at all simply an expedient to dispose of "onerously large case loads."

Martin Levin (1977: 87) states that "a large caseload is not the major factor behind plea bargaining. It may be a necessary factor, but it does not seem to be a sufficient one."

Researchers such as Malcolm Feeley insist that "The criminal court must be seen as an *open* system...." (1979: 19) whose primary actors "do not operate in isolation" (1979: 20) but reflect the norms of the legal profession. The practitioner of law, be he/she employed by a large national law firm, corporation, engaged in civil or criminal practice, views the trial process as problematic because of its inherent *uncertainty*. The trial process lacks the level of predictability favored by those in the business of law (as well as those in many other types of business). The trial process requires lawyers, whose professional education is based on the need to reason through issues and problems, to give up control of case outcome to a group of persons (a jury) with no legal training. Whether it is in civil or criminal court, this prospect is not one that would normally be pleasing to an attorney.

Feeley also rejects the assembly-line metaphor and the notion that adversarial justice has been replaced by the courts acting merely as case processing bureaucracies (1979: 16):

> The antithesis of bureaucracy is discretion, the ability to base decisions on individual judgments rather than on rules. And it is the discretionary capabilities of prosecutor and judge and the many options of the defense which facilitate rapid processing of vast numbers of cases.*

William McDonald and his colleagues (1979: 187) point out that

> the existing literature had overstated the nonadversarial nature of plea negotiations. While it is true that defense attorneys act cooperatively with prosecutors in plea bargaining and do lean on clients to plea bargain when the client would prefer to go to trial, it was not our impression that this was usually done with improper motives or that this usually involved a sacrifice of the client's interests. We do not feel that cooperation between defense attorneys and prosecutors precludes an adversarial relationship. It may just make the adversarial characteristics of the interaction more difficult to see.

David Neubauer (1974: 78) points out that normative behavior on the part of lawyers requires that they be outgoing and congenial:

> if defense and prosecution are on good terms, this does not mean the adversary process has broken down. It may be only a reflection of the normal rules of conduct expected of lawyers. The "cooperation" of defense and prosecution is a product of such general expectations about how lawyers should conduct themselves.

Feeley (1979: 29) adds:

---

*Lief Carter (1974: 42) finds little substance to the description of criminal justice as an "assembly line" since that would require "considerable capacity to turn out products of uniform quality by controlling or programming the type of inputs, their rate of movement, and the sequence in which they are combined." The prosecutor, unlike the assembly line, "cannot fully specify in advance what materials they will have and how they will combine them."

To infer the lack of an adversarial stance and the existence of bargained settlement—for the pure purpose of administrative convenience—from the absence of trials is to ignore altogether the importance of these other "truthtesting" and highly combative processes. . . . combativeness—short of trial—does in fact exist.

We have seen that two sets of observers evaluating the same system and using the same basic variables have reached different conclusions. On one side are those who view the system as *closed* and pathological, decrying the loss of the adversarial model of justice. On the other side are those who view the system as *open,* who argue that the adversarial model remains the norm, plea bargaining notwithstanding (Buckle and Buckle, 1977: 158):

> The primary reason for the acceptability of the adversary process as a norm for bargaining is that these norms of behavior generally seem less addressed to what strategy participants might select than to matters of style. For example, personal hostility, especially if expressed in open court, was strongly sanctioned. In turn, the participants who were most rewarded by the system were those who were seen as cooperative and "on the ball."

> In contrast to these behavioral norms, which tended to focus on the minimization of tension through fostering cooperation, the values that informed the interests of the bargainers were more nearly those espoused by the respective professional groups in the court. Judges, for example, did value efficiency and rapid processing of cases, but seemed even more concerned with the equity of outcomes of cases and the protection of their communities through what they hoped would be effective correction. Lawyers too, when they articulated their values, focused on vigorous advocacy, holding themselves and their colleagues to that standard of professional behavior. In selecting their strategies, they appeared to be guided by values growing out of their professional training. . . .

PLEA BARGAINING: THE PROCESS AND THE LAW

Plea bargaining has been subjected to a variety of legal tests. In *Santobello v. New York* (92 S.Ct. 495, 1971) the Supreme Court ruled that a prosecutor's plea bargain promise must be kept. In this case the defendant was indicted for felony gambling violations and agreed to plead guilty to a lesser offense in return for the prosecutor's promise to make no sentencing recommendation. However, at the sentencing hearing another prosecutor appeared and recommended the maximum sentence of one year (which the judge imposed). The court held that the prosecutor's actions violated an agreement which is binding. The decision stated:

> The disposition of criminal charges by agreement between the prosecutor and the accused, sometimes loosely called "plea bargaining," is an essential

component of the administration of justice. Properly administered, it is to be encouraged.

In *Bordenkircher v. Hayes* (No. 76-1334, 1978) the defendant was informed by the prosecutor that if he plead guilty to an indictment charging uttering a forged instrument, the prosecutor would recommend a sentence of five-years. Hayes refused, and, after a jury trial, was found guilty of uttering a forged instrument. In addition, at a separate proceeding, he was found to be an habitual offender under state law. As such he was sentenced to a term of life imprisonment. After a U.S. Court of Appeals ruled in favor of Hayes' appeal, the case reached the Supreme Court which upheld the life sentence:

> There is no doubt that the breadth of discretion that our country's legal system vests in prosecuting attorneys carries with it the potential for both individual and institutional abuse. And broad though that discretion may be, there are undoubtedly constitutional limits upon its exercise. We hold only that the course of conduct engaged in by the prosecutor in this case, which no more than presented the defendant with the unpleasant alternatives of forgoing trial or facing charges on which he was plainly subject to prosecution, did not violate the Due Process Clause of the Fourteenth Amendment.

Malvina Halberstam (1982: 47) notes: "In rejecting challenges to plea bargaining, the Court has argued that the defendant's decision to plead guilty is voluntary, that he is represented by counsel and, perhaps, most importantly, that the plea is a reliable admission of guilt." Furthermore (1982: 46):

> The Supreme Court has sanctioned the use of promises of leniency to induce guilty pleas. It has sustained guilty pleas induced by fear of harsh penalties, including fear of the death penalty. It has also sustained the imposition of far more severe penalties on defendants who were convicted after refusing to plead guilty.

Plea bargaining can occur at a number of different junctures in the criminal justice process (and this has an affect on plans to control, reduce, or abolish plea bargaining). In any event, plea bargaining cannot commence until the prosecutor's office becomes involved in a case. In some jurisdictions the lodging of formal charges against a defendant is accomplished by the police who made the arrest.

> In Buffalo, New York, for example, the police arrest the defendant, take him before the committing magistrate where his bond is set, the complaint filed, defense counsel appointed, if necessary, and the case set for preliminary hearing. It is only prior to the preliminary hearing that the prosecutor is made aware of the case and the files are sent to him. Thus, the preliminary hearing provides the first opportunity for case review and witness interviews. The result is to place the prosecutor in a reactive position since he does not

exercise the charging function which controls the intake into the system. This contrasts sharply with the prosecuting attorney's office in Michigan where state law mandates that no charge or warrant shall issue without prosecutorial approval. (Jacoby, 1982: 26).

The police require only evidence of probable cause to effect a lawful arrest, while a prosecutor must evaluate cases based on a need for significantly higher levels of proof, including that necessary for a successful trial outcome: "Beyond a reasonable doubt." Richard Schuster (1979: 7) points out, however, that police departments often reward their officers for the quality of the arrest—not for quality of case outcome. Thus, "many officers see the arrest of a suspect as the end of his/her job with little thought to the needs of future processing." McDonald (et al., 1982: 24) observes:

> If the initial prosecutorial review occurs a few days after the arrest, the process can be based on more complete information thereby increasing the prosecutor's ability to select out additional problematic cases and more accurately prioritize the rest. However, delaying the review to this time has several disadvantages. The cases that would have been screened out earlier have now been allowed to enter the court system thereby creating a variety of costs to the court and to the defendants. In addition the police will now control the decision regarding initial charges. This means that cases will usually be charged at higher levels than they would have been by prosecutors [because police are rewarded for the "quality" of arrests, not convictions]. This in turn means that bail will probably be higher than it would have been; the official criminal records will be misleading; and in some places the prosecutor's discretion in charging will have been constrained.

A prosecutor must be concerned with conserving the resources of his/her office by rejecting or downgrading (felony to misdemeanor, misdemeanor to offense) cases which are trivial or which cannot be successfully prosecuted as felonies. In California, for example, prosecutors rejected about 17 percent (or 86,033) of the felony cases referred to them by the police during a four-year period (Stewert, 1982: 10). The practices and abilities of police agencies and personnel vary, and a prosecutor usually has to work with a number of different police agencies. In his study of one midwestern prosecutor's office, David Neubauer (1974: 125–26) found that while "prosecutors *agreed seventy-five percent* with the city police, they *disagreed seventy-five percent* of the time with the sheriff's arrest designations." He notes that the police were more active in screening their arrests and that the sheriff's office had a tendency to arrest large numbers of teenagers for matters seen as trivial by prosecutors. The police often make arrests as part of their "order maintenance" responsibilities. These arrests are usually considered a nuisance or too trivial to be worthy of prosecutorial resources and are terminated by *nolle prosequi* (sometimes referred to as "nolle" or "nol pross), declining to proceed after a case has been filed in court.

SCREENING AND CHARGING

Joan Jacoby (1977, 1979) delineates between four screening and charging policy models commonly used by prosecutor's offices. (The four are neither mutually exclusive nor meant to cover every possible policy type).

1. *Legal Sufficiency Model.* Cases in this model are screened only to determine if the legal elements of the case are present—little more than probable cause. If no obvious defects are found the case is accepted for prosecution. Since rejection rates are low and caseloads are, correspondingly, high, the prosecutor relies on the courts to dismiss weak cases and uses extensive plea negotiations to minimize the number of cases that have to be tried. This model is one routinely used in misdemeanor courts, so that a prosecutor's office may actually use two models: one for misdemeanors and one for felonies. It is this model that brings charges of "rough justice" and "assembly-line justice" because of the need to move large numbers of cases quickly and efficiently.

2. *System Efficiency Model.* This model is usually found in systems characterized as chronically overburdened. The focus is on speedy and early dispositions and pre-trial screening is extensive. A variety of methods will be used to accomplish the goals of this model including overcharging (to encourage a guilty plea), diversion (where a defendant is offered a social program alternative to prosecution), or charge reduction for handling in misdemeanor courts. If the case is boundover for felony processing the emphasis is on plea bargaining. However, in the event plea bargaining is unsuccessful, prosecutors usually win the resulting trials since only serious and strong cases will reach the trial stage in this model.

3. *Defendant Rehabilitation Model.* In practice this model utilizes many of the methods described in the System Efficency Model. However, the purpose is quite different. In this model the prosecutor's office attempts to separate out the more serious offenders from those who can benefit from rehabilitative programs. The focus is upon avoiding the use of the criminal justice system to deal with social and psychological problems that can be dealt with more appropriately by other agencies. An observation by the President's Commission on Law Enforcement and Administration of Justice set the stage for this model (1968: 331–32):

> Prosecutors should endeavor to make discriminating charge decisions, assuring that offenders who merit criminal sanctions are not released and that other offenders are either released or diverted to noncriminal methods of treatment and control by:

> Establishment of explicit policies for the dismissal or informal disposition
> of the cases of certain marginal offenders.
> Early identification and diversion to other community resources of those
> offenders in need of treatment, for whom full criminal disposition does not
> appear required.

David Aaronson and his colleagues (1977: 3) refer to this as "Alternatives
to conventional adjudication:"

> A central thesis of the alternatives movement is that our criminal courts,
> patterned on an adversary model for the resolution of social conflicts, are an
> imperfect—and often inappropriate—societal response to the processing of
> many offenders, especially those charged with minor criminal offenses or
> offenses involving no substantial factual disputes. In many lesser criminal
> cases the process of conventional adjudication may be too time-consuming,
> too expensive, somewhat irrelevant to, or even inconsistent with, achieving
> effective dispositions. Recently, the overwhelming workload placed upon
> criminal courts by increasingly efficient law enforcement creates a new
> impetus for the adjudicatory alternatives movement. Alternatives seek imme-
> diate relief for the overburdened criminal justice system: through simpler,
> less expensive, more effective and fairer dispositions.

Extensive screening focuses on the offender and then on the offense in an
effort to divert as many defendants as possible from the criminal justice
system. Those defendants with prior histories who evidence no potential for
rehabilitation are subjected to vigorous prosecution.

   4. *Trial Sufficiency Model.* This is the model that usually is operative on
the federal level where U.S. Attorneys do not file charges until they are
virtually certain that a conviction will be obtained. The basic criterioron is
the legal strength of a case and it is the model Neubauer (1974: 118) found in
"Prairie City" (a pseudonym), Illinois:

> When presented with a case, the Prarie City prosecutor asks: "Is this case
> prosecutable?" As one assistant commented, "When I examine the police
> report I have to feel that I could go to trial with the case tomorrow. All of the
> elements of prosecution must be present before I file charges." A prosecut-
> able case differs from the more familiar legal benchmark, probable cause . . .
> From the prosecutor's perspective, however, probable cause is too gross a
> yardstick; it may be present but a case still may be weak legally. Thus the
> concept of a prosecutable case . . . is the standard of trial—what must be
> proven in order to secure a conviction. The state's attorney's office in Prarie
> City sees no advantage to filing charges on a legally weak case that will survive
> a preliminary hearing but will lose at trial. They prefer to weed out such
> weak cases as soon as possible, before the arrest even becomes an official case.

There are some basic variables that influence the charging decision:
seriousness of the offense, legal strength of the case, and such extra-legal

items as the defendant's prior criminal history, personal characteristics (age, health, marital status), and the amount of publicity and public reaction to the offense and the offender. The status of the victim—his/her standing in the community, any criminal record—can also be a significant factor that is *extra-legal.*

We can conceive of four different *factor-combinations:*

    I Weak Case-Offense Not Serious.
    II Strong Case-Offense Not Serious.
    III Weak Case-Offense Very Serious.
    IV Strong Case-Offense Very Serious.

To these factor-combinations we would also have to consider extra-legal factors.

  (a) offender characteristics:
      —prior criminal history;
      —age, health, sex;
      —marital status, children.
  (b) community sentiments:
      —publicity about case;
      —attitude toward the defendant;
  (c) victim characteristics:
      —criminal record;
      —status in the community.

If we put aside the extra-legal factors and refer to the four factor-combinations:

1. Factor-combination IV cases would always be prosecuted vigorously, while factor-combination I cases would usually not be prosecuted.
2. The charging decision for factor-combination II cases and factor-combination III cases would be most susceptible to the influence of extra-legal factors, and would also be the cases most likely to be plea bargained.

John Kaplan, a former federal prosecutor, presents a set of standards used by his office (Northern District of California) which, although unwritten and tacit, were a "real set of standards for making the prosecutorial decision" (1965: 178).

1. Belief in the defendant's guilt.
2. Could a conviction be expected? Would prosecution be an efficient use of time and provide for enhancement of one's "batting average?"
3. Would prosecution bring criticism of the U.S. Attorney, who is highly political, for "fruitless prosecution?"

4. Possible suppression of evidence (exclusionary rule) would not necessarily deter prosecution since this was the fault of law enforcement agents, not the U.S. Attorney's Office.
5. More serious cases would be prosecuted although the same evidence in a lesser case would not result in prosecution.
6. Occasionally, at the request of a federal agent, a "courtesy prosecution" would occur in cases that otherwise would not be prosecuted.
7. Each case was carefully examined for its "jury appeal."
8. The ability of the law enforcement agent(s) involved was considered.
9. The attitude of the probable judge toward the case was considered.
10. The ability of the defense attorney was very seldom part of the case evaluation.
11. The case would be examined to see if the likely punishment was too severe for the offense being charged.

Frank Miller (1969: 42) notes that the usual standard for charging is "only if prosecutors are convinced of the guilt of the suspect and are convinced that a jury or judge will share that belief on the basis of the same evidence and if the judge and jury will not be prevented from considering that evidence [by the exclusionary rule, for example]." He points out that there are instances where there is no doubt about the facts, but there may be uncertainty about the legal consequences: "Has a crime been committed?" For example, in cases of alleged fraud there is a thin line of distinction between the matter being criminal or civil in nature; in cases of negligent vehicular homocide the matter centers on the nebulous issue of the degree of care exercised in operating a motor vehicle. In other cases there may be doubt about the facts—will a jury be convinced?— or about the motives of the complainant—revenge? The prosecutor needs to evaluate the impact of the case on a judge or jury: for example, what about the state's chief witness? Is he/she considered immoral or has he/she been engaged in illegal activities? The victim may be "guilty," as in a case where a john paid a prostitute but did not receive the services promised, nor his money back. A prosecutor will often be reluctant to prosecute respected or popular (e.g., local sports hero) members of the community for non-serious matters. Finally, but no less important, is the question of resources. Miller (1969: 159) states: "Enforcement practices designed to utilize resources most efficiently are adopted by prosecutors everywhere."

A report on the impact of "Proposition 13" in California (which reduced available tax revenues) concluded (Jan Chaiken, et al., quoted in Cockrell, 1983: 1):

Fiscal limitations inevitably lead to a rethinking of what the criminal justice system should and should not do. We observed trends that we think portend a less humane and less responsive system.

Agencies generally respond to reduced budgets (in real dollars) by shedding demand: They stop performing certain kinds of activities that they previously would have undertaken on their own initiative or at the request of a citizen or criminal justice agency.

Tom Cockrell (1983: 1) notes:

What the researchers found, for example, was that district attorneys reduced the categories of offenses they would prosecute and cut back on investigations into matters such as official corruption and consumer fraud, both of which are costly in terms of staff time. Police departments screened out reported crimes that they determined were unlikely to be solved, and concentrated investigative resources on the remaining crimes.

ORGANIZATION FOR PLEAS AND TRIALS

Once screening and charging have been accomplished, a case will be assigned according to two basic designs:

1. *Vertical Prosecution.* Each assistant prosecutor is assigned total responsibility for a number of cases—his/her caseload. The assistant picks the case up after charging and stays with it until the final disposition. (Those who are familiar with basketball will recognize this as a "man-to-man defense".) This design has the advantage of providing the victim/complainant the comfort of having his/her own prosecutor to relate to throughout the prosecutorial process/ordeal. The major disadvantage of this design is that it is quite costly in terms of staff time, as opposed to the horizontal design.

2. *Horizontal Prosecution.* Assistant prosecutors (and public defenders) are assigned to courtrooms, each of which handles a different step in the prosecutorial process. (Those who are familiar with basketball will recognize this as a "zone defense".) Thus, "in the lower court there may be bond settings, preliminary hearings and misdemeanor trials. In the felony court there may be arraignment court, motions and pretrial conference parts and finally, trial courts" (Jacoby, 1982: 33). With this design a defendant's case (and the victim/complainant) may be handled by different assistants at each of the various court appearances. This can be costly in terms of witness/ victim/complainant cooperation.

There is also "a mixture of vertical and horizontal prosecution so that some cases would be handled throughout by the same assistant while the remainder would be handled in an assembly line fashion." David Weimer (1980: 369) also notes: "Although prosecutors' offices serving populous jurisdictions often do employ mixed systems, the proportion of vertically prosecuted cases is usually very small. A typical pattern is to handle all cases horizontally except for homocides or otherwise notorious cases."

Horizontal prosecution predominates for logistical reasons. The assignment of assistants to court rooms permits a maximum of court time per lawyer with a minimum of scheduling difficulties. Assigning assistants to cases on the other hand, involves much more out-of-court time. Even if court appearances could be scheduled back-to-back, court time would be lost when defendants failed to appear or the defense was granted continuances. Travel time between court appearances increases the costs of vertical prosecution in jurisdictions where the preliminary stages of prosecution occur in decentralized local (municipal) courts that feed cases to a county (superior) court for trial preparation and final disposition. . . .

Vertical prosecution . . . [allows] continuous contact with the case [and] may enable the assistant to gather more or better evidence, increasing the chances of gaining a conviction if the case goes to trial.

ACCOMPLISHING THE PLEA BARGAIN

Lewis Katz (1972: 194) notes:

The etiquette of plea bargaining differs from city to city. It may occupy several months, if the practice of the attorneys is to become involved in a series of offers and counteroffers. Or it may be a one-time effort by the prosecutor to reduce the charge or recommend a lenient sentence, in return for a plea of guilty, or a single offer by the defense attorney to plead his client guilty, in return for reduction. In some situations, it may be done prior to the scheduled trial date; in others, it may normally occur on the first date set for trial. Occasionally it happens before the defendant in the courtroom, but more often the lawyers negotiate out of the defendant's presence. Although the absence of the judge during the negotiations avoids undue pressure upon the attorneys, often the judge is present and serves as an outside factor forcing attorneys to come to terms.

James Mills (1975: 139) provides the scenario for a plea bargain in the New York City Criminal Court:

"Your honor," Lowe [prosecutor] says, looking over his file, "this is a robbery, no weapon, two victims. It's a woman who beats up old people in the subway and robs them. One of the complainants is eighty-one years old." He hands Schweitzer [judge] her three-page record of drugs, prostitution and assaults.

"Injuries?" Schweitzer asks.

"Just light, your honor. Nothing serious."

"In these times," Erdmann [legal aid attorney] says, "people ought to be grateful when they're not injured while being robbed."

Schweitzer looks up. "What about a year and a year consecutive?" Erdmann
and Lowe agree.

In the next case Mills (1975: 140) notes that the defendant is "tried, convicted
and sentenced before his lawyer even knew what he looked like."

"Jose Sanchez!" the clerk calls. A drug-sale case.

"Your honor, he hasn't been seen yet," Erdmann says.

"Let me see the file," Schweitzer says to Lowe.

"Your honor," Erdmann protests, "he hasn't even been interviewed. I
haven't seen him."

"Well, just let's look at it Marty," the judge says. He goes over to Lowe's
file. "It's one sale, Marty. He doesn't have any robberies. Burglaries, petty
larceny. Mostly drugs. I'll tell you what, Marty, I'll give him an E and a flat
[Class E felony with a one-year sentence]." Lowe agrees.

Plea bargaining can also be accomplished in a judge's chambers as part of
a formal pre-trial conference at which the judge, prosecutor, public defender
and defendant are present. (Kerstetter and Heinz, 1979: 177–78). Other
participants may include the victim and arresting officer.

Participants: Judge, Public Defender, Assistant State Attorney, Victim
Location: Judge's Chambers
Charge: Larceny

Speaker	*Person Addressed*	
Judge	Defense Counsel	What is this case?
Def. Coun.	Judge	This is a shoplifting case. There was another woman associated with her who is a known shoplifter. The stores involved are _____, _____, and _____. Baby clothes, dresses, housecoats, and purses were taken. The defendant has no prior record.
Judge	All	Is she married?
Def. Coun.	Judge	Yes.
Judge	Def. Coun.	Any children?
Def. Coun.	Judge	One daughter.
Prosecutor	Judge	She was carrying a large shopping bag, cruising the store with this other person who has a record of shoplifting.
Judge	Prosecutor	The record ought to list what was stolen.
Judge	Victim	What was stolen?
Victim	Judge	Baby goods and women's apparel. The items have been recovered.

Judge	Prosecutor	Would PTI* be acceptable? What would you recommend?
Def. Coun.	Judge	When the security officer stopped her she didn't give any trouble and said she needed clothes for her family.
Judge	All	I think PTI should be tried. She has no prior record.
Judge	Victim	What would you recommend?
Victim	Judge	When I talked to the defendant it was clear she knew these other shoplifters well. I think she planned this—it wasn't any whim. It is my personal belief that this is not the first time for her although she may well not have a prior record.
Def. Coun.	Judge	The police talked with me yesterday and said the defendant has given them information about the other shoplifters. I'm not arguing that no prior record means she hasn't done this before. I know the realities.
Prosecutor	Judge	I think you should give probation.
Judge	All	That's all right with me. If she violates it then she will get time.
Judge	Victim	What's your name?
Victim	Judge	_____
Judge	Victim	What was your loss?
Victim	Judge	About $100 worth of goods.
Judge	Victim	I want you to know I shop there too. (Laughter as victim and defense counsel leave.)

Time elapsed: 5 minutes.

Conference Status: tentative settlement with disposition probation (no length specified)

---

*PT = Pretrial Intervention Program—diversion program for first offenders run by State Attorney's Office.

Participants: Judge, Assistant State Attorney, Public Defender, Defendant, Arresting Police Officer
Location: Judge's chambers
Charge: Aggravated Assault

Speaker	*Person Addressed*	
Judge	Public Defender	Who is the defendant and what are the facts in this case?
Pub. Def.	Judge	The charge is aggravated assault, and the defendant is alleged to have threatened the victim with a knife.
Pub. Def.	Defendant	Explain the facts of this case to the judge.
Defendant	Prosector	The guy claims that I attacked him, but I didn't. We just had an argument.
Pub. Def.	Judge	The victim claimed that my client had a knife.
Judge	Public Defender	Were there any eye witnesses?
Pub. Def.	Judge	No, there were no witnesses. The neighbors heard the argument but didn't see it.
Judge	Defendant	Did you, in fact, have a knife?
Defendant	Judge	No, Your Honor, I did not.
Judge	Police	What do you know about this case?
Police	Judge	We responded to a neighbor's call. The defendant's parked car had been struck by the victim's car. The two got into an argument. The victim says the defendant got a knife from the glove compartment and started waving it at him.

Judge	Police	Did you find the knife?
Police	Judge	No.
Judge	Public Defender	Does this man have any prior record?
Pub. Def.	Judge	Well, yes, there is a pending charge in another case.
Judge	Defendant	Have you had any prior convictions?
Defendant	Judge	Yes.
Pub. Def.	Defendant	Back in 1969, there was a charge of breaking and entering in the Carolinas, was there not?
Defendant	Public Defender	That's correct.
Pub. Def.	Defendant	How much time did you serve on that charge?
Defendant	Public Defender	Two and a half years.
Prosecutor	Defendant	Did you have two robbery charges in that case?
Defendant	Prosecutor	Yes, but they were dismissed. I was only charged with breaking and entering.
Judge	All	That is not a very good record
Judge	Defendant	Are you married?
Judge	Defendant	Do you have a job?
Defendant	Judge	I worked at _____ for 14 months but was laid off two months ago.
Judge	Prosecutor	What do you think should happen?
Prosecutor	Judge	The State wants three years.
Judge	Public Defender	What do you think should happen?
Pub. Def.	Judge	We were looking for time served and probation.
Judge	Police	Do you have a recommendation?
Police	Judge	Whatever you think is appropriate is all right with us.
Judge	All	I can't let him walk on probation. This is a serious charge and I need to protect society as well as look out for the defendant. I am thinking of 18 months and 3 years probation.
Pub. Def.	Judge	I'd like to see jail time but not prison. The victim was involved in the argument, too.

Judge	Prosecutor	Where is the victim?
Prosecutor	Judge	The victim is ill today.
Judge	All	The defendant's record is pretty bad. If the defendant pleads guilty I have to give 18 months and probation. This is not the first time he has been in trouble.
Pub. Def.	Judge	I'll have to discuss this with my client.
Judge	Public Defender	When can you report back?
Pub. Def.	Judge	I'm back here on April 14th.
Judge	Prosecutor	What about you?
Prosecutor	Judge	Okay with me.
Judge	All	Let's reschedule it for sounding on April 6. Thanks for coming.

> Time elapsed: 14 minutes
> Conference status: Tentative settlement with disposition of 18 months in prison
> followed by 3 years probation.

Plea negotiations can occur in the courtroom, the judge's chambers, or, as in Detroit, in a hallway (McIntyre, 1967: 132–33):

> A hallway about 20 feet long and 4 feet wide running between two court-rooms is used as conference quarters by the assistant prosecuting attorney and the various defense attorneys who line up to talk with him and discuss pleas and sentences during the judge's first docket call or immediately thereafter. . . .

> One typical hallway negotiation involved a defendant charged with being in possession of 19 capsules of heroin, a crime carrying a maximum sentence of 10 years. The assistant prosecuting attorney offered him an added count as a user, which would carry a 1-year maximum. Defense counsel asked the assistant prosecuting attorney if he would not also recommend probation on the one year maximum as a user, since the defendant was 28 years old and had no prior record and the heroin was only for his own use. The assistant prosecutor argued that anybody having 19 caps had some to sell; no user would have that much for his own use alone. After some arguing back and forth, the assistant prosecuting attorney said that he would neither favor nor oppose probation, but if the defense counsel could get the inspector in charge of the narcotics bureau to agree to it, he would go along. The defense counsel shrugged his shoulders, saying that the inspector will not favor probation. But defense counsel finally agreed to plead his client to the reduced charge.

Plea bargaining can be accomplished in a variety of settings: from court-rooms to offices, hallways to washrooms—this writer has seen plea negotia-tions completed in front of urinals. How can these matters be discussed and settled in such informal settings? How can they be completed in so

short a time—seconds, minutes? David Sudnow (1965) provides an answer:
Normal Crimes. The term as used by Sudnow indicates "typifications," or
"routinizations." In the course of routinely encountering persons charged
with "normal" offenses (theft, burglary, robbery, rape, murder), the public
defender and prosecutor gain knowledge about the typical manner in which
each of these "normal" crimes is committed, the social characteristics of the
persons who regularly commit them, and the features of the settings in which
they occur, the type of victims often involved, etc. The "regular players" in
the criminal courts operate in accord with an unwritten schedule of what
each "normal" crime is "worth"—the sentence—as long as it is *normal.* Any
variety of elements can move a case out of the "normal" category: e.g., if the
victim is a prominent public person or perhaps a police officer; when a
victim is injured without provocation or perhaps tortured; crimes against
children, clergymen, the blind, etc. As long as the features of the crime are
viewed as "normal," negotiating a plea and sentence is quite simple, perhaps
only an exchange of a few words: "We'll take the usual." the public defender
to prosecutor. "O.K." she responds.

Plea negotiations can vary according to judicial involvement. Martin
Levin (1977: 73) states that during his research in Minneapolis negotiations
did not involve the prosecutor who "is present but merely as a 'third-party'
witness." Discussions center on the sentence, not the level of charges, and
charges are rarely reduced. Generally, he found, in Minneapolis the sentencing decision is completely within the purview of the judge, and assistant
prosecutors rarely make sentencing recommendations either informally or
in open court. If a prosecutor does make a sentencing recommendation in
open court, his/her move has usually been suggested by the judge. Levin
notes that the judge is also a central figure in plea negotiations in Pittsburgh.
In this city negotiations center on the sentence, not the charges, and typically occur between defense counsel and judge.

The role of the judge in plea bargaining is often dependent on the type of
sentencing mandated by the statutes in a particular jurisdiction. Determinate sentences usually enhance the plea bargaining authority of the prosecutor,
while indeterminate sentences usually increase the discretionary powers of
the judge. (The types of sentences and their implications for discretion will
be examined in the next chapter.)

Research conducted more than a decade ago in New York City provides
some insight into the charging and plea bargaining process. The research
was the result of criticism leveled at the court system in 1972 by Police
Commissioner Patrick V. Murphy. Murphy claimed that while his police
officers were making arrests for serious crimes, the courts were allowing
offenders off with only a "slap on the wrists." The Vera Institute of Justice
(1977: 134) concluded that Murphy was correct:

(a) 43% of the cases commenced by felony arrest and disposed of in the Criminal Court were dismissed.

(b) 98% of the cases that ended in conviction were disposed of by guilty pleas rather than trial.

(c) 74% of the guilty pleas were to misdemeanors or lesser offenses.

(d) 50% of the guilty pleas were followed by "walks" (no incarceration), and 41% by sentences to less than one-year in jail.

(e) Only 9% of the guilty pleas were followed by felony time sentences (of more than one-year in prison).

(f) Only 2.6% of the cases were disposed of by trial.

However, while the research confirmed Commissioner Murphy's criticism, it also provided an explanation for its findings that the Commissioner did not anticipate (1977: 135):

> The reason why so many cases that come into the system as felonies are not prosecuted as charged is . . . that a high percentage of them, in every crime category from murder to burglary, involve victims with whom the suspect has had prior, often close, relations. Logically, suspects who are known to their victims are more likely to be caught than strangers because they can be identified more easily by the complainants. And this very fact of a previous personal relationship often leads a complainant to be reluctant to pursue prosecution through adjudication. The study found that tempers had cooled, time had passed, informal efforts at mediation or restitution might have worked, or, in some instances, the defendant had intimidated the complainant.

> The study found an obvious but often overlooked reality: criminal conduct is often the explosive spillover from ruptured personal relations among neighbors, friends and former spouses . . . Judges and prosecutors, and in some instances police officers, were outspoken in their reluctance to prosecute as full-scale felonies some cases that erupted from quarrels between friends or lovers.

Ilene Bernstein and her colleagues (1977: 374) found that in cases of assault investigated in New York City an overwhelming majority "were alleged to have occurred between friends and relatives." These cases were treated leniently, and Bernstein (et al., 1977) suggest that "leniency accorded to assault cases may additionally reflect the courts' adoption of a street-wise definition of assaults as routine for the lower class culture. . . ." Frank Miller (1969: 175) states: "If, within certain cultural subgroups, objectively more serious assaults are routinely regarded as not serious, it is not surprising that police and prosecutors tend to accept the group judgment. . . ."

THE TRIAL AND JURY SELECTION

When plea bargaining is not attempted (the case may be too serious or too sensitive) or does not succeed, the alternative is a trial by jury (jury trial) or by judge (bench trial). Each criminal defendant is guaranteed the right to a jury trial by the Sixth Amendment: "In all criminal prosecutions the accused shall enjoy the right to a speedy* and public trial by an impartial jury...." In 1968 (*Duncan v. Louisiana* 391 U.S. 145) and 1970 *Baldwin v. New York* 399 U.S. 66, 69) the Supreme Court ruled that this right to a jury trial applies only to crimes punishable by a term of imprisonment of six months or more. (Some states such as California provide a jury trial for anyone accused of *any* criminal charges). For crimes punishable by at least six months of imprisonment the defendant can exercise his/her discretion to have a bench trial or a jury trial. In a bench trial the judge acts as both referee, determining matters of procedure and law, and a one-person jury determining matters of fact and guilt or innocence. (Juries in Indiana and Maryland have limited power to determine questions of law).

While most states and the federal government use twelve-person juries, the Supreme Court (*Williams v. Florida* 399 U.S. 78, 102) in 1970 declared that the number twelve was an "historical accident" and thus not constitutionally required. The *Williams* decision upheld the six-person jury used in Florida in all but capital cases, but ruled against a five-person jury (*Ballew v. Georgia*

---

*While the Supreme Court has not quantified the meaning of a "speedy trial," it has set down four factors to be considered when assessing whether a particular defendant was denied his Sixth Amendment right (*Barker v. Wingo*, 407 U.S. 514, 1972):
1. the length of the delay;
2. the prosecution's reasons for the delay;
3. the defendant's demand for a speedy trial; and
4. the degree of prejudice to the defendant caused by the delay.

Peter Lewis and Kenneth Peoples (1978: 673) point out:
   The length of the delay is dependent upon the particular circumstances of each case (e.g., a complex conspiracy case would justify a longer delay than would an ordinary street crime). A purposeful delay by the prosecution in an attempt to handicap the defense would weigh heavily in favor of the defendant, whereas a more neutral reason (e.g., crowded court docket) would weigh less heavily. Although it is not absolutely necessary that a defendant assert his right to a speedy trial, his failure to do so will usually count strongly against him.

They point out further, that in the *Barker* decision the Court was interested in the need to prevent oppressive pretrial incarceration, to minimize the anxiety and hardship of the defendant, and to avoid hampering the defense. "The greatest weight is to be assigned to the latter category since an unusually lengthy delay can result in a denial of a fair trial in violation of the Due Process Clauses of the Fifth and Fourteenth Amendments" (1978: 673).

   In 1974, Congress passed the *Speedy Trial Act* which provided for a gradual reduction of the amount of time permitted between arrest (or summons) and trial. By 1979 federal prosecutors were required to bring defendants to trial within 100 days. States have followed the federal lead by adopting similar rules. Illinois requires that a defendant in custody be brought to trial within 120 days; a defendant out on bail 160 days. The "clock" starts running as soon as the defense makes a demand for trial.

435 U.S. 233) in 1978 even though the case only involved a misdemeanor. In most states jury decisions are required to be unanimous, or else a "hung jury" results, requiring either a re-trial or dismissal of the charges. However, Louisiana, whose legal system reflects French, not English, influence, has permitted verdicts of 9-3, and in 1934 Oregon enacted a law permitting 10-2 verdicts in all but capital cases. The Supreme Court (*Johnson v. Louisiana* 406 U.S. 356; *Apodaca v. Oregon* 406 U.S. 404) in 1972 ruled the Louisiana and Oregon laws constitutional. However, in 1979 the Court ruled that if six jurors are used the verdict must be unanimous (*Burch v. Louisiana* 441 U.S. 130).

The *jury trial* is a time-consuming process beginning with the selecting of jurors. While the procedures vary, there are ten general steps.

1. *First Master List.* This can include voting rolls, lists of persons having driving licenses, and those on the tax rolls. Most, if not all, jurisdictions use the voting rolls, and many supplement it with driving or tax lists (to reach persons who deliberately fail to register to vote to avoid jury service).

2. *First Juror List.* Names are selected at random from the master list.

3. *Questionnaires.* Persons on the first juror list are sent questionnaires to determine if they are qualified. In order to be qualified most jurisdictions require that a person be at least eighteen, have no felony convictions, be a U.S. citizen and have lived in the court's jurisdiction for a minimum period of time, e.g., one-year, be able to read, write and understand English, and be devoid of any mental or physical disability that would make the person unable to render jury service. Otherwise qualified persons may be exempted: for example, law enforcement officers, doctors, lawyers, teachers during the school year, mothers of infants, farmers during the harvest season. Jurors may also be excused from service based on personal hardship: owners of small businesses, students, etc. Persons may receive a temporary postponement based on a hardship that is time-limited.

Evasion of jury service is a serious problem in some jurisdictions. In Cook County (Chicago is the county seat), Illinois "Court officials say that as many as 65 percent of those receiving questionnaires do not bother to answer them" (Mount and Taylor, 1983: 1). In New York City, on the opening of the 1983 fall term of the state courts, 27 percent of those summoned failed to appear and some trial courts had to be shut down for lack of jurors (Shenon, 1983).

4. *Second Master List.* Based on the questionnaires, a second master list is developed and summonses are mailed out. Those responding to the summons are screened: disqualified, exempt, excused and qualified.

5. *Report for Service/Jury Pool.* Those who are qualified are directed to report to a central jury room.

6. *Impaneled.* Those who report to the central jury room and are not excused are sworn in as jurors.

7. *Voir Dire.* A panel of sworn jurors is selected for a hearing during which each prospective juror is questioned by the judge, defense counsel and prosecutor. In some jurisdictions the judge conducts the questioning and defense and prosecution are allowed to submit questions they want asked. The judge decides which questions are appropriate. The purpose of the questioning is to determine those jurors who would not be able to render an impartial verdict. Such persons can be discharged by the judge on his/her own authority, or challenged by one of the attorneys for *cause:* for example, if the juror is related to the defendant or the victim, or expresses negative feelings about the defendant, or has heard or read a great deal about the case (the problem of pre-trial publicity). The judge determines if the challenge for cause is valid. Defense attorneys and prosecutors also have a number of *peremptory* challenges by which they can dismiss a juror without having to provide any reason. The number of these challenges can vary from two to twenty-six depending on the jurisdiction and the seriousness of the case—murder cases usually entitle attorneys to more peremptory challenges. The final trial jury will usually consist of twelve jurors and one or two alternate jurors, persons who hear the case along with the regular jurors but do not participate in the deliberations unless a juror is incapacitated or becomes disqualified.*

Before turning to the trial process, let us look briefly at the problem posed by *scientific jury selection* (Hunt, 1982; Andrews, 1982). Morton Hunt (1982: 70) summarizes the approach:

> . . . a few dozen sociologists, psychologists, market researchers and others—use public-opinion surveys, in-depth interviews, computer analyses correlating jurors' backgrounds and attitudes and laboratory simulations of impending trials to help lawyers select jurors likely to favor their side, exclude those likely to be hostile to it and present their cases in ways psychologically designed to benefit from the unconscious needs and motives of the jurors.

Scientific jury selection attempts to identify the type of person most likely to be favorable to their side, as well as those most likely to be hostile, for use at voir dire hearings. In some programs a simulated jury selection process is conducted and the "jurors" selected are paid to participate in a mock trial. After the mock trial the "jurors" are questioned to determine the best trial approach, that most likely to convince a real jury. The attorneys are advised

---

*In 1984 the Supreme Court (*Press-Enterprise v. Superior Court,* No. 82-556) ruled unanimously that trial judges must ordinarily permit the public and news media to attend jury selection proceedings. The court stated that only in "rare" circumstances, when less drastic alternatives are not available, can the jury selection process be closed: "Closed proceedings, although not absolutely precluded, must be rare and only for cause shown that outweighs the value of openness."

about questions to ask, how to speak, what clothes to wear in order to enhance their influence on a jury.

There are a number of firms that will provide this service and it is expensive. For that reason, except in isolated instances, scientific jury selection usually occurs in civil cases where the outcome can involve millions of dollars. The best-known criminal case utilizing scientific jury selection involved Joan Little, a 20-year-old black woman inmate in a rural North Carolina jail who in 1974 killed a 62-year-old white jailor with an icepick. The defendant claimed self defense. She stated that the jailor had forced her to commit oral sex by threatening her with the icepick with which she eventually killed him. A public opinion survey in the Beaufort area enabled the defense to gain a change in venue, moving the case to Raleigh. Further research enabled the defense to develop a profile of the type of person who would be a friendly juror and this information was utilized during the voir dire hearing. The five-week trial ended with a jury deliberation that lasted only 78 minutes—Joan Little was found "not guilty."

Scientific jury selection has the potential of exacerbating already existing inequities in the criminal justice system. The estimated cost of these services for Joan Little, which was contributed, is in excess of $300,000.

THE CRIMINAL TRIAL PROCESS

Before the trial begins (if there is a jury), the judge instructs the jury on the basic rules of conduct: e.g., do not discuss the case among yourselves before deliberations; do not discuss the case with anyone else until you are discharged; do not read or listen to any accounts of the case; report immediately any attempt by anyone to influence you or any other member of the jury. The judge also explains how the trial is conducted, and the jury's role: to determine the facts; to decide what weight is to be given to any evidence; to determine the credibility of witnesses. The trial is ready to begin.

1. *Opening Statements.* The trial begins with an opening statement by the prosecutor who provides an overview that explains the nature of the case and what he/she intends to prove. Next, the defense can present an opening statement, although some jurisdictions permit him/her to do so after the prosecutor has presented his/her case and "rests." The defense attorney may waive the opening statement: he/she need not prove anything, the prosecution has the obligation to prove guilt "beyond a reasonable doubt."

2. *Calling Witnesses.* Evidence can only be entered via the direct testimony of a witness. First, the prosecutor calls a series of witnesses, e.g., police officer, victim, forensic experts. Through direct examination of each witness the prosecution builds his/her case. After each witness has testified under direct examination, the defense lawyer can cross-examine. During cross-

examination the attorney can ask leading questions requiring a "Yes" or "No" response: e.g., "Isn't it true, that on the night you said you saw the defendant, that you had been drinking for several hours?" The attorney will also try to discredit the witness, if possible, by impeaching his/her credibility: e.g., "Isn't it true that you have several criminal convictions?" After each cross-examination is completed, the prosecutor may question the witness again—a redirect—usually limited to clarifying or developing material that was raised during the cross-examination. If new matters result from the redirect, the judge can permit the defense to re-cross-examine the witness.

After the prosecution rests, the defense counsel may call witnesses for direct testimony, subject to cross-examination by the prosecutor, redirect by the defense, and re-cross-examination. The defendant need not testify (Fifth Amendment), but may choose to waive his/her right to silence and, in effect, become a witness on his/her own behalf. As a witness, information about a prior criminal history, which ordinarily would not be allowed entry, can be brought out by the prosecutor in his/her cross-examination efforts to impeach the credibility of the *defendant-as-witness.* Finally, the prosecution may call witnesses in rebuttal to defense testimony. If the prosecutor presents rebuttal witnesses, the defense may also.

3. *Closing Arguments.* This part of the trial provides the attorneys with an opportunity to sum up their views of the case and try to persuade jurors to adopt their view. The summation by the prosecutor includes a review of the testimony that established the *corpus delicti,* evidence to prove that a crime actually occurred. If the defendant chose not to testify, the prosecutor may not comment on that fact in his/her summation. Final arguments must be based on evidence developed during the trial—inadmissable evidence cannot be discussed. The defense attorney usually bases his/her final argument on the failure of the prosecution to establish guilt beyond a reasonable doubt.

4. *Charging/Instructing the Jury.* After closing arguments are completed, the judge must charge the jury: instruct them on matters of applicable law and their responsibilities as determiners of fact. He/she will admonish them against considering any matter that was ruled out of order. If the defendant chose not to testify, the judge will direct them not to consider that as any indication of guilt or innocence. In some states the judge will read from a standardized form; in other jurisdictions the prosecutor and defense counsel will be consulted by the judge prior to his/her charge to the jury. At the conclusion of the testimony the judge may (it is infrequent) render a *directed verdict* of acquittal based on the lack of a *prima facie* case as presented by the prosecution: the minimum level of required evidence is not present for any finding of guilty.

5. *The Verdict.* The jury now retires to deliberate. In some cases the judge

may order the jury sequestered: guarded from any improper contact. This may be done when there is concern that attempts to tamper with the jury may be tried, or when the amount of news media coverage is so extensive that jurors may easily be exposed to it. Jurors may also be sequestered from the very beginning of a trial, although this is rare. If, after lengthy deliberations and encouragement from the judge, the jury is unable to reach a verdict, there is a "hung jury," and the judge will order the jury discharged. The prosecutor must subsequently determine if he/she wishes to try the defendant again. A verdict of "Not guilty" means that the defendant cannot be tried again on these same charges (although defendants acquitted in state courts have been tried in federal court for "civil rights" violations based on the same evidence). A verdict of guilty (on one or more counts) moves the case into the sentencing stage which will be discussed in the next chapter.

As we can easily see, the jury trial is a time-consuming process. It increases the uncertainty inherent in the criminal justice system, uncertainty that defense and prosecution attempt to reduce through plea bargaining. In addition, it is trying, if not traumatic, for the victim who must recount in detail all of the elements of the crime and be subjected to rigorous cross-examination: "They treated me like *I* was the criminal," is not an uncommon assertion from victims at a trial. Police officers involved with the case, of course, will have to spend a great deal of time away from their usual posts or assignments.

POLICE-PROSECUTOR RELATIONS

As we have already noted, the police usually serve on a municipal level with resources far in excess of that enjoyed by a prosecutor who usually serves on a county level. One prosecutor will have to deal with a number of different police agencies. There are important social and educational differences between police officers and prosecutors, and "Police are more likely to see their job as a career whereas many, if not most, prosecutors see law enforcement as a stepping-stone for a private law career" (Schuster, 1979: 6). The police have a singular role—law enforcement—when the offense is serious and there exists probable cause. The prosecutor has a dual role: (a) law enforcement *and* (b) "justice:" protecting the rights of those whose guilt is in doubt or against whom there is insufficient evidence to warrant prosecution. Thus, the police may be required to arrest in cases where the prosecutor is obliged to decline prosecution. Richard Schuster (1979: 8) notes: "Police officers do not understand the prosecutor's need for plea bargaining and may become alienated from the prosecutor's office. This situation is accerbated even more when . . . prosecutors do not inform the police of reasons for plea bargaining (some of which may have to do with

sloppy police work." McDonald (et al. 1982: vi) points out that "the police
are more sensitive to the immediate demands for crime control and prosecutors are more sensitive to the legal constraints on government action."

McDonald (et al., 1982: viii) points to a conflict over the boundary line
between police discretion and that of the prosecutor:

> Prosecutors have been expanding the scope of their activities into the earli-
> est stages of the justice process to include control over the initial charging
> decision. Although this change has been endorsed by national commissions
> it has been resisted . . . by the police . . . In 51% of jurisdictions over 100,000
> population the police still control the initial charging decision. This has two
> significant consequences: (1) the police decision regarding initial "police"
> charges substantially affects the pretrial release decision. (2) The social and
> financial savings to defendants and the state that might be achieved by
> prosecutorial screening prior to initial filing are not being realized.*

However, no matter when the prosecutor enters the process, the police are
still able to exert a great deal of control: "Police departments are able to
control this [prosecutorial] review by controlling information that is sent
forward in the organization of prosecution" (Litrell, 1979: 173). W. Boyd
Littrell (1979: 173) notes: "Detective bureaus eliminate some information
and reshape other information, putting it in legal form. In this way, detectives gain a great deal of control over dispositions."

Littrell explains that the police, by controlling the initial charging decision,
are able to determine the sentence (1979: 174). In this case the detective

> charged three offenses in the first case: armed robbery, larceny from the
> person, and larceny. When I asked why, he replied: "We'd try it on armed
> robbery; we'd be happy with larceny from the person and satisfied with a
> larceny, a misdemeanor—a three-year misdemeanor." . . . the detective knew
> . . . that the defendant would receive the punishment he deserves: a three-
> year sentence that would amount to something less than a year of real time.

McDonald (et al., 1982: 6) summerizes police complaints about prosecutors:

> they are too "conviction-oriented" by which the police mean that prosecutors
> are only willing to take very strong, winnable cases to trial and are too ready
> to plea bargain, dismiss or reject the rest.

> . . . They feel that prosecutors are just using their office as a stepping stone

---

*Aaronson (et al., 1977: 62) provides an example of just how far the scope of the prosecutor's
activities can reach into the earliest stages of the criminal justice process: placing an assistant
prosecutor in a police station. This is done in Houston, Texas "where representatives of the
Harris County District Attorney's Office are assigned on a twenty-four hour basis. . . . The
prosecutor reviews the appropriateness of the charge and, depending on the case, the adequacy of
the supporting evidence in the presence of the police officer. The prosecutor must place his
initials on the appropriate documents before the police officer can complete the papering process
and obtain an expected court date."

on a legal career and therefore lack an appropriate level of dedication to law enforcement; that prosecutors are too "political" which means that they are overly concerned with their personal and organizational "track records;" that they are afraid of offending members of the local power structure; that prosecutors are too inexperienced and lack the competence to obtain appropriate dispositons either at trial or through negotiations....

... they do not understand or appreciate police work, problems and priorities ... do not "know the street" and therefore are naive about the real world of crime....

On the other side (McDonald, et al., 1982: 7):

The main complaint prosecutors have about the police is that they do not provide prosecutors with the amount and kind of information (evidence) they need. Investigations and case reports are insufficient for the purposes of prosecution. Prosecutors say the police are too arrest-oriented. That is, they terminate their role in a case as soon as they have probable cause and an arrest; and it is difficult to get them to continue to investigate a case once ... they have gotten their arrest and clearance statistic out of it.... *

... police do not ask for prosecutorial advice before acting, or fail to warn prosecutors about weaknesses in cases, or the police are not easily accessible to discuss cases, or too many police officers get involved in a case thereby unnecessarily complicating its prosecution.

CONTROL OF DISCRETION

James Vorenberg (1976: 679) points out that the courts have been reluctant to limit the discretionary powers of a prosecutor except when it involves discrimination—"an unjustifiable standard"—based on race, religion, political beliefs or other arbitrary classification. However, "a number of courts have set aside convictions or enjoined prosecutions where the defendants were arbitrarily selected..., even without a showing of discrimination...." He notes that courts have also set aside prosecutions when they were viewed as intended for the purpose of intimidation or harassment. These instances have generally involved "vice" or similar offenses where most of the cases known to law enforcement are simply not subjected to prosecution (prohibition against "selective enforcement"). Precedent or tradition can also limit discretion. Earlier in this chapter it was noted, for example, that federal prosecutors developed largely tacit, but nonetheless real, standards that exerted control over prosecutorial decision-making (Kaplan, 1965). Let us

---

*Fredric Waldstein (1983: 14) found that in one jurisdiction that he studied "the police frequently exaggerated the seriousness of an offense beyond what the evidence warranted. In such instances the police received credit for solving a 'major' crime, but the prosecutor's office was left with a case it had little chance of winning as charged given the quality of the evidence in hand."

review the three official methods for controlling discretion: statutes, rules/regulations, supervisory review.

1. *Statutes.* Vorenberg (1976: 681) states that it is unrealistic to expect legislative bodies to enact effective legislation dealing with plea bargaining since it would require a great deal of legislative specification:

> It is clearly unrealistic, except perhaps in the very long run, to assume that such legislative specification would take place. Certainly the slow process of state legislatures and Congress in enacting coherent criminal codes suggests that pursuing such an approach for the purpose of encouraging greater specification in the criminal codes would be quixotic.

Aaronson (et al., 1977: 70) notes that "Proposals to abolish plea bargaining derive from the belief that its deficiencies cannot be remedied by reforms designed to regulate its use, and that the criminal justice system can work effectively without it." These are dubious propositions. He (et al., 1977: 70–71) points out that "Effective limitation of plea bargaining can only be implemented by prohibiting characteristics of the plea bargain, because the legislature cannot specify the subject matter of the charge but rather the elements that constitute plea bargaining. Guilty pleas, for example, cannot be eliminated." New York attempted this approach, specifying and controlling by statute the elements that constitute a plea bargain.

THE NEW YORK EXPERIENCE

When Governor Nelson Rockefeller failed to win the Republican nomination for President in 1972, he moved from his previous liberal orientation toward criminal justice issues to a "law and order" approach. New York, under Rockefeller, had attempted to deal with the problem of drug addiction through an extensive treatment response orchestrated by the New York State Narcotic Addiction Control Commission (for which this writer worked as a Senior Narcotic Parole Officer). In 1973, the Governor decided on a new approach: severe mandatory penalties for drug offenses at *all* levels. In order to accomplish the goals of the new approach—deter drug offenses and incarcerate the others for long terms—plea bargaining had to be curtailed.

The "Rockefeller Laws" created three categories in the State's class A felony:

1. Class A–I with a minimum of between 15 and 25 years and a maximum of lifetime imprisonment.
2. Class A–II with a minimum of between 6 and 8.4 years and a maximum of lifetime imprisonment.
3. Class A–III with a minimum of between one-year and 8.4 years and a lifetime maximum.

The statute prohibited any person *indicted* for a class A–III offense from pleading guilty instead to a lesser charge. Those *charged* with class A–I or A–II offenses could plead guilty to a class A–III felony, but no lower, guaranteeing imprisonment for an indeterminate period of from one-year to life (as determined by the parole board—discussed in the next chapter). In addition, a person paroled after serving (at least) the minimum sentence for any class A drug offense would remain under parole supervision for life, thereby subjecting that person to the real possibility of being returned to prison at any time for violating the technical rules of parole. There was also a "predicate felony" feature of the law which prescribed mandatory sentences for all (not only drug) offenders. Any person who had previously been convicted of a felony and who was subsequently indicted for a felony, was prohibited from pleading guilty, instead, to a misdemeanor.

A research study by the Joint Committee on New York Drug Law Evaluation (1977: 17) revealed that "the demand for trials rose sharply," and noted that "A trial took up to ten to fifteen times as long to complete as a non-trial disposition." The report notes that "defendants in class A–III were forbidden to plead guilty to a lower charge," and so "they had a major incentive to demand a trial rather than simply to plead guilty." In an effort to deal with the growing backlog of cases demanding trial, some prosecutors offered class A–III cases short prison minimums in exchange for a guilty plea. Under the predicate felony provisions persons indicted for a class D felony with a minimum of between 2 and 3.6 years and a maximum of between 4 and 7 years, could only plead down to a class E felony with a minimum of between 1.6 and 2 years and a maximum of between 3 and 4 years. Since these differences, between class D and class E felonies, were often mitigated by the parole board (which was not party to the plea bargain process), there was very little incentive for offenders to plead guilty.

Aaronson (et al., 1977: 71) points to the reasons the 1973 laws were subjected to significant changes by the state legislature in 1976, at the insistence of prosecutors and judges:

> First, it is ineffective; drug traffic has not declined. Second, not only has the law failed as a deterrent, but those most likely to obtain long sentences are the low-level drug pushers. Third, the courts are becoming clogged with cases as more defendants who cannot plea bargain come to trial, even with the addition of new judges. Fourth, some prosecutors expect to avoid the problems posed by the mandatory life sentences by offering lesser charges to defendants at the preindictment stage not covered by the law. . . . The difficulties with such rigid legislative attempts to regulate plea bargaining—which so directly limited prosecutorial and judicial discretion, while leading to such unfair, irrational, and non-humane dispositions—suggest that ways will be found to circumvent the law.

The basic way the law was circumvented by prosecutors is sometimes referred to as *front-loading:* plea negotiations and screening at the earliest stages of the process—well in advance of the indictment, perhaps even at the charging stage.

2. *Administrative Policy/Rules.* Vorenberg (1976: 681) states that while legislatures are currently inadequate for the task of setting standards for prosecutors, "there is no reason why they should not require prosecutors' offices to issue and keep current public guidelines that describe the circumstances under which they will charge less than the maximum and that deal with the multiple charge issue." Aaronson (et al., 1977: 63) believes that rulemaking should involve a cooperative venture between police and prosecutors:

> whereby each devises a set of internal departmental rules that are complementary and consistent. Each makes its rules known to and participates in the rulemaking process of the other. The police devise rules on the substantive regulation of arrest discretion, and the prosecutor focuses on the regulation of charge discretion. Its purpose is to establish rational rulemaking by improving the character and quality of cooperation and communication.
>
> . . . establish an ongoing law revision committee whose activity would be visible and which would involve the support and participation of the citizenry.
>
> . . . participants would consist of both senior and line officials and would receive advisory citizen participation.

While it is difficult to argue against a public agency having rules and guidelines governing its operational behavior, the promulgation of written rules and guidelines for public consumption is controversial with prosecutors. Norman Abrams (1971) points out that the publication of prosecutorial policy can encourage litigation of "side-issues" by giving the defense an issue, i.e., that his/her prosecution violates the prosecutor's *written* guidelines. In addition, once written these guidelines tend to take on a "statutory" quality making it difficult to change or adjust to special circumstances. It may also have the affect of providing immunity for behavior prohibited by law (e.g., a policy against prosecuting certain consensual sex offenses or non-commercial gambling). Abrams cautions against legislation requiring prosecutors to publish their policy, since this may cause them to hesitate to articulate *any* policy with respect to a controversial issue. Vorenberg (1976: 682) takes note of this issue:

> such an approach would have to include consideration of whether the individual defendants could challenge the prosecutor's rules and their fair application in particular cases. The extent to which an administrator's violations of his own guidelines provides a basis for judicial relief may affect not only the

punctiliousness of his compliance, but also his willingness to issue the guidelines, since permitting such challenges would open up a new major level of litigation, with more resulting delay and a need for greater resources.

Aaronson (et al., 1977: 77–78) argues that a variety of rules can be devised to formalize the charging process:*

> some absolute rules might specify conditions under which charging will or will not occur, particularly where a great volume of cases uses up the resources of the prosecutor's office. [For example] . . . if persons are arrested with a certain amount of a drug, they will be charged with a simple possession; if a greater amount, the charge will be increased to a higher level.

> Devising rules for other categories of crime such as burglary and larceny is more difficult. For some serious cases, guidelines may be applicable.

> A point system might be established that lists characteristic aspects of any given offense, and crimes would be weighted according to their seriousness.

A major effort to structure the decision-making process of U.S. Attorneys was completed in 1980 with the publication of *Principles of Federal Prosecution* by the United States Department of Justice. This 56-page document is intended "to assure regularity without regimentation, to prevent unwarranted disparity without sacrificing flexibility" (page i). Page one of the document explains that it is intended "to promote the reasoned exercise of prosecutorial discretion by attorneys for the government with respect to:

(a) initiating and declining prosecution;
(b) selecting charges;
(c) entering into plea agreements;
(d) opposing offers to plead nolo contendere [equivalent to a plea of guilty but cannot be used as an admission of guilt elsewhere, e.g., in a civil action for damages];
(e) entering into non-prosecution agreements in return for cooperation; and
(f) participating in sentencing."

The *Principles* must be adhered to by each federal prosecutor (page 2); however, "A United States Attorney may modify or depart from the principles set forth herein as necessary in the interests of fair and effective law enforcement within the district" (page 3). Only situations in which a modification or departure is contemplated as a matter of policy or regular practice need permission be secured from the Attorney General's Office (page 3).

The principles provide guidelines, not directives or rules, for the decision

---

*Through tight control of the charging process, a prosecutor can eliminate plea bargaining. Using the *trial sufficiency model* each case is subjected to intensive screening by experienced assistant prosecutors. Cases which cannot withstand the evidentiary requirements of a trial are screened out (Mellon, et al., 1981: 66).

to prosecute: "if he believes that the person's conduct constitutes a federal offense and that the admissible evidence will probably be sufficient to obtain and sustain [on appeal] a conviction, unless in his judgment, prosecution should be declined because:

(a) no substantial federal interest would be served by prosecution;
(b) the person is subject to effective prosecution in another jurisdiction; or
(c) there exists an adequate non-criminal alternative to prosecution" (pages 6–7).

The *Principles* than go on to break down each of the three reasons for declining to prosecute and offers guidelines on each. For example, the lack of a substantial federal interest is to be determined by such items as (page 7):

(a) federal law enforcement priorities;
(b) the nature and seriousness of the offense;
(c) the deterrent effect of prosecution;
(d) the person's history with respect to criminal activity;
(e) the person's willingness to cooperate in the investigation or prosecution of others.

The *Principles* then goes on to detail out each of these considerations in making a decision to charge or decline to charge. For example, Federal law enforcement priorities (page 8):

> Federal law enforcement resources and federal judicial resources are not sufficient to permit prosecution of every alleged offense over which federal jurisdiction exists. Accordingly, in the interest of allocating limited resources so as to achieve an effective nationwide law enforcement program, from time to time, the Department establishes national investigative and prosecutorial priorities.... In weighing the federal interest in a particular prosecution, the attorney for the government should give careful consideration to the extent to which prosecution would be in accord with established priorities.

Most importantly, the *Principles* require that the reason(s) for not prosecuting be reduced to writing and maintained as part of the prosecutor's records (page 14):

> Whenever the attorney for the government declines to commence or recommend federal prosecution, he should ensure that his decision and the *reasons* therefor are communicated to the investigating agency involved and to any other interested agency, *and are reflected in the files of his office.* (emphasis added)

The *Principles* provide guidelines for plea bargaining and make note of the possibility that a defendant may agree to plead guilty while actually maintaining innocence. Such pleas require the approval of the Attorney

General's Office and the *Principles* suggest (page 30) that the federal attorney "make an offer of proof of all facts known to the government to support the conclusion that the defendant is in fact guilty."

Leslie Donavan (1981: 992) argues that the *Principles* leave "Too many gaps," and thus they cannot "foreclose disparate treatment of similarly situated defendants," and they "provide no assurance of objectivity." She states (1981: 958fn) that the very generality of the *Principles* "has defeated the purposes of establishing such guidelines" in the first place. Thus, "While strict rules designed to meet every conceivable situation would be impossible, detailed outlines, explicit hypotheticals, and mechanisms for accountability are feasible and needed" (1981: 961).

3. *Supervisory Controls.* The manner in which a prosecutor sets up his/her organizational structure will impact on the exercise of discretion. For example, centralizing the case review function will insure a degree of consistency over filing and charging decisions. If there is adequately articulated policy, a centralized case review process can insure adherence to policy. Waldstein (1983) reports that in one jurisdiction, a newly elected prosecutor centralized routine administration into the hands of some top echelon staff and thereby was able to reduce the discretion over case disposition that had heretofor been enjoyed by assistant prosecuting attorneys. He argues that the most effective way to fashion a clear, consistent prosecutorial policy is to adopt a centralized bureaucratic approach to prosecutorial management. The two key stages for internal supervisory review are: *intake:* where decisions to prosecute or not, as well as the charges are made; and *plea agreements:* whether to reduce a felony to a misdemeanor, or to drop charges approved at intake, or to agree to recommend a particular sentence to the judge.

Aaronson (et al., 1977: 78) notes:

> Successful review requires a system for arranging the flow of cases—not just problem cases, but all cases. An adequate support staff also is needed. To maintain some degree of consistency, reviewers ought not rotate too often. Moreover, the reviewer must have regular access to the office head, since the charge decision reflects on the policy of the office; the reviewer must ensure that the charging decision conforms with the policy of the office. This . . . cannot work, however, without the cooperation of the assistants whose discretion it will diminish.

Aaronson (et al., 1978: 78) cautions: "Bad decisions made by a central review authority may have graver consequences than if the function were never centralized."

Aaronson (et al., 1977: 78–79) advocates consulting with the defense counsel in less serious cases before the filing of final charges: "It represents a corrective procedure designed to improve prosecutorial screening by giving more equal access to defendants." Miller (1969: 349) supports expanding the role of the defense attorney:

> extend the role of the defendant's counsel in the charging decision beyond his now recognized duty to guard the defendant's right to remain silent and to force the state to supply its own evidence. By presenting to the prosecutor all the alternatives available, by using his skills as an advocate, the defense counsel could contribute to a more rational and uniform basis for selecting charging alternatives as well as alternatives to charging.

Plea bargaining can also be reduced, usually inadvertently, by destabilizing the *courtroom workgroup* (Eisenstein and Jacob, 1977: 26):

> All members of the courtroom workgroup are interested in disposing cases, although the reason for this interest varies. Judges and prosecutors want high disposition rates in order to transmit an aura of efficiency and accomplishment. Prosecutors also prefer speedy dispositions because as cases age, memories dim and witnesses scatter, weakening the evidence and lowering the chances of conviction.

> Retained attorneys face a more complicated set of incentives. Most attorneys who specialize in criminal cases depend on a high turnover of clients who can afford only modest fees. Without high volume and the investment of a modest amount of time in each case, many a private defense counsel would go broke. Yet private counsel must maintain a reputation for vigorous defense in order to attract new clients. Public defender organizations charged with representing all indigent defendants prefer quick dispositions because their manpower barely suffices to handle their case load. But they also seek to establish a reputation for effective representation of defendants.

The key actors in the courtroom workgroup share a singular goal: reducing or controlling uncertainty—developing norms that are designed to make behavior and, thus, one's work, more predictable. The ability of the workgroup to achieve this goal is dependent on the degree and frequency of interaction. Thus, negotiations are fostered and facilitated by the stability of the workgroup "and the knowledge they acquire of each others' values and probable behavior" (Eisenstein and Jacob, 1977: 309). "Bustup" the workgroup by shifting or rotating members—judges, prosecutors, defenders—and the stability will be destroyed reducing that ability to negotiate—less plea bargaining and more trials will result.

ALASKA BANS PLEA BARGAINING (RUBINSTEIN, ET AL, 1980)

On July 3, 1975, Avrum Gross, the Attorney General of the State of Alaska, issued an order to the state's district attorneys which read in part:

... District Attorneys and Assistant District Attorneys will refrain from engaging in plea negotiations with defendants designed to arrive at an agreement for entry of a plea of guilty in return for a particular sentence. ...

In order to prevent the subversion of the sentence-bargaining ban, the Attorney General instructed prosecutors that, except in certain limited circumstances, they were to make absolutely no recommendation concerning the length of a defendant's sentence or to recommend any specific form of dispostion such as a fine or probation.

While bargaining over the sentence was relatively easy to discourage, the Attorney General found it considerably more difficlut to curtail bargaining over the charges. Despite this difficulty, Michael Rubinstein and his colleagues conclude that plea bargaining in general was clearly curtailed.

There was no statewide policy on the screening of cases, and various localities experienced different rates of case rejection after 1975: in Anchorage, felony case rejection went up only 1.7 percent; in Fairbanks, however, it more than doubled. In general, however, the new policy did not substantially increase the number of cases rejected by prosecutors. One explanation can be found in Alaska's rules of criminal procedure which require defendants to be brought before a judge no later than 24 hours after arrest, giving the prosecutor very little time and information upon which to make a filing decision.

Despite the new policy against plea bargaining, pleas of guilty continued at about the same level as before 1975 — most defendants pled guilty even when the state offered them nothing in return. Rubinstein (et al.) notes that an important reason for this is that no lawyer likes to make a fool of him/herself in public. If the defendant simply has no credible response to the state's case, the contest of a trial seems quite one-sided, if not foolish. On the other hand, a plea of guilty does avoid tying up the court's time and holds out the possibility of eliciting some leniency from the judge. In practice, this often occured. Since there was no decline in guilty pleas and prosecutors did not have to waste time on negotiations, the system became much more efficient.

There were some unanticipated results of the new policy:

— there was absolutely no change in sentences for cases involving violent crimes such as rape, robbery and felonious assault;
— there was very little change in sentences for most serious property crimes, particularly those involving offenders with prior felony convictions;
— the major change was the increased severity of sentences imposed on less serious property offenders, the "cleanest" of the defendants suffered the most as a result of the new policy.

Rubinstein and his colleagues conclude (1980: 243):

Although the Attorney General got what he asked for in that responsibility for sentencing was restored to judges, he probably did not expect what he got: a denial of leniency to the minor offenders . . . without any increase in the severity of punishment for violent or dangerous criminals. The Attorney General proved that it was possible to make large and significant statewide changes in an institutionalized plea-bargaining system, that this could be done rather quickly and without spending a lot of money, and that the curtailment of plea bargaining would not necessarily bring about a break-down in the administration of justice.

Efficiency increased; did *justice?*

REVIEW QUESTIONS FOR CHAPTER 3

1. Prior to the twentieth century, what was the level of legal training required of lawyers?
2. What is meant by the "case method?"
3. How is the legal profession stratified and where do criminal attorneys appear, in what stratum?
4. What are the major problems of a private criminal law practice?
5. Why do criminal defendants dislike being represented by the Public Defender?
6. What is the singular role of the defense counsel, and the dual roles of the prosecutor?
7. Why is the prosecutor the most powerful person in criminal justice?
8. How does the role of a judge differ from that of a jury?
9. What are the purposes of bail?
10. How can the police influence a bail decision?
11. What are the disadvantages for a defendant of being unable to make bail?
12. What are the advantages and disadvantages of early prosecutorial case review/screening?
13. What is the difference between an *information* and an *indictment?*
14. Why do some persons view plea bargaining as symptomatic of a closed or pathological criminal justice system?
15. Why do some persons view plea bargaining as a rational response to problems in criminal justice; an open system balancing the needs of law enforcement and due process?
16. What has been the Supreme Court's position with respect to plea bargaining?
17. What are all of the possible reasons for plea bargaining?

18. What are the four models for screening and charging by a prosecutor's office?
19. What is the difference between vertical and horizontal prosecution?
20. How does the concept of "normal" crimes help to explain why plea bargaining can be accomplished in a few minutes or even a few seconds?
21. What are the various roles that can be played by a judge in plea bargaining?
22. What are the various trial steps leading to a verdict by a jury?
23. What has the Supreme Court determined with respect to the size of a criminal jury and the size of a majority verdict?
24. What is meant by scientific jury selection?
25. What are some of the problems in police-prosecutor relations?
26. When have the courts acted to limit prosecutorial discretion?
27. What are the ways that prosecutorial discretion can be controlled, and what are the shortcomings of each approach?
28. What is meant by the courtroom workgroup and what is its significance with respect to plea bargaining?

CHAPTER 4

SENTENCING, PROBATION
AND AUXILIARY PERSONNEL

After a finding of guilt, by a plea, bench trial or jury trial, the defendant, now officially a *convict,* enters the sentencing stage of the criminal justice process and a number of theoretical and practical matters need to be considered.

PURPOSES OF SENTENCING

There are four oft-cited purposes for sentencing an offender:

1. *Retribution.* This ancient notion is expressed as *lex talionis*—"an eye for an eye"—and includes such concepts as vengence, punishment, and deserts, to "pay" for one's transgressions. (In biblical days *lex talionis* actually meant compensation for any injuries caused.) Ernest van den Haag (1975: 12) argues that "retributive punishment is indispensible to the maintenance of any social order. . . . " He notes that "Laws threaten, or promise, punishment for crimes. Society has obligated itself by threatening." Thus, "It owes the carrying out of its threats" (1975: 15). The constitutional prohibition against cruel and unusual punishments (Eighth Amendment) limits punishment to fines, imprisonment and (with restrictions) capital punishment—execution.

2. *Incapacitation.* This obviously, in our society, refers to imprisonment. (Nations governed by Islamic law cut off the hands of thieves.) During the period of incarceration the offender is prevented from victimizing others (who are neither fellow inmates nor prison staff). James Q. Wilson (1975: 200) argues that a sizable reduction in crime would ensue if *every* person convicted of a serious crime were imprisoned for three years.

3. (a) *General Deterrence.* This refers to the fear of being punished; its purpose is to deter law-abiding citizens from violating the law. "This is the concept that if one man is punished with a degree of severity for committing a crime, his publicized example will deter other would-be criminals from the same offense" (Gaylin, 1974: 18–19).

(b) *Specific Deterrence.* This assumes that if an offender is punished with a degree of severity for his/her offense, he/she is less likely to repeat this (or other) offense.

4. *Rehabilitation.* This refers to efforts at correcting the behavior of an offender from law-violator to law-abider through the application of "treatment." Willard Gaylin notes that this approach conceives of the offender "As a kind of social malfunctioner" who "needs to be treated or to be re-educated, reformed, or rehabilitated." He states: "Rehabilitation is the opposite of punishment. . . . " (1974: 20).

In order to understand how these "purposes" are operationalized in the sentencing process, it is necessary to look at the contrasting philosophies of the *classical* and *positive* schools of thought.

CLASSICAL SCHOOL

The classical philosophers of the 18th century offered a radical concept of law and justice — *equality.* Revolutionary in its time, classical thought helped to spark a revolution in the American colonies with the declaration "that all men are created equal" (July 4, 1776). Thirteen years later a revolution in France adopted a "Declaration of the Rights of Man and Citizen" which asserted the equality of all men. Both revolutionary documents were influenced by Jean Jacques Rousseau (1712–78) whose *Social Contract* (1762) conceives of a mythical state of affairs wherein each person agrees to a pact whose basic stipulation is that the conditions of law are the same for all: "The social contract establishes among citizens an equality of such character that each binds himself on the same terms as all the others, and is *thus* entitled to enjoy the same rights as all the others" (Rousseau, 1954: 45). With respect to crime and criminal justice Rousseau stated: "One consents to die — if and when one becomes a murderer oneself — in order not to become a murderer's victim" (1954: 48). In order to be safe from crime, we have all, via a "social contract," consented to punishment if we resort to criminality. Punishment, however, consistent with the stress on equality, must be meted out without regard to station — all are equal and all shall suffer equally for equal crimes.

Another aspect of classical philosophy incorporated into our legal system is the concept of *free will.* This view insists that every person has the ability to choose between right and wrong — criminal behavior is a deliberate choice by a rational actor. Since every person is rational, endowed with free will, punishment is not to be varied to suit the person or the circumstances of the criminal. From these philosophical roots developed the *determinate sentence.*

POSITIVE SCHOOL

Auguste Comte (1798–1857) is the French founder of a school of philosophy known as *positivism.* He argued that the methods and logical form of the natural sciences (e.g., physics, chemistry) are applicable to the study of man as a social being—he coined the term "sociology." The scientific study of *criminal* man (*L'uomo delinquente*) was the life work of Cesare Lombroso (1835–1909), a Venetian physician, whose research centered on physiological characteristics believed indicative of criminality (although his later work recognized environmental factors that explain crime).

Positivism denies the (classical) belief in "free will," which is a philosophically-based legal construct, but not scientific. Instead, positivists seek to explain criminality by utilizing the methods of science, the *social* sciences, particularly sociology and psychology.

Positivism argues that a legal (classical) response to criminals is not adequate to deal with the problem of crime. The causes of criminal behavior must be studied and the results of this research operationalized in the form of treatment designed to rehabilitate criminals. From these roots developed the concept of *corrections* and the *indeterminate sentence*.

DETERMINATE VS. INDETERMINATE SENTENCES

In its purest form, the *determinate* sentence provides for a set amount of time (years, months, days) as a penalty for each specific crime. The legislature determines the exact amount of time for each offense and the judge *must* impose it—no judicial discretion. An *indeterminate* sentence, on the other hand, does not have an exact amount of time but, instead, has a minimum amount and a maximum amount. For example, the crime of burglary could result in an indeterminate sentence of no less than 1.6 years and a maximum of no more than 9.6 years (written: 1-6-0/9-6-0). With the indeterminate sentence a parole board decides exactly when a person is to be released from prison, sometime between the minimum and the maximum. (Parole and parole boards will be discussed in detail in the next chapter.) Let us briefly review the historical development of determinate and indeterminate sentences in which discretion is a central issue.

America has been a pioneer in the development of prisons. (The French author of *Democracy in America,* Alexis de Tocqueville, 1805–1859, actually came to our country to study the American prison system). This pioneering effort led to the widespread construction of the stone-fortress, Auburn-type prison (named after the first institution of this type built in Auburn, New York). This large, walled institution proved to be very expensive to construct, but the cost was offset by contracting or leasing out inmate labor to private employers—some prisons actually made a net profit. Opposition to the use of very cheap inmate labor reached a peak during the great depression which began in 1929. As a result, laws were enacted that eliminated the profitable use (exploitation) of prison labor. At the same time there was very little money available to construct new prisons which were needed to relieve the dangerously overcrowded American prison system. At this point, philosophy and more practical concerns coincided and the indeterminate sentence (and parole) emerged. The indeterminate sentence and parole were presented as rehabilitative efforts. Inmates who had behaved satisfactorily would be paroled to the supervision of a parole officer who would aid them to "go straight."

A variety of "treaters" with college degrees, social workers, psychologists, psychiatrists, clergymen, teachers, entered the correctional institution in an effort to "treat" the "illness" that was crime. *Corrections* became the model for every state and the federal government. State after state re-named their prisons, e.g., Sing Sing Prison in New York became the Ossining Correctional Facility. After the treaters completed their work, the parole board would evaluate the inmate and determine when he/she would be released. By the 1970s, however, this system came under increasing criticism as an abuse of discretionary powers.

On the right of the political spectrum there had always been criticism— indeterminate sentences result in the paroling of dangerous criminals before they complete their (maximum) sentence. But criticism in the 1970s came from the left of the political spectrum. The American Friends Service Committee (1971: 29) declared that the indeterminate sentence results in a degree of uncertainty for inmates that constitutes "one of the more exquisite forms of torture." They criticized (alleged) rehabilitation arguing that this was just an excuse to keep inmates incarcerated for longer periods of time— made to stay in prison until they are "treated" or "cured." This attack on positivism as expressed through the indeterminate sentence had only minimal impact. In 1974, however, the results of an extensive research effort was published (Martinson, 1974: 25) and its conclusion devastated the positivist/corrections model: *"With few and isolated exceptions, the rehabilitative efforts that have been reported so far have had no appreciable effect on recidivism."*

Other critics stepped up the attack: David Fogel (1975), Andrew von Hirsch (1976) and the Twentieth Century Fund (1976) decried the sentence disparity caused by the indeterminate sentence and urged alternatives to the wide discretionary powers exercised by judges and parole boards. In 1976, Maine became the first state to abolish the indeterminate sentence and by 1983 eight other states (California, Colorado, Connecticut, Illinois, Indiana, Minnesota, New Mexico, North Carolina) had done the same. Each state, however, adopted a different form of the determinate sentence, and in several states (e.g., Maine, Indiana, Illinois) the wide discretionary powers of the sentencing judge were continued.

Let us now summarize the various sentencing systems in order to assess their impact on discretion:

SENTENCING RANGES FOR SELECTED FELONY OFFENSES*

(a) *Forcible Rape/Prior Convictions:* Maine (0–20 years) California (4–6 years) Indiana (6–50 years) Illinois (6–60 years).

(b) *Forcible Rape/First Offense:* Maine (0–20 years) California (3–5 years) Indiana (6–20 years) Illinois (6–60 years).

(c) *Narcotic Offense/First Offense:* Maine (0–10 years) California (3–5 years) Indiana (20–50 years) Illinois (4–30 years).

(d) *Simple Burglary/Prior Convictions:* Maine (0–5 years) California (28–48 months**) Indiana (2–38 years) Illinois (6–60 years***).

(e) *Simple Burglary/First Offense:* Maine (0–5 years) California (16–36 months) Indiana (2–8 years) Illinois (3–14 years).

---

*From Lagoy, et al., 1978: 399.

**Under the California code, one year is added to the base term for each prior prison term for a nonviolent offense; three years are added for violent offenses if the current offense is also violent. This example assumes that one prior prison term was served for a nonviolent felony.

***Persons convicted of a class 1 or class 2 felony with two prior convictions of class 1 or class 2 felonies are sentenced as class X offenders under Illinois law.

(a) *Indeterminate.* The legislature provides a range of minimum sentences and a range of maximum sentences. For example: a sentence of no less than 1-0-0 (one-year, no months, no days) nor more than 15-0-0. This means the judge can set the minimum between one-year and fifteen years, and the maximum between one-year and fifteen years, e.g., 1-0-0/15-0-0, 2-0-0/14-0-0, etc. (The exact amount of time served is determined by a parole board.)

(b) *Determinate/Narrow Discretion.* The legislature provides for a specific sentence (no minimum, no maximum — an exact number of years) for each offense, e.g., 9-0-0 for a Class B crime. Thus, *any* person convicted of a Class B crime *must* be sentenced to 9-0-0.

(c) *Determinate/Wide Discretion.* The legislature provides a range of sentences (no minimum, no maximum — an exact number of years) for each offense, e.g., 4-0-0 to 30-0-0 for a Class A crime. This means that a judge can set the sentence at 4-0-0, or 5-0-0, or 6-0-0 . . . , all the way up to 30-0-0.

(d) *Determinate/Presumptive.* The legislature limits discretion to a narrow range of sentences (no minimum, no maximum — an exact number of years) for each offense. For each criminal category, however, there is a *presumed* sentence from which the judge cannot deviate (no discretion) except for *mitigation* or *aggravation.* For mitigation, usually based on a motion by defense counsel, the judge can lower the presumed sentence by some limited amount, e.g., one-year. For aggravation, usually based on a motion by the prosecution, the judge can increase the presumed sentence by some limited amount, e.g., one-year. If the amount of time is substantial (e.g., for a Class B crime in Indiana: presumed sentence is 10-0-0; aggravation is plus 10-0-0; mitigation is minus 4-0-0) this can be considered a *Determinate/Presumptive/Wide Discretion.*

DISCRETION AND SENTENCING PRACTICES

Discretion can be compared to a balloon which is filled with water and closed: you can shift it around quite easily, but the total amount remains the same. Advocates of the determinate sentence intended to shift from positivism to a more classical approach to criminals based on "just deserts." The classical stress on equality would be operationalized through determinate sentencing which would reduce judicial discretion and thus sentence disparity. However, the only system capable of approaching this goal is a determinate sentence with narrow discretion. In practice, no system of determinate sentencing has narrowed discretion, "rather it is transferred to the prosecutor who uses it in charging" (Mellon, et al., 1981: 62).

We pointed out in the last chapter that an important reason for the continuation of plea bargaining is that it reduces the uncertainty inherent in the criminal justice system. Indeterminate sentencing requires that the judge agree to the "bargain" since he/she retains the discretion to set sentence minimums and maximums. However, the parole board is not a party to the deal and, therefore, continues the uncertainty over when a defendant will actually be released from prison. Determinate sentencing with narrow judicial discretion "locks-in" the judge—he/she must impose a specific sentence based on the charge to which an offender pleads (or is found) guilty. Since the prosecutor controls the charging decision, the prosecutor actually determines the sentence and, thus, when the defendant will be released from prison. This enhances the ability of a prosecutor to bargain: he/she can guarantee the date of release (assuming good behavior in prison) in exchange for a plea of guilty—no uncertainty.

In determinate sentencing systems in which the judge retains wide discretion, e.g., Illinois, the judge becomes directly involved in plea negotiations. A typical felony case in Cook County, Illinois will procede in the following manner:

> A preliminary and informal discussion will take place between defense counsel and prosecution. In open court and for the record, the defense attorney will request that the judge participate in a plea discussion. The judge will warn the defense that should he/she agree, in the event information is revealed which ordinarily the judge should not hear, he/she will not

disqualify himself/herself from presiding over the trial that will result if no plea agreement is reached. If all agree, a negotiating session(s) is held in the judge's chambers. In some cases, before a judge will agree to a plea bargain he/she may request a pre-sentence investigation (psi) by the probation department. If all agree, the court convenes for the defendant to enter a plea. The agreement is revealed in open court and for the record, and the prosecutor states the nature of the case and the evidence he/she was prepared to present. The defendant stipulates that the facts as presented by the prosecutor are essentially correct, and then enters a plea of guilty.

In most jurisdictions there are statutes that *require* (no judicial discretion) the imposition of a prison sentence of a certain duration for particular offenses or offenders, e.g., persons convicted of murder or rape, for habitual offenders, or for certain drug and weapons offenses. However, by controlling the charging decision, the prosecutor can avoid having a mandatory sentence imposed on a defendant in exchange for a plea of guilty. The mandatory sentence, in other words, often becomes just another piece of leverage in the plea bargaining process.

Lagoy, et al., (1979: 230) point out that "when changes are made in the sentencing system, accomodative responses are likely to occur which act to undermine the intent of the changes."

PROBATION

Probation is several things (all of which can be seen as part of a positivistic approach to crime and criminals): a sentencing alternative, an agency assigned to carry out the supervision of a person sentenced to a term of probation, and a report (also known as a presentence investigation, psi) drafted for the benefit of the sentencing judge. (The role of probation and probation officers in juvenile court will be examined in Chapter 6).

(a) *Presentence Investigation* (PSI). The psi report will vary with respect to length and quality of content. In some states every person convicted of a felony (and sometimes even a misdemeanor) will have a psi unless he/she waives this right. In other states the psi is at the discretion of the sentencing judge. In either event, the psi report will contain basic information about the offender and the offense (in addition to such biographical data as name, age, residence):

— circumstances of the offense (essentially the police version);
— defendant's version of the offense (an opportunity to offer mitigating or extenuating circumstances);
— remarks of complainant(s), witnesses, victim(s);
— prior juvenile and adult criminal history (often determines if the

defendant is eligible for probation or an enhanced, more severe, sentence, e.g., an habitual offender);

— family history (parents, siblings, spouse, children);
— military service (if any);
— education;
— health/physical;
— health/mental (includes the results of any psychological or psychiatric testing/evaluations, hospitalizations, drug or alcohol addiction);
— employment history;
— probation officer's analysis and recommendation (very important when a sentence of probation is being considered).

The length and quality of the psi (e.g., the amount of substantiation and verification of information) will be determined by:

1. the ability of the probation agency to provide adequate staff time to conduct a thorough psi and the capability of the individual probation officer; and
2. the attitude of the judge (does he/she even bother to read the report?) toward information in the psi and the degree to which the judge supports the probation officer's recommendation when imposing a sentence.

There has been a great deal of research on the relationship between the probation officer's recommendation and the sentence imposed by the judge. The research invariably concludes that there is an extremely high correlation, 60–96 percent, between the probation officer's recommendation and the judge's sentence. However, there is a problem with *causal order*. In other words, it may be the judge who is, directly or indirectly, explicitly or implicitly, influencing the probation officer's recommendation and not the other way around. In addition, police officers and prosecutors and, perhaps, defense counsel, can influence the recommendation of the probation officer. Indeed, the psi and the recommendation may be used to provide justification for the plea bargain that has already been agreed upon. This should serve "to remind us that the probation officer is simply one actor in a rather complex setting. How much influence he/she can exert often depends on procedural or structural variables, or perhaps the probation officer's force of personality" (Abadinsky, 1982: 76).

Since most cases entering the criminal justice system and making it to the judicial stage are settled by a plea bargain, a post-conviction psi is often superfluous and waived. In states utilizing a determinate sentencing system with narrow discretion, the psi would be of little value.

(b) *Sentence of Probation.* After a conviction (as a result of a trial or a plea) the judge has a limited number of options available in rendering a sentencing decision:

— fines and/or restitution;
— incarceration in jail or prison;
— suspended sentence;
— probation (a suspended sentence with supervision).

(These are not necessarily mutually exclusive. Fines and restitution can be combined with any of the other alternatives, and a short period of imprisonment followed by probation supervision—"shock probation"/"split sentence"—is also possible).

Most states have some statutory limitations on which defendants are eligible for a sentence of probation, precluding such a sentence for second or third felony convictions, murder, rape, kidnapping, robbery, etc. When probation is a lawfully permitted option the sentencing judge, quite naturally, will place great weight on the probation officer's recommendation (usually contained in the psi, but may be conveyed to the judge in some other manner).

Unfortunately, the probation agency may be influenced by the number of cases they are already supervising. In other words, a recommendation of incarceration may be based, not on the needs of the defendant and the case, but on the needs of the probation agency. Since probation only costs about 10–15 percent of what it costs to incarcerate a defendant, this self-serving recommendation has both human and economic costs. However, in the first chapter we noted the problem caused by criminal justice agencies operating at different levels of government. In this case, probation is often a county function, funded by county tax dollars. Prisons, on the other hand, are state institutions. It is easy to see that a county can experience a savings by having offenders sent to state-funded institutions instead of probation or the county jail. (This would not be a problem in the 26 states where adult probation is a state-level function, often combined with parole services.)

(c) *Supervision of Probationers.** The defendant whose sentence is suspended in lieu of imprisonment is placed under the aegis of a probation officer (po) for a term of supervision that varies with the level of the offense (misdemeanor, felony) and the laws of the particular jurisdiction. During the period of supervision the po is available to assist his/her client with a variety of problem areas: residence, employment, education, marital problems, drug or alcohol abuse, etc. The po also has a role in controlling the offender—to protect the community—and this involves the client conforming to a set of conditions or rules of probation. These rules are similar from

---

*About three-fourths of all adult offenders under "correctional" authority in the United States are in the community on probation or parole. At any given time there are about 1.5 million persons under probation supervision in the U.S. (Bureau of Justice Statistics).

jurisdiction to jurisdiction (and they are similar to rules of parole—see chapter 5). They caution the offender against violating the law, associating with criminals, possessing weapons, using controlled substances, or leaving the jurisdiction without advance permission from the po. The probationer is required to seek and maintain lawful employment, support his/her dependents, report in person, by telephone or letter to the po weekly, monthly, as directed, and to keep the po advised of any changes in residence or employment.

There is a great deal of (potential) discretionary authority inherent in the role of a po: How close will the client be monitored? How strictly will the rules be enforced? Most probation agencies are overwhelmed by the number of cases they must supervise (in addition to preparing presentence reports). As a result there is neither close monitering of client behavior, nor strict enforcement of the rules of probation, except when the behavior results in an arrest for a crime. In many agencies probationers who do not conform to the rules, but who avoid arrest for criminal behavior, are discharged—as "unimproved"—from supervision. Supervision is terminated, in effect, for poor behavior—hardly a punishment.

Probation violation is often invoked when a probationer absconds (fails to keep in contact with his/her po, ignores directions to report), or is arrested for a new crime. The case for a violation may be prepared by the probation agency or referred to the prosecutor's office. The violation of probation procedures are governed by the 1973 Supreme Court decision in *Gagnon v. Scarpelli* (411 U.S. 77) which requires two hearings:

1. *Preliminary Hearing.* At the preliminary hearing the probationer has an opportunity to respond to the charges against him/her. It takes place in court before the judge who imposed the original sentence (if practical). The probationer can deny the allegations or plead guilty to them, perhaps offering mitigating circumstances. If he/she pleads guilty, the judge may deal with the case at once, or wait until a violation of probation report is prepared. If the charges are denied, a revocation hearing is scheduled. Pending the second hearing the judge may remand the probationer to jail, release to bail, or his/her own recognizance. The probation department will prepare a violation of probation report detailing the charges and providing a summary of the probationer's adjustment while under supervision for the judge.

2. *Revocation Hearing.* At this second hearing the probationer may be represented by counsel and the probation agency by the prosecutor's office. The probationer can testify and present witnesses. If the judge finds no *substantial* violation of the conditions, the probationer is restored to supervision. If the judge sustains any charge(s) that amounts to a serious violation of probation, supervision is terminated and probation revoked;

FEDERAL CONDITIONS OF PROBATION

It is the order of the Court that you shall comply with the following conditions of probation:

(1) You shall refrain from violation of any law (federal, state, and local). You shall get in touch immediately with your probation officer if arrested or questioned by a law-enforcement officer.

(2) You shall associate only with law-abiding persons and maintain reasonable hours.

(3) You shall work regularly at a lawful occupation and support your legal dependents, if any, to the best of your ability. When out of work you shall notify your probation officer at once. You shall consult him prior to job changes.

(4) You shall not leave the judicial district without permission of the probation officer.

(5) You shall notify your probation officer immediately of any change in your place of residence.

(6) You shall follow the probation officer's instructions.

(7) You shall report to the probation officer as directed.

(8) You shall not receive, possess or transport any firearms or dangerous weapons.

The special conditions ordered by the Court are as follows:

---

the probationer is imprisoned to serve the suspended sentence.

Probation violation varies slightly from one jurisdiction to another, particularly with respect to "street time." This refers to the amount of time a probationer spends under satisfactory supervision. In some states it is credited against the sentence(s) he must serve. In other states he/she gets no "street time" or it is left to the discretion of the judge.

AUXILIARY PERSONNEL

In addition to the lawyers (judge, prosecutor, defender) and police officers, the courtroom "workgroup" includes clerks and bailiffs (whose official title may be court officer or deputy sheriff):

The clerk keeps records. Although judges and lawyers may keep their own, the clerk's record is the official one. He records decisions, the dates when they occurred, and the motions and appearances that are filed with him. Together with the stenographic record of the proceedings, the clerk's file is the official record of the case and is used by everyone in the courtroom to

PROBATION VIOLATION PROCESS
IN COOK COUNTY, ILLINOIS*

It is mandatory that a probation officer institute a petition charging the probationer with a violation of probation when:
1. there is a commission of a criminal offense; or
2. there is possession of a firearm or other dangerous weapon.

When a probationer has failed to maintain contact with his probation officer for a 30-day period the officer should proceed as follows:
(a) Contact the probationer by telephone informing him of his failure to comply.
(b) Send a delinquent letter directing the probationer to report to the assigned probation officer on a certain date.
(c) Contact by telephone or mail those personal references given by the probationer to ascertain or verify the whereabouts of the probationer.

In the event of a probation violation, the following procedures shall be followed:
1. Upon Supervisor's review, the Probation Officer submits a written directive to the Clerical Staff indicating to the court the reason(s) for the violation request.
2. The appropriate clerical staff member types the petition from the information supplied by the Probation Officer.
3. The appropriate clerical staff member notifies the Clerk of the Court in order that the case may be set before the Judge on a specific court date.
4. The Probation Officer presents the petition along with the Adult Probation Department's and the Clerk's case material to the sentencing Judge.
5. The Judge rules on the petition, either resentencing, recommitting (no change in length of sentence), incarcerating, or issuing a warrant on the probationer in the event that the subject fails to appear.
6 In the event that a warrant is issued, the Probation Officer returns the signed and sealed warrant to the main office of the Adult Probation Department.
7. The warrant is then noted in our record keeping system and directed to the Sheriff's Fugitive Section which is located in the same building, along with any pertinent identifiers we are able to provide. The Probation Officer makes a determination to proceed with any violation proceedings only after consultation with and approval from the designated supervisor.

---

*SOURCE: Cook County Probation Department

determine what happened in the past and what still needs to be done to
complete disposition of the case (Eisenstein and Jacob, 1977: 29).

James Eisenstein and Herbert Jacob (1977: 24) point out that if the dockets
are not arranged by computer, the clerk will usually determine the order in
which a case is called. This is particularly important for lawyers who want to
avoid waiting for hours until their case is called for a preliminary ritual that
may only require a few minutes of his/her time. Clerks will often move cases
up on the docket in order to expedite those involving females with young
children (who may be disruptive to courtroom decorum), invalids, or intoxicated persons. Eisenstein and Jacob state that, insofar as one case can have an
effect on the outcome of another, "the clerk's decision may also lead to more
or less severe results for the defendant" (1977: 24).

Melvin Lewis and his colleagues (1978: 153) state: "It is also well known
that court officials such as clerks and bailiffs play an important role in the
bail process. They may provide information regarding the background of an
individual to the judge or magistrate and sometimes the actual administration of the bail procedures is delegated to them." The clerk and bailiff may
be assigned a variety of administrative tasks by the judge. Martin Levin
(1977: 81) notes that in Pittsburgh "sometimes the attorney asks the court
clerk as a 'favor' to reschedule the case with a particular judge. . . . It is easily
within the clerk's power and authority to do so because his scheduling of
cases is completely discretionary and the judges give little attention to such
administrative details." Levin also notes that judges often accept information
or seek advice about procedural or substantive matters from clerks and
perhaps knowledgeable bailiffs. This, of course, is not surprising. Clerks and
bailiffs often work together with the same judge day after day; they may even
be part of the same political organization—judges, the chief clerk, and the
sheriff are often elected officials.

The bailiff (court officer or deputy sheriff) performs a variety of *ministerial*
functions (those with no discretion):

> Ensures the security of court buildings, enforces judicial rules and regula-
> tions (e.g., prevents the use of cameras in court), guards and escorts prisoners,
> and maintains courtroom decorum. He/she assists in the processing of jurors
> and provides security for judges, jurors and witnesses (based on a job descrip-
> tion for Deputy Sheriffs in Cook County, Il. which this writer developed).

The exercise of discretion in what is essentially a ministerial position can
occur in the courtroom. Here, the bailiff controls access to the bench area
containing (in addition to the judge's bench) the clerk and prosecutor who
are capable of providing a great deal of information to persons, defense
lawyers, defendants, complainants, witnesses, and the friends and family of
defendants. If the judge has not set down any specific instructions, the bailiff

decides who has access to these persons while court is in session and during brief recesses when they remain in the courtroom. In addition, visitors will often ask the bailiff (who as a uniformed employee has high visibility) for information concerning court matters. The quality and quantity of the response is clearly discretionary. (The bailiff is also in a unique position to make a referral to private attorneys, usually for a "kick-back"—illegal—fee.)

CONTROL OF DISCRETION

The judiciary has been subjected to severe criticism because of sentencing disparity. When he was U.S. Attorney General Robert J. Jackson stated:

> It is obviously repugnant to one's sense of justice that the judgment meted out to an offender should depend in large part on a purely fortuitous circumstance: namely the personality of the particular judge before whom the case happens to come for disposition (quoted in President's Commission on Law Enforcement and Administration of Justice, 1972: 357).

Edward H. Levi, when he was U.S. Attorney General, criticized sentencing that "appears to be fickle—a matter of chance" or "appears to be unequal with respect to socioeconomic groups" (speech before Governor's Conference on Employment and the Prevention of Crime, Milwaukee, February 2, 1976). Psychiatrist and author Willard Gaylin (1974: 3) declared: "One of the most glaring and provocative of inequities in a world not known for fairness is a disparity in punishment: when like individuals, committing like offenses, are treated differently."

Leslie Wilkins and his colleagues (1978: 1) argue, however, that

> dispositional variation which is based upon permissible, rationally relevant and understandably distinctive characteristics of the offender and/or the offense is wholly justified, beneficial and proper, so long as the variable qualities are carefully monitered for consistancy and desirability over time. Moreover, since no two offenders are identical, the labeling of variation as disparity necessarily involves a value judgment—what is disparity to one person may simply be justified variation to another.

When does *justified variation* in sentencing become sentencing disparity? "It is only when such variation takes the form of differing sentences for *similar* offenders committing *similar* offenses that it can be considered disparate" (Wilkins, et al., 1978: 1; emphasis added).

In order to structure sentencing discretion the President's Commission (1968: 357–58) recommended sentencing councils and appellate review:

> The sentencing council consists of several judges of a multijudge court who meet periodically to discuss sentences to be imposed in pending cases...
> Foremost among their advantages is the opportunity they give for discussion

of sentencing attitudes. From such a discussion a consensus on sentencing may emerge.... The ultimate responsibility for determining sentence rests with the judge to whom the case is assigned, although the discussion and need to state reasons for a sentence tend to restrain the imposition of unreasonably severe or lenient sentences.

Appellate review would encourage the development of uniform and considered sentencing policies within a jurisdiction. It leads both the trial court and the appellate court to give sustained and explicit consideration to the justification for particular sentences. It provides a workable means of correcting unjust and ill-considered sentences, particularly those in which the punishment imposed is grossly inappropriate ... [and possibly] should have authority to increase as well as decrease sentences appealed by the defendant....

Wilkins and his colleagues conclude that both sentencing councils and appellate review are unlikely to achieve any overall reduction in sentencing disparity since they involve a time-consuming process that can only affect a small number of cases. Instead they recommend sentencing guidelines: a system which "functions as a tool in assisting decision-makers in arriving at individual and policy determinations" (1978: 4). The "tool" consists of a sentencing grid based on scores for the seriousness of the crime and offender characteristics (prior criminal history, employment, etc.).

The difficulty with using the guideline approach is that it does not deal

---

FELONY SENTENCING GUIDELINES

Each possible crime is placed in one of five categories. Each of the categories has four possible time spans based on the rehabilitative potential of the offender (as indicated in the psi).

1. *Greatest:* very good (4–6 years) good (5–7 years) fair (6–8 years) poor (7–life).
2. *Very High:* very good (3–5 years) good (4–6 years) fair (5–7 years) poor (6–8).
3. *High:* very good (2–4 years) good (3–5 years) fair (4–6) poor (5–7).
4. *Moderate:* very good (probation) good (probation) fair (2–4 years) poor (3–5 years).
5. *Low:* very good (probation) good (probation) fair (probation) poor (2–4 years).

Thus, for example, an offender whose crime category is rated as *High* and whose prognosis (rehabilitative potential) is "good" would receive a sentence of between 3 and 5 years.

with a major, perhaps the major, factor causing sentence disparity: plea bargaining. (The "guideline" approach will be examined in greater detail when parole is discussed in the next chapter.)

Typical of the critics of the discretionary powers (of judges and parole boards) inherent in the indeterminate setence is Richard Singer. He argues (1978: 402) that sentence disparity "often seems tinted [sic] with racisim" and the solution he proposes "as a possible means of correcting many of these disparities" is the *presumptive sentence:*

> a sentencing scheme by which the "normal" sentence for the "normal" burglar, for example, would be predetermined, and sentencing judges could vary from that norm only in exceptional cases, justified by a written opinion. Appellate review would follow....

Like other critics of the indeterminate sentence, he fails to account for the discretion exercised by prosecutors who can influence, if not control, the length of a sentence through the charging powers enjoyed by all prosecutors. Nowhere in his 27-page article does Singer mention the prosecutor or plea bargaining.

(Control of discretion in probation supervision will be discussed in Chapter 5.)

REVIEW QUESTIONS FOR CHAPTER 4

1. What are the purposes of sentencing an offender?
2. What is meant by the Classical School approach to crime and criminals?
3. What is meant by the Positive School approach to crime and criminals?
5. What type of sentencing scheme is the Classical School associated with and why?
6. What type of sentencing scheme is the Positive School associated with and why?
7. What is the difference between indeterminate and determinate sentencing?
8. What are the criticisms of the indeterminate sentence?
9. What is meant by a presumptive sentencing scheme?
10. How does the determinate sentence increase the ability of the prosecutor to plea bargain?
11. What is a presentence investigation (psi); what does it contain; what is its purpose?
12. What is the relationship between the sentencing recommendation in a psi and the judge's sentence? Does this mean that the probation officer is, in reality, setting the sentence?
13. How can the size of a probation agencies' caseload influence the sentencing recommendation in a psi?

14. How can a recommendation of a prison sentence in a psi save the county money?
15. What are the discretionary powers of a probation agency and why are they often not utilized?
16. What are the procedures for a probation violation?
17. What is the discretionary power enjoyed by clerks and bailiffs?
18. What is the difference between sentence *disparity* and sentence *variation?*
19. How can sentence variation be justified using a positivistic approach to crime and criminals?
20. Why do recommendations for the control of judicial discretion need to consider prosecutorial discretion?

CHAPTER 5

JAILS, PRISONS, PAROLE AND PARDONS

JAILS

Most, but not all, jails are administered on a county level by an elected sheriff. Some cities (e.g., New York), have their own jails (city prisons) operated by a commissioner appointed by the mayor. There are a few jails operated by state governments: Alaska, Connecticut, Delaware, Rhode Island, Vermont. Of the approximately 3,500 local jails in the United States, 2900 are county (usually administered by a sheriff) and the rest are municipal (except in five states). On any given day, American jails house in excess of 210,000 persons, most of whom, about 60 percent, are legally innocent—they have not been convicted.

Throughout most of their history, jails have been described in the most pejorative of terms: depressing, disgraceful, inhuman, squalid, dangerous. Those responsible for administering jails admit to the inadequacies, while placing the blame on inadequate resources. Jails do not rate high on the priority list for scarce tax revenues and the resulting neglect has caused the federal courts to intervene, to prevent the continuation of what often amounts to "cruel and unusual punishment." In New York, for example, a federal judge ordered one jail (the Manhattan-based Men's House of Detention—the "Tombs") shut down, and at the end of 1983, 610 inmates were ordered released from New York City jails to ease overcrowding. As was noted in Chapter 3, jail conditions serve a latent (unintended, but beneficial nevertheless) function: helping to pressure defendants to plead guilty. The writer (as a New York State Parole Officer) experienced parole violators being held in jail beg to be sent to prison to "escape" the jail—and New York State prisons are not country club environments.

Under the best of conditions jails are difficult institutions to administer. Inmates spend a relatively short time in jail—less than a year and often only a few days or weeks; the population is always unstable. There is a vast amount of traffic in and out on a daily basis: new prisoners, police officers, lawyers, probation and parole officers, and the relatives of inmates. Every day inmates are transported to court, to hospitals, to state institutions, and many return to the jail. Because this heavy traffic (out) can facilitate escape, jails are preoccupied with security. Prisoner movement is highly restricted and there are few recreational facilities available to them. Jail time is always "hard time." The serious implications of the discretion exercised by police, prosecutors, judges, and sometimes probation and parole officers, that can result in jailtime are obvious.

Discretion exercised in jails is essentially the same as that exercised in prisons. Therefore, the issue of discretion for both types of institution will be reviewed in the following discussion of prisons.

PRISONS

As noted in the last chapter, the prison is a peculiarly American development inspired by the classical thinkers (particularly the Italian Cesare Bonesana, Marchese de Beccaria, usually referred to as Cesare Beccaria, 1738–94, and the Englishman Jeremy Bentham, 1748–1832). In America, Quaker reformers succeeded in having the Pennsylvania legislature establish the Walnut Street Jail in Philadelphia. Consistent with Calvinist tradition, Walnut Street featured a bible, hard labor combined with solitary confinement. Other institutions, based on the Walnut Street model, were built; Newgate in New York City and in Pennsylvania Western and Eastern Penitentiaries (1826 and 1829) were built in the pentagonal design suggested by Jeremy Bentham. The requirements of solitary confinement, however, made the construction of these institutions quite expensive and led to the development of the Auburn-style prison.

Auburn prison, built in upstate New York, became the world's most frequently copied prison. This fortress-type institution features large stone walls with gun-towers facing a prison yard. Hard work and strict discipline were maintained, but instead of solitary confinement inmates moved together in the infamous lock-step shuffle wearing grotesque black and white stripped uniforms; they walked and worked together in total silence. The exploitation of inmate labor enabled prisons to be self-supporting and some actually earned a profit for the state. The great depression, which began in 1929, eventually resulted in federal legislation which curtailed the use of inmate labor, increasing the costs of imprisonment. The Auburn-type prison was expensive to construct and the last one was completed in Attica, New York in 1931—the most expensive prison ever built in the United States.

Beginning in 1944, the California prison system underwent changes that influenced the direction of penology in the United States for several decades. California adopted *rehabilitation* as the primary goal of imprisonment and to operationalize this goal adopted the indeterminate sentence, an extreme version of indeterminacy that handed over enormous discretionary powers to the Adult Authority (parole board). Prisons became *correctional institutions,* wardens became *superintendents,* and guards became *correction officers.* The purpose of incarceration was *treatment* and each inmate would earn release by providing evidence to the Adult Authority that he/she was rehabilitated. As noted in the last chapter, every state eventually adopted a form of this model, but in 1977 California helped to lead the way back to the goals of *retribution* and *deterrence*—"just deserts"—by abolishing the Adult Authority and adopting the determinate sentence. In a 33-year cycle, California had moved from a clasical approach to the positive and back to the classical.

MODERN AMERICAN PRISONS*

Most American prisons are located in rural areas and are staffed primarily by rural whites, while the inmate population is heavily urban, black and hispanic. Since the custodial staff of a prison is vastly outnumbered by inmates, staff has traditionally depended on inmate cooperation to operate a prison in a relatively smooth and orderly manner. The traditional *rapprochment* ("I scratch your back, you scratch mine") between correction officers and inmates began to come apart in the 1960s, and the revolt at Attica in 1971 was symptomatic of this problem. Younger (and "darker") and more aggressive inmates, often organized into gangs, have made the prison a very dangerous place for both staff and inmates. Add to this the problem of overcrowding and declining resources for prisons, and it is easy to understand what is called the "prison crisis." It is against this background that discretion in prison must be understood.

Neal Shover (1979: 245) notes that the 1960s and 1970s was characterized by an "increased willingness of correctional clientele to define their situation in legal and political terms."

> Consistent with this new awareness, they have pressed litigation challenging a wide variety of the conditions of their treatment by the police and correctional personnel. Newly cognizant of their rights and how to seek redress for violations of them, prisoners not only have won decisions from the courts expanding their formal rights but modifications of the administrative laws of corrections in virtually every state.

The courts have traditionally been reluctant to interfere with the discretionary powers of prison officials; such interference could conceivably make more difficult an already difficult task—running a prison. In addition, there was fear that once involved, it would be difficult, if not impossible, to extricate the courts from prison operations and the judiciary is not equipped for such an assignment. However, the activities of prison officials were often

---

*The prison population in the United States (the world's third largest per capita—behind the Soviet Union and South Africa) has been rising steadily since the mid-1970s. On any given day there are slightly less than a half-million adults in state and federal prisons.

so arbitrary and capricious that they cried out for intervention, and by the late 1960s the time was ripe.

During the 1960s anti-war activists, civil rights workers, members of radical, and sometimes violent political, groups began entering the nation's prisons. They were politically conscious and better educated than their fellow inmates and assumed advisory, if not leadership, roles amongst the prison population. The political climate in Washington throughout most of the 1960s was decidedly liberal and activist, and this was reflected in judicial appointments and the activities of the Department of Justice. Federal funding was made available for legal services for the poor and Law Enforcement Assistance Administration funding was available for prison research and improvements. The result was a surge in prison-related litigation.

The "Civil Rights Act of 1871" (particularly section 1983), which was enacted during Reconstruction days to enable blacks who were deprived of their civil rights to avoid the state courts, provided a basis for prisoners to move directly into federal court. In 1968 the Supreme Court ruled in *Lee v. Washington* (390 U.S. 333) that the racial segregation of prisoners violated the Fourteenth Amendment. In 1969 the court ruled in *Johnson v. Avery* (393 U.S. 483) that prison officials must permit prisoners ("jail house lawyers") to assist other prisoners with legal work. Prison officials had argued that such activity was prohibited to those who were not licensed lawyers. The court responded by offering prison officials the option to provide licensed attorneys — or else permit inmates to help other inmates. The court expanded on this decision in 1971, *Younger v. Gilmore* (404 U.S. 15) by ordering prison officials to provide legal materials, books, etc., for inmates. The Supreme Court was beginning to limit the discretion that prison officials could exercise over inmates. The court limited the discretion of prison officials to censor inmate letters (*Procunier v. Martinez,* 417 U.S. 817, 1974), but in 1977 rejected the notion that inmate's had a First Amendment right to organize a prisoner union (*Jones v. North Carolina Prisoners' Labor Union, Inc.* 433 U.S. 119).

There has been a great deal of litigation dealing with the constitutionality of conditions of imprisonment. Federal courts have ordered state officials to engage in extensive and expensive prison revisions in order to comply with constitutional standards. In 1976, Federal District Court Judge Frank Johnson found the state of Alabama's entire prison system in violation of the Eighth Amendment and appointed a committee to oversee sweeping changes. However, in 1979 (*Bell v. Wolfish,* 441 U.S. 520) and 1981 (*Chapman v. Rhodes,* 101 S.Ct. 2392) the Supreme Court overturned lower court decisions which had found overcrowded prison conditions to be unconstitutional. The Supreme Court ruled that the Constitution does not require inmates to be housed in single cells; it permitted "double-bunking" even for detainees awaiting trial. The court ruled in *Chapman* that prison conditions are constitutional, including double-bunking, as long as the totality of prison conditions does not "involve the wanton and unnecessary infliction of pain," but conditions cannot "be grossly disproportionate to the severity of the crime warranting punishment," as in *Hutto v. Finney* (437 U.S. 678, 1978). In *Hutto* the court ruled that solitary confinement in a harsh setting for more than 30 days constitutes cruel and unusual punishment.

In 1974 (*Wolf v. McDonnell,* 418 U.S. 539) the Supreme Court ruled that inmates are entitled to (only) a minimum of procedural due process before the imposition of punishment for disciplinary violations: solitary confinement, the loss of privileges, or the loss of time off (the sentence) for good behavior ("good time"). The court ruled that inmates must be given written notice of the alleged infraction(s) at least 24-hours before a disciplinary hearing and the hearing officer must give written reasons for his/her decision. However, the court ruled that the right to counsel and the right to cross-examine adverse witnesses is not a constitutional right in such proceedings. (Prisoners are typically subjected to dozens of rules governing all aspects of institutional life. In the Attica Correctional Facility, for example, there are 229 such rules, 157 more than in other New York prisons. An inmate "may be punished for talking, smoking or putting his hands in his pockets when walking through the halls or for not standing up when guards pass his cell for the twice-daily head counts" (Anderson, 1983: 22.)

Good time refers to a system used to control inmate behavior. In states utilizing an indeterminate sentencing system a prisoner is usually eligible for one day of good time for every three days of his/her sentence (one-third off). Thus, an inmate serving a sentence of 1-0-0/9-0-0 could receive up to three-years off his/her maximum:

$$
\begin{array}{ll}
9\text{-}0\text{-}0 & \text{(maximum)} \\
-3\text{-}0\text{-}0 & \text{(good time)} \\
\hline
6\text{-}0\text{-}0 & \text{(actual time served)}
\end{array}
$$

(In some states good time may also be deducted from the minimum, thus moving up the parole eligibility date).

In states utilizing a form of determinate sentence, prisoners usually receive one day of good time for every two days served (half-off). Thus, an inmate receiving a sentence of 12-0-0 could receive up to six-years off his/her sentence:

$$
\begin{array}{ll}
12\text{-}0\text{-}0 & \text{(determinate sentence)} \\
-6\text{-}0\text{-}0 & \text{(good time)} \\
\hline
6\text{-}0\text{-}0 & \text{(actual time served)}
\end{array}
$$

In practice good time is usually subtracted from the sentence when the defendant is first received by the department of corrections. For example, an inmate sentenced on January 2, 1984 to a (determinate) term of 12-0-0 would be scheduled for release on January 1, 1990 (good behavior is presumed). Any loss of good time as a result of infractions adds time to this projected release date. Thus, the loss of thirty-days good time would cause the inmate's release date to be moved to February 1, 1990. (In no event could the inmate be held beyond January 1, 1996, except if convicted of additional crimes.) In most states, whether they use an indeterminate or determinate sentencing system, inmates released on good time (referred to as *mandatory release* or *conditional release*) are placed under the supervision of a postrelease agency, usually referred to as *parole* supervision (even when the parole board was not responsible for the inmate's release). Such persons remain under supervision (of a "parole" officer) for a period of time determined by statute and can be returned to prison for violations of the conditions of their good time (mandatory/conditional) release. The conditions are similar to, or exactly the same as, parole rules/conditions, and the procedures used to return violators are the same as used for parolees (to be discussed later in this chapter).

CORRECTION OFFICER AS POLICE OFFICER

The correction officer in a prison is a uniformed employee responsible for protecting staff, inmates and property, maintaining peace and order, and enforcing rules and regulations; his presence serves as a deterrent to rule violative or criminal behavior. In many important respects his/her responsibilities are similar to that of a police officer working in a limited physical space. However, while inside the institution the correction officer carries no firearms and rule enforcement, as opposed to law enforcement, is a primary function. These rules often seem petty, although they may be quite necessary to orderly life in a prison environment: rules control what an inmate can wear, how it is to be worn, when to eat, sleep, shower, talk, walk, work and play. As is the case with police agencies, in prisons lower echelon officers exercise a great deal of discretion in dealing with the persons being policed. Like their police counterparts, the correction officer usually responds to minor infractions by avoidance, threat or reprimands—something short of official disciplinary action ("arrest").* Informal dispositions are the rule, while formal enforcement is usually reserved for more serious violations such as assaults, stealing, insolence, refusals to obey orders to work or maintain a clean cell, etc. However, while the police officer can

---

*For example, the New York State Department of Correctional Services advises correction officers to "deal with minor infractions, or other violations of rules and policies governing inmate behavior, that do not involve danger to life, health, security or property by counseling, warning, and/or reprimanding the inmate, and the employee need not report such minor incidents" (Section 251.5: "Procedures for Implementing Standards of Inmate Behavior").

THE ROLE OF A CORRECTION OFFICER*

The core of the work of a correction officer is the supervision, in one form or another, of the inmate population. Because of the abnormal environment of the intitution, inmates cannot safely be left to themselves—they must be supervised. Their supervision by the officer personnel must be adequate and effective before any of the other departments of the institution can go into action. Therefore, the entire institutional program depends upon the way in which correction officers carry out their duties.

INMATE SUPERVISION

The first object of inmate supervision is the maintenance of order and prevention of escapes. The uniform is to the inmate the visible symbol of the power and authority of the state. Any challenge to this authority must be decisively dealt with by the officer, whose responsibility in such case is single and absolute. Officers must be careful, however, not to invite the flouting of the authority vested by the state by the careless or excessive use of it. Moderation is good counsel.

In addition to preventing escapes and maintaining order, supervision assists the educational and recreational programs of the institution—in fact, it supports the entire rehabilitative process which could collapse in the absence of supervision. From this point of view supervision is as necessary to the inmate as it is to the administration of the institution. An inmate obviously cannot rehabilitate himself if careless custodial supervision invites him to attempt to escape; nor will his rehabilitation be facilitated by the confusion and general turmoil which inevitably results from lack of supervision. However, one must not lose sight of the fact that SELF–DISCIPLINE is the ultimate goal, and often times this cannot be achieved by a series of "do's" and "don'ts," followed by rigid penalities.

Inmates must comply with rules and regulations. These are often a source of irritation to the inmate, constituting some of the annoyances and inconveniences of institutional life. However, you will realize that no rule or regulation is established merely for the purpose of annoying somebody. Its necessity or advisability has been plainly indicated by experience, and for every rule or regulation, no matter how annoying or irritating it may be in specific cases, there should be a definite and valid reason. Above and beyond the specific necessity for observance of specific rules, there is also the general necessity for observance of rules and regulations as a disciplinary measure. Discipline is not divisable; it exists as a complete entity or it does not exist at all. To permit inmates, therefore, to pick out for observance such rules and regulations as do not particularly bother them, and violate others, would be to destroy completely the entire custodial and rehabilitative structure.

---

*SOURCE: American Correctional Association, 1975: 19.

expect many victims of robbery, assault, rape and theft to report these crimes, the strength of the inmate code against informing ("ratting") usually precludes this level of cooperation. The inmate code and the norms of prison behavior are part of the world with which both inmate and officer have to understand and contend as part of prison life.

The "criminal justice system" of a prison often parallels that of the outside society. Thus, correction officers patrol, issue "summons," make "arrests," and inmates are put in detention, released to bail and appear in "court" for "trial" (without the right to counsel, cross-examination of witnesses, or a jury of one's peers). When the misbehavior of an inmate constitutes a crime, particularly a felony, it is usually referred to the prosecutor of the county in which the institution is located.

Inmates in institutions operated by the Illinois Department of Corrections are required to abide by a set of 23 standard rules and regulations:

1. Obey all orders from institutional staff.
2. Vulgar, abusive, insolent, threatening or improper gestures are not acceptable.
3. No intimidating group behavior is acceptable.
4. When an inmate is moving around the institution, unless he is in possession of an authorized Call-Ticket or on free-flow movement, he must be escorted by an institutional staff member, and is expected to walk in proper formation. Excessive noise, smoking and general horseplay are not acceptable.
5. No trafficking is allowed. This means inmates will not loan their property to other inmates. Anything found in the possession of an inmate during a general shakedown is *that* inmate's responsibility.
6. Inmates may not engage in pressuring activities or any other unlawful activity. This includes trafficking in contraband, stealing, forgery, use of intoxicants, drugs or medication which is unauthorized. In addition, inmates may not possess weapons or U.S. Currency, and may not engage in gambling, sexual assault or physical assault upon any inmate or employee.
7. Lying or giving false information to an institutional staff member is not acceptable behavior.
8. Inmates may not alter or tailor any clothing or bedding issued to them.
9. If an inmate involves himself with any gang, or is found in possession of gang paraphernalia, he will be dealt with through the disciplinary process, and will not be retained at the Lincoln Correctional Center.
10. No blankets, sheets or any other obstructions are allowed in the dormitories.
11. It is not mandatory that inmates attend meals. All inmates will be given the opportunity to eat three (3) meals per day. If an inmate does not want to eat, he will not be compelled to go to the Inmate Dining Room. Inmates choosing to go to the dining room will go there in formation and will not roam around the dining room during the meal.
12. Inmates are required to make their own beds after rising in the morning, and to keep their living area clean and neat at all times.

DISCIPLINE IN A CORRECTIONAL INSTITUTION*

HANDLING OF SERIOUS INFRACTIONS

The more serious infractions of the rules should be handled either by the disciplinary officer or by the Disciplinary Committee. Although the membership of the Disciplinary Committee must vary, it should generally be composed of the following: The Warden or Superintendent as chairman; Associate Warden-Custody; Associate Warden-Classification and Treatment; Classification Officer; Institutional Phychiatrist or Psychologist; and the Captain. It is important for the good administration of the disciplinary program that adequate, complete, impartial and factual reports be prepared by the correction officer observing the infraction. This report is the basis for any corrective action that the Disciplinary Officer or Committee may take.

There is fairly widespread feeling and recognition among administrators that there is some value in having the deputy or associate warden, rather than the warden, serve as Chairman of the Disciplinary Board. This reserves the warden from personal involvement in line discipline, and places him in a position to serve as a reviewing or "appeals" authority, and in a position to have some theropeutic value in discipline and treatment. Also the Warden is a rather busy person.

All punishment for the infraction of rules or because of misconduct must be in accordance with the Penal-Code provisions, and the rules established by the proper authorities within the frame work of the organization. The inmate may be subjected to one or more of the following punishments by order of the Disciplinary Committee subject to the approval of the Warden or Superintendent.

1. Reprimand.
2. Temporary or permanent loss of one or more privileges.
3. One or more Sunday or holiday lockups.
4. Assignment to a special work detail.
5. Confinement in isolation cells on regular or restricted diet.
6. Recommendation to the proper authority appropriate action regarding loss of part or all of the discretionary reduction of sentence (commonly referred to as loss of "good time") or redetermination of parole or discharge date.
7. Forfeiture of part or all of camp or correctional industries earnings.
8. Suspended sentence or action on any of the above.

The Disciplinary Committee should only recommend to parole authorities regarding time status rather than have final authority.

*SOURCE: American Correctional Association, 1975: 65.

13. Personal hygiene will be exercised at all times. Tattooing of the body or piercing of the ears is not acceptable.
14. Inmates are required to reside by their appropriate living space during the 7:00 a.m., 3:45 p.m., 11:00 p.m. to 7:00 a.m. count with the exception of the first count on that shift.
15. Inmates are required to familiarize themselves with and be governed by all safety rules of their respective assignment or dormitory.
16. Inmates are required to read the institutional bulletin board in their dormitory and assignment, in order to have knowledge of any changes in institutional policy or rules.
17. All Administrative Rules of the Department of Corrections and general laws of the State of Illinois will be enforced at the institution. Inmates are prohibited from violating any of those regulations.
18. All sound equipment will be used with headphones at all times. Anyone abusing this privilege will be dealt with through the existing disciplinary procedures, and if continued violation exists, the offending item of sound equipment will be locked in personal property.
19. Portable radios should not be transported to work assignments. Portable radios should be used during leisure times only and with head phones.
20. The only exception to the above regulation is using a mutual radio in the weight room or recreational areas. This will be allowed only with the consent of other inmates in the areas. Once again, inmates must be governed by common sense. Extremely loud playing of any radio is not acceptable.
21. Inmates will not verbally or physically signal to any resident of the Developmental Center or private citizens.
22. Inmates will not draw attention to themselves while in the yard area. Abusive language or loud horseplay, music etc., will not be tolerated.
23. Inmates will not be allowed to receive or pass any items through the fence.

Correction officers are given wide discretion in enforcing minor violations, while major violations require a "Disciplinary Report:

In the event an inmate violates an Administrative Regulation, Departmental and/or Institutional Rules, the provisions of Administrative Regulation 804 will be complied with.

a. In the event of a minor rule violation such as smoking in line or loud playing of radios, an informal means of resolving the inmate's behavior may be used, such as counseling the inmate and warning him that further violations will result in disciplinary action.
b. Repeated minor rule violations by an inmate indicate the need for disciplinary actions, and an Inmate Disciplinary Report will be issued to the offending inmate.
c. In the event of any major rules violation by an inmate, disciplinary action is necessary, and an Disciplinary Report will be issued to the offending inmate.

The Illinois Department of Corrections provides guidelines for its officers:

If the infraction is one of those listed . . . [as minor], the employee may use discretion in regard to the preparation of an inmate disciplinary report [which results in a disciplinary hearing and possible punishment]. Where the employee determines that a verbal reprimand of the inmate will be sufficient to resolve the situation, preparation of a disciplinary report is not necessary.

The Illinois Prisoner Review Board (which replaced the parole board), sitting in panels of three, is responsible for hearing and deciding cases brought by the Department of Corrections against inmates for alleged violations of rules with respect to good time credits if the amount of time at issue exceeds 30 days or when, during any 12-month period, the cumulative amount of credit revoked by prison officials exceeds 30 days.

The Board may:
1) Concur with the Department's request.
2) Deny the request.
3) Reduce the amount of time on the request. The reduction cannot go below 30 days.

Criteria include:
1) Mitigation surrounding the incident.
2) Past record involving discipline.
3) Is the request consistent with past practices.
4) Is the recommendation consistent with the Department's Administrative Regulations 804 and 845.

The Board:
1) Conducts hearings on a monthly basis in conjunction with appearances for parole hearings.
2) Gives inmates face-to-face hearings.
3) Reserves the right to call witnesses.

Each prison (correctional institution) in New York State develops a set of rules which must be in accord with the "Standards of Inmate Behavior" promulgated by the Department of Correctional Services. These rules deal with every conceivable aspect of an inmate's life and are distributed to each inmate as he/she is received at the institution. For example, the Auburn Correctional Facility (Auburn, N.Y.) requires prisoners to abide by 192 rules including:

— A weekly shower is mandatory for each inmate.
— Facility I.D. cards must be carried at all times.
— The inmate's name and/or number must be clearly marked on each article of clothing. Green shirts, chino jackets and coats must have a name tag on the left breast.

The Clinton Correctional Facility (Dannemora, N.Y.) has an "Inmate Rule Book" with more than 185 rules including:

— Shirts with tails must be worn inside of the trousers and must be buttoned to the second button from the top.
— Inmates shall walk in columns of two and to the right of the corridors and shall move as quietly and orderly as possible while being escorted about the facility.
— In the Visiting Room: No petting or fondling will be tolerated. Inmates may embrace a visitor once when entering the Visiting Room and once when leaving.

The New York State Department of Correctional Services empowers correction officers to confine inmates:

251.6 Confinement. (a) Where an officer has reasonable grounds to believe that an inmate should be confined to his cell or room because he represents an immediate threat to the safety, security or order of the facility or an immediate danger to other persons or to property, such officer shall take reasonable and appropriate steps to so confine the inmate.

(b) An inmate also may be confined to his cell or room where such action appears reasonably necessary for protection of the inmate. In any such case, however, the inmate shall not be so confined for more than 72 hours, and within such time period the inmate shall either be:

(1) transferred to another housing unit;
(2) scheduled for transfer to another facility;
(3) released from such confinement.

(c) An inmate who is unable or who refuses to participate in an assigned activity may be confined to his cell or room and, if such inmate has not been excused for medical reasons, the officer having charge of the inmate shall report such incident to the superintendent in the manner provided in section 251.4 of this Part.

(d) If the officer having charge of an inmate or if any superior officer has reasonable grounds to believe that an inmate's behavior in his cell or room is disruptive or will be disruptive of the order and discipline of the housing unit, or is inconsistent with the best interests of the inmate or of the facility, such fact shall be reported to the superintendent and the superintendent may order confinement in a special housing unit. Any such order shall be in accordance with Part 304 of Chapter VI of the rules and regulations of the department.

(e) (1) An employee who places an inmate in confinement in his cell or room or who places an inmate in a special housing unit pursuant to the provisions of this section shall report such fact, in writing, to the superintendent as soon as possible, but in any event before going off duty. Where an inmate is placed in confinement or in a special housing unit in connection with an incident required to be reported in the manner provided in section 251.4 of this Part, the report of confinement shall be entered upon and made part of the report of the incident.

(2) Reports of confinement shall be made even where confinement was authorized or directed by a superior officer, but need not be made where confinement:

(i) is necessitated by a medically excused inability to participate in an assigned activity; or

(ii) was directed by the adjustment committee or by a decision in a superintendent's proceeding.

(f) The provisions of this section shall not be construed so as to prohibit emergency action by the superintendent of the facility and, if necessary for the safety or security of the facility, all inmates or any segment of the inmates in a facility may, on the order of the person in charge of the facility, be confined in their cells or rooms for the duration of any period in which the safety or security of the facility is in jeopardy. In any such case the superintendent shall immediately notify the commissioner.

The rules and regulations of the department provide for the complaining officer to draft a "Misconduct Report" consisting of "a written specification of the particulars of the alleged incident of misbehavior involved, a reference to the inmate rule book number and a brief description of the violated rule. . . . " The report is reviewed by a "Review Officer" (staff member of the rank of lieutenant or above) who, according to the seriousness of the allegations, decides on who will hear the case:

1. Violation Hearing (presided over by a sergeant or above);
2. Disciplinary Hearing (presided over by a lieutenant or above); or
3. Superintendent's Hearing (presided over by the superintendent, deputy superintendent, or captain).

The inmate is given a copy of the Misconduct Report and can request that a prison employee assist him to prepare for the hearing. The inmate can present testimony, documents, written statements and call witnesses at the hearing. The following are the procedures for the Superintendent's Hearing which considers only the most serious allegations:

Notice and assistance to inmate.

(a) The person appointed to conduct the hearing shall designate an employee to furnish assistance to the inmate. This assistance shall be solely of an investigatory nature. The employee is not intended to and may not act as an advocate for the inmate. If the inmate elects, such employee shall be of the inmate's choice selected from a list of available employees established by the superintendent, or any other employee upon approval of the superintendent.

(b) Such employee shall deliver a copy of the charge to the inmate at least 24 hours prior to the commencement of the superintendent's proceeding. He shall explain the nature of the proceeding and the charge to the inmate. He also shall ask the inmate whether there is any factual matter that can be presented in his behalf and he shall investigate any reasonable factual claim the inmate may make.

(c) A written report of the action taken and the results of the investigation, if any, including documentary evidence and statements of witnesses interviewed, by the person designated to furnish assistance to the inmate shall be delivered to the person appointed to conduct the proceeding prior to the commencement of the procedure for determination of the charge.

Decisions

Right to judicial review

Held that although the decisions of the Correction Department are not judicially reviewable if made according to law, where petitioner prisoner's claim that he was denied a hearing conducted in accordance with the provisions of the rules and regulations of the department before being deprived of 90 days good time is uncontroverted, an issue is presented requiring a hearing in the Supreme Court to determine whether such decision was made in violation of lawful procedure.

Method of determination.

(a) The person appointed to conduct the proceeding shall first interview the inmate and ascertain that he understands that no statement made by him in response to the charge or information derived therefrom may be used against him in a criminal action or proceeding.

(b) Then the person conducting the proceeding shall ask the inmate whether he admits or denies the substance of the charge. If the inmate admits the substance of the charge, or admits any variation of the charge that is acceptable to the interviewer, the inmate shall sign his name in the place indicated for that purpose. Where the admission accepted differs from the charge made, the points of difference shall be noted on the charge by the interviewer before the inmate signs. After the inmate has signed, as hereinabove provided, a disposition shall be made. If the inmate does not make any such admission, or refuses to sign, the proceeding shall continue as provided in this section and all further interviews shall be recorded stenographically or by an electronic recording device.

(1) The inmate shall be permitted to call witnesses on his/her behalf, provided that so doing does not jeopardize institutional safety or correctional goals.

(2) Where the inmate is illiterate, or where the charges are especially complex, the person conducting the proceeding may allow the inmate to select an employee to assist him at the hearing.

(c) The person conducting the proceeding shall interview one or more employees who witnessed or have direct knowledge of the incident and he may also interview any other person who can be of assistance in contributing relevant information.

(d) In any case where there are written reports on the incident, or where the matter has been before the adjustment committee, the reports and the records of the adjustment committee shall be deemed to be incorporated into the record of the proceeding. . . .

In any case where the person conducting the proceeding is not satisfied after considering all available evidence that the record of the proceeding contains substantial evidence to support the charge, he shall either:

(1) dismiss the charge and so advise the inmate; or

(2) affirm such state of facts related to the charge made as may be supported by substantial evidence, record the state of facts affirmed, and so advise the inmate.

(i) A written disposition including a statement of the evidence relied upon and reasons for the disciplinary action shall be provided to the inmate following the proceeding.

Disposition.

(a) Where the inmate admits and signs, or where the person conducting the hearing affirms on the basis of substantial evidence, a charge or state of facts within the criteria set forth . . . one or more of the following dispositions may be made:

(1) reprimand;

(2) loss of one or more specified privileges for a specified period;

(3) temporary or permanent change of program;

(4) confinement to cell or room or in a special housing unit continuously or on certain days or during certain hours for a specified period; provided, however, that any such disposition amounting to a period of more than 60 days is subject to the approval of the commissioner for that portion which exceeds 60 days;

(5) Confinement as authorized in paragraph (4), but on a diet that is not the same as the diet of other inmates; provided, however, that the inmate shall at all times be supplied with a sufficient quantity of wholesome and nutritious food;

(6) restitution for loss of or intentional damage to State property, to be made from existing and future funds standing to the credit of the inmate;

(7) loss of a specified period of good behavior allowance ('good time'), subject to restoration as provided in Subchapter B of this Chapter; or

(8) referral to the adjustment committee for such action or further action as may be deemed appropriate by the committee (within the limits of the action the committee is authorized to take).

(b) Where the inmate admits and signs, or where the person conducting the hearing affirms on the basis of substantial evidence, a charge or state of facts which, although not within the criteria set forth in section 253.1, nevertheless amounts to a breach of rules and regulations or established standards governing inmate behavior, one or more of the following dispositions may be made:

(1) reprimand;

(2) any action that the adjustment committee would have been authorized to take;

(3) temporary or permanent change of program;

(4) restitution for loss of or intentional damage to State property, to be made from existing and future funds standing to the credit of the inmate;

(5) loss of a specified period of good behavior allowance ("good time"), subject to restoration as provided in Subchapter B of this Chapter; or

(6) referral to the adjustment committee for . . . further action. . . .

PAROLE

The term parole derives from the French meaning to "give one's word," a promise by prisoners of war that if released they would not take up arms. In modern times parole also refers to a form of conditional release, usually from prison (although the term "bench parole" is sometimes used to refer to release without bond—on one's word that he/she will return to court). As noted earlier in this chapter, most states use an indeterminate form of sentencing in which the judge sets a minimum and maximum term (e.g., 1-0-0/9-0-0) and a parole board determines if the inmate is to be released (paroled) in 1-0-0, 2-0-0, 3-0-0 . . . years, all the way up to 9-0-0 (not accounting for good time).

Parole is an outgrowth of two concerns: rehabilitation and prison over-crowding, although not necessarily in that order. A review of the early parole literature (Abadinsky, 1982) indicates that while reformers viewed parole as a means to rehabilitate, prison officials and legislators were concerned with the problem of prison overcrowding, and they tended to see parole as a legal "escape valve." In any event, while parole definitely helps to relieve prison overcrowding, its usefulness as a method of rehabilitation has been challenged (a challenge that caused a number of states to abolish parole and switch to a determinate form of sentencing).

Parole boards are made up of from 3 to 12 members, usually appointed by the governor for four to six years. States differ in how much they pay board members and the qualifications for the position. Most often members have some background in criminal justice (in addition to political connections). Parole boards have been under severe attack by conservatives (for releasing criminals "too soon") and by liberals (for holding offenders too long—until they are "rehabilitated"). They have been criticized for being unable to determine when, and if, an inmate is rehabilitated or to predict behavior. Liberals and conservatives have ridiculed the rehabilitative (positive) model as inappropriate: liberals tend to see criminal behavior as symptomatic of larger social problems, e.g., poverty, discrimination, while conservatives tend to see criminal behavior as the ("free will") choice of "evil" persons. Both sides have favored a more classical (e.g., determinate sentence) approach and the abolition of parole boards.

In response to these criticisms parole boards have adopted a "guidelines" approach which stresses "just deserts" while also considering "social" factors when making release decisions. (There has been little consideration of using the parole board as a mechanism for alleviating prison overcrowding). The New York State Board of Parole describes its guidelines approach:

a. The Board may consider aggravating and mitigating circumstances associated with the particular crime. The guideline model merely establishes a general factor index. It is up to the Board members to look at specific factors that comprise the case. A few examples may help:

(1) You may have been convicted of three offenses or three counts of one offense. The guideline offense severity score would only consider the *highest* felony score. It is up to the Board members to decide if these multiple offenses or counts should be considered.

(2) The offense severity score takes into consideration the degree of forcible contact with the victim. It is up to the Board members to consider whether the characteristics of the victim or the nature of the contact should be considered as a mitigating or aggravating factor concerning the guideline range.

(3) The prior criminal history score takes into consideration the *number* of prior felonies and misdemeanors, but does not consider the *nature* and *type* of these offenses. This may be considered by the Board, so that a more serious background may be an aggravating factor leading the Board to go above the guidelines, while a less serious background may be grounds to go below the guidelines.

(4) The prior criminal history takes into consideration the number of prior prison terms and prior probation/parole revocations. In these situations, the Board may also consider prior adjustment within the institution, on parole, or on probation and the circumstances for the revocations.

In all examples, the attempt is to find a balance between the desire to consider the individual aspects of each case and the desire to bring consistency and uniformity to the parole decision-making process; on the one hand to allow flexibility for the consideration of individual cases, while on the other hand to develop a general frame of reference for the decisions.

b. The Board also considers for the parole release decision such factors as:

(1) Institutional adjustment, including (but not limited to) program goals and accomplishments, academic achievements, vocational education, training or work assignments, therapy, and interpersonal relationships with staff and inmates.

(2) Performance (if any) as a participant in a temporary release program.

(3) Availability of adequate release plans, including community resources, employment, education and training, and support services.

The United States Board of Parole has been a pioneer in the development of parole guidelines. The board provides six classes of "Severity of Offense":

1. *Low:* e.g., Immigration law violations; minor theft.

2. *Low Moderate:* e.g., Alcohol law violations; marijuana law violations (under $500); forgery fraud (under $1000); income tax evasion (under $3000); theft from mail (under $1000).

3. *Moderate:* e.g., bribery of a public official; possession of drugs (under $500); embezzlement (under $20,000); receiving stolen property to resell (under $20,000).

4. *High:* e.g., burglary from a bank or Post Office; sale of hard drugs to support habit; sale of marijuana (over $5000); embezzlement ($20,000–100,000); organized vehicle theft; robbery (no weapon or injury); theft, forgery, fraud ($20,000–100,000).

5. *Very High:* e.g., robbery (weapon or injury); possession of hard drug by nondrug dependent user; sale of hard drugs for profit (no prior conviction for selling drugs); extortion; sexual act by force.

6. *Greatest:* e.g., aggravated felony (weapon fired or serious injury); aircraft hijacking; sale of hard drugs for profit (prior drug conviction for sale); espionage; kidnapping; willful homicide; explosives (detonation).

For each of the six "Severity of Offense" categories there is a corresponding set of categories (very good, good, fair, poor) indicating the board member's judgment of the likelihood of the inmate not reverting to criminal behavior. Each of the four categories of this "Parole Prognosis" (or *salient factor score*) has a time span (e.g., 6–10 months) which allows a board member to select the actual amount of time an inmate must serve before being released on parole.

1. *Low:* very good (6–10 months) good (8–12 months) fair (10–14 months) poor (12–16).

2. *Low Moderate:* very good (8–12 months) good (12–16 months) fair (16–20 months) poor (20–25 months).

3. *Moderate:* very good (12–16 months) good (16–20 months) fair (20–24 months) poor (24–30 months).

4. *High:* very good (16–20 months) good (20–26 months) fair (26–32 months) poor (32–38 months).

5. *Very High:* very good (26–36 months) good (36–45 months) fair (45–55 months) poor (55–65 months).

6. *Greatest:* Greater than the above. However, specific ranges are not given due to the limited number of cases and the extreme variations in severity possible within this category.

Thus, for example, an inmate who had bribed a public official ("Severity of Offense" *High*) but whose parole prognosis was very good could be paroled after serving as little as 16 months or as much as 20 months.

A parole board typically holds release hearings in panels of one to three members. The panel convenes at correctional institutions and interviews inmates being considered for parole. The board hearing takes only a few minutes. The board members have a copy of institutional reports and the presentence report, if one has been done. They usually ask the inmate about his/her criminal history, institutional adjustment, and release plans. David Stanley (1976: 42) argues: "The atmosphere at such a hearing is full of tension and latent hostility. Under these circumstances the hearing is an ineffective way to elicit information, evaluate character traits, and give advice, all of which parole boards try to do." Despite this criticism, Stanley (1976: 43) points out:

> Given the present parole system, hearings are necessary as an expression of our national tradition and culture. A man has his day in court before he is convicted and sentenced. In all sorts of situations we feel outraged if a person is not even confronted with the evidence before something adverse is done to him. In the hearing the prisoner is at least given a chance to state his case, correct erroneous statements, and impress the board with his determination (real or alleged) to reform.

Some jurisdictions utilize *examiners* to conduct parole hearings. Typically, the examiner conducts hearings at correctional institutions and summerizes his/her findings with a recommendation to the parole board. The board then votes on the examiner's findings and recommendations. In some hearing examiner models, if the inmate is dissatisfied with the examiner's decision, he/she can appeal to the parole board. In whatever hearing examiner model is used, the board does not interview or deal directly with the inmate.

PAROLE SUPERVISION*

Inmates released by a parole board or mandatory/conditional (good time) releasees are usually placed under the supervision of a parole officer. As is the case with probation supervision, the offender is required to abide by a set of rules/conditions. A violation of any of these rules can subject the offender to a violation of parole/release and possible return to prison.

The parole officer (sometimes called a parole agent or some other title) may also be responsible for supervising probationers in some states and in the federal system. He/she attempts to help the client with diverse problems: residence, employment, marital, drugs or alcohol. Because caseloads are usually high (in excess of 100; 50 is considered moderate), the time spent with each client is quite limited and, of course, the help that can be rendered. This places the offender at a disadvantage, while also

---

*At any given time there about three-quarters of a million adults under parole supervision (includes mandatory, "good time," releasees).

STATE OF ILLINOIS RULES GOVERNING PAROLEES AND MANDATORY SUPERVISED RELEASES

You are obligated to comply with all rules, regulations and orders and subsequent amendments thereto of the Prisoner Review Board and of the Adult Parole Services of the Department of Corrections.

1. You must comply with the instructions of your Department of Corrections agent (if paroled or released out of the state, obedience to the rules of both states is required) and the following Board special orders:
2. You must obey all municipal, county, state and federal laws and ordinances.
3. You must consult and follow the advice of your agent before visiting or writing to correctional center residents.
4. You shall not leave the state or county without prior written permission of your agent.
5. You are to:
   (a) Maintain employment and support your dependents; if not employed, you are to seek work or participate in educational or vocational training.
   (b) Notify your agent prior to any change in residence or employment.
   (c) Submit a written report on forms provided, on the first day of every month.
   (d) Report all arrests to your agent.
6. You shall not own, possess, use, sell, or have under your control any firearms or other dangerous weapons.

---

causing the officer to neglect his/her control functions—rule enforcement.

As with probation, rule-violative behavior is often undetected or simply overlooked—exercise of discretion. When the violation is serious, absconding or new criminal activity, for example, parole/release violation procedures will be invoked. These are governed by the guidelines set down by the Supreme Court in *Morrissey v. Brewer* (408 U.S. 471, 1972) and they are similar to the procedures used in probation violation with one important difference: probation and probation violation are judicial functions; parole and parole violation are administrative functions divorced from the courts.

PRELIMINARY HEARING

Once in custody, the parolee (or releasee) is presented with a list of the allegations against him/her and advised of the right to a preliminary hearing.

If this right is waived, the parolee is held in custody pending a revocation hearing. At the preliminary hearing the offender may present witnesses and confront adverse witnesses. He/she may be represented by counsel. The hearing officer determines if there are reasonable grounds to believe that the offender has violated one or more of the conditions of release in a serious manner, referred to as "probable cause." If probable cause is found the parolee will be held in custody pending a revocation hearing. If probable cause is not found, the parole warrant will be cancelled and the parolee restored to parole supervision.

REVOCATION HEARING

The revocation hearing follows the same format of the preliminary hearing except that it is more comprehensive. In addition to the allegations, the hearing officers (often parole board members) will consider the totality of the parolee's situation: mitigating circumstances, employment while on parole, etc. Thus, the allegations may be sustained and the parolee can still be returned to supervision—or to prison.

PARDON—EXECUTIVE CLEMENCY

All states and the federal government have provisions for clemency. In 31 states and the federal government the chief executive holds the final clemency power, and in most of these states the parole board investigates requests for clemency. Clemency includes:

(a) *Reprieve.* A temporary suspension of the execution of sentence. Rarely used today except in cases of a "stay of execution" in cases of capital punishment to provide more time for legal action.

(b) *Commutation.* A modification (reduction) of sentence usually granted for meritorious acts, e.g., providing assistance to prison staff in emergency situations, or it may be granted to inmates with fatal illnesses.

(c) *Pardon.* The power of pardon derives from the English concept of the king as a fountainhead of justice and mercy. After the American Revolution this concept shifted to state and federal governments, and it eventually was transferred to the chief executive. The power of the President to grant pardons for federal crimes is without any limitations, e.g., President Ford's pardon of Richard Nixon who was not even tried, no less convicted, for any federal offense. Pardon has historically been used as a form of "parole" in the United States and, thus, it is not surprising that parole boards are often involved in the exercise of executive clemency.

The basis for a pardon varies from state to state, and it is not used

EXECUTIVE CLEMENCY IN NEW YORK STATE*

1. WHAT IS EXECUTIVE CLEMENCY?

The State Constitution (Article IV, Section 4) provides the Governor "the power to grant reprieves, commutations and pardons after convictions, for all offenses except treason and cases of impeachment upon such conditions and with such restrictions and limitations, as he may think proper . . . "

Clemency is a matter in the sole discretion of the Governor. It constitutes extraordinary relief and is granted in only the most compelling of circumstances.

2. WHEN ARE PARDONS CONSIDERED?

Pardons may be considered if no other adequate administrative or legal remedy is available:

1. to permit a judgment of conviction to be set aside where there is overwhelming and convincing proof of innocence not available at the time of conviction;
2. to relieve a disability imposed upon a judgment of conviction for an offense (but this reason will rarely be considered since relief may generally be obtained by means of a Certificate of Good Conduct or Certificate of Relief from Disabilities);
3. to prevent deportation or to permit reentry into the United States.

3. WHEN IS COMMUTATION OF SENTENCE CONSIDERED?

Commutation (reduction) of your minimum period of imprisonment may be considered to enable you to appear before the Board of Parole for release consideration at a time earlier than permitted by the court-imposed sentence.

Absent an exceptional and compelling circumstance, a case will be reviewed for possible commutation of sentence only if:

1. your term or minimum period of imprisonment is more than one year;
2. you have served at least one-half of the minimum period of imprisonment;
3. you will not become eligible for release on parole within one year from the date of application; and
4. you are not eligible for release on parole in the discretion of the Board of Parole.

---

*SOURCE: New York State Division of Parole

extensively anywhere. In some states, e.g., Georgia, a conditional and limited form of pardon may be granted which has the effect of removing certain restrictions that result from felony conviction, e.g., to hold certain licenses.

STATE OF ILLINOIS RULES GOVERNING PETITIONS FOR EXECUTIVE CLEMENCY (PARDON OR COMMUTATION OF SENTENCE)*

1. All applications for pardons, reprieves and commutations of sentence or adjudication shall be made by written petition, addressed to the Governor and filed in the office of the Prisoner Review Board at Springfield. The original and four copies of the petition must be filed at least thirty (30) days prior to any scheduled meeting of the Board for the purpose of hearing petitions for executive clemency. The petition shall conform to the following requirements:
   (a) The petition shall contain a brief history of the case, a brief biography of the petitioner, setting forth his full and correct name, any aliases he may have used during his lifetime, his age, place of birth, the different places where he has resided, the years of residence in each place, the occupations pursued in each locality, and the specific reasons why a pardon or commutation of sentence should be granted.
   (b) It shall be signed by the applicant or other person in his behalf.
   (c) If signed by another person, the full address of such person shall be given, and his relation to the applicant stated.
2. Copies of the petition shall be furnished to the Sentencing Judge or, if for any reason this is not possible, to the Chief Judge of the Circuit in which sentence was imposed, and the Prosecuting State's Attorney, if available, and also to the present State's Attorney of the county from which the petitioner was committed in each case. Proof of such service may be made by a receipt of such official, or affidavit that it was posted, or a receipt of the United States Post Office if sent by registered or certified mail. Such proof of service shall accompany the petition.
3. Publication of intent to petition for executive clemency shall be made in a newspaper of common circulation in the county of commitment on at least two occasions no less than two weeks apart. Said notice shall contain the name of the petitioner, the offense for which he was convicted, the date of sentencing and the sentence imposed. Said notice shall invite any interested party to communicate their views to the offices of the Prisoner Review Board prior to the scheduled hearing date.
4. Where circumstances warrant or the exingencies of the case suggest, the Board may waive the requirement of publication of intent to file for executive clemency.
5. For each meeting of the Board, a docket shall be prepared listing all petitions filed thirty (30) days or more before the date of the meeting which have not been previously considered and which petitions comply with the applicable statutes of Illinois and these rules. Counsel and

*SOURCE: Illinois Prisoner Review Board

those who wish to be heard in favor of or in opposition to the respective petitions on the call of the docket, must register in person at the meeting of the Board.

6. The Board or a designated panel thereof will hear counsel or any other persons who appear in support of or in opposition to the petition at the scheduled public hearing. The Board will also consider petitions on the docket on which there are no appearances and may elect to hear petitioners who are in confinement.

7. No requirement herein shall preclude the Chairman or the Governor from calling a special session of the Board for the purpose of giving a hearing and consideration to any petition deemed to be of an emergency nature. All usual requirements shall be met insofar as is practical.

8. The Board will determine by majority vote in conference what its recommendation is on each petition and shall advise the Governor by a written report without publicity.

CONTROL OF DISCRETION

Jails/Prisons. The nature of correctional institutions makes the control of discretion very difficult. Jails and prisons are relatively isolated from the outside world. Inside, however, correction officers are continuously outnumbered; they do not have enough coercive force at hand to control a determined inmate population. Thus, corrections personnel depend on inmate acquiescence, if not cooperation. Prisoners keep the institution clean, they maintain and repair the facility and its grounds, cook and serve the food, sew the uniforms and help with the paper work; in some institutions inmate trustees would even guard other prisoners: "There are many jobs and services that *must* be performed by prisoners on a day-to-day basis in order to maintain an institution" (American Correctional Association, 1975: 119; emphasis added).

While the American Correctional Association (ACA) maintains that the correctional institution should be geared "to rehabilitate the offender" (ACA, 1975: 114), this is not a priority concern. Prison administrators are not judged on their ability to deliver rehabilitative services, nor are they expected to rehabilitate prisoners. A sound administration is one that, first of all, prevents inmates from escaping; second, protects staff; and third, protects inmates. Escapes, riots, staff injuries or inmate deaths (not the failure to rehabilitate—whatever that means), are the central concerns of prison administrators (and the executives who appoint them): peace and security are the only *meaningful* goals of a jail or prison.

To accomplish the goals (peace and security) each correction officer is empowered to use a great deal of discretion. The exercise of this discretion, however, must be in accord with the security needs of the institution, not the convenience of the officer; it must contribute to, at least, inmate acquiescence or cooperation. Favored inmates find institutional life a little more bearable and the favored inmate may be in a position to influence, if not control, the behavior of other inmates. "Straw bosses" or "cell tenders" or "trustees" usually occupy favored positions as a result of their (unofficial) ability to instill fear in other inmates. Such inmates have a stake in maintaining the peace and security of an institution. Transfers or release of a number of such persons can easily destabilize an institution leading to anarchy or a power struggle among inmates or inmate groups.

In some institutions leaders of inmate gangs or organized crime figures (Abadinsky, 1983) may be able to exert an influence over other inmates that can help maintain the peace of an institution. Unfortunately, when the official mechanism of discipline becomes dependent on the unofficial, the goals become so distorted that prison officials may actually abdicate their responsibilities except for the need to prevent escapes. Perimeter control is assured, but the internal operation of the institution is effectively in the hands of the inmates. Inmate discipline and justice often has little restraint and, obviously, need not conform to such abstractions as the rule of law or constitutional standards.

Because the correction officer, as opposed to the police officer, carries out his/her responsibilities in a limited physical space, supervisory control is more easily accomplished. Combined with carefully drafted rules/regulations, supervision can provide a realistic basis for controlling the exercise of discretion by correction officers. A further check on the improper use of discretion is the inmate grievance or advisory council/committee, an elected group of inmates that meets regularly with the superintendent.

The exercise of discretion by correctional administrators has been subjected to extensive judicial review (as we have seen earlier in this chapter). Administrative review can be accomplished by the use of in inspectional unit that is outside the control of the sheriff or corrections commissioner. These units are often referred to as board of visitors or corrections board/commission. Their effectiveness is dependent upon:

(a) statutory powers
(b) resources/funding
(c) quality of staff
(d) support of the chief executive (governor/mayor)
(e) public support (e.g., civic organizations, bar association, media)

PAROLE BOARD AS SENTENCE REVIEW PANEL

Parole boards have responded to criticism by developing internal controls—"guidelines" (or "salient factor scores") for making release decisions. The role of a parole board in reducing sentence disparity has been given scant attention.

In every state dozens of judges representing a cross-section of opinion and philosophy impose sentences for a variety of crimes. The results: sentence disparity. Judges with wide sentencing discretion impose significantly different sentences for similar criminal behavior. The parole board, because it has the opportunity to review the sentence of all prison inmates, can make adjustments necessary to reduce unwarranted disparity. For example:

I. Three offenders commit the crime of robbery with a firearm and all three are arrested:

(a) at the scene of the crime;

(b) several seeks later with some of the stolen money; and

(c) several months later as the result of being identified by one eye-witness.

- The first offender (a) insists on a jury trial and is convicted in Western Court of Robbery in the First Degree and an indeterminate sentence of 5-0-0/15-0-0 is imposed.

- The second offender (b) requests a bench trial. He is found guilty of Robbery in the Second Degree and an indeterminate sentence of 4-0-0/12-0-0 is imposed in Central Court.

- The third offender (c) agrees to plead guilty to Assault in the First Degree which results in a sentence of 3-0-0/9-0-0 in Eastern Court.

Each offender appears before the state parole board. The parole board members take note of the actual criminal behavior (robbery with a firearm). Assuming the role of a sentence review panel whose primary purpose is *equity* (reducing sentence disparity), the three offenders are paroled after serving 5-0-0.

In a state utilizing a system of determinate sentences, in our hypothetical example the sentences would be:

(a) 10-0-0

(b) 8-0-0

(c) 6-0-0

There would be no parole board, no sentence review—disparity. With 50 percent good time, each offender would be released after serving: (a) 5-0-0; (b) 4-0-0; and (c) 3-0-0.

PROBATION AND PAROLE SUPERVISION

While police officers and correction officers are uniformed personnel organized along military lines, probation and parole (p/p) officers work in conventional dress and receive no out-of-office (field) supervision. P/p officers report their activities to supervisory staff, verbally and in written reports. Supervisory review is necessarily limited by the large caseloads usually carried by each p/p officer. The degree to which a p/p officer moniters client behavior and reports violations of the conditions of p/p are subject to a great deal of discretion and only limited review.

Typically, a p/p case will be subjected to intensive supervisory review as the result of adverse information about a probationer/parolee being received from outside the agency, e.g., from the police or client-relatives, particularly spouses, or girlfriends. Thus, p/p officer activity is subjected to some control by the realization that at any time one of his/her cases can be brought to the attention of supervisory staff—a situation over which the p/p officer has little, if any, control. Random or spot checks of p/p officer activity reports may be used for the same purpose in the absence of "outside" information. However, in such instances the supervisor knows only what the p/p officer has chosen to provide.

Agencies attempt to subject officer-discretion to some control by requiring a minimum amount of contact with each case, or cases may be classified according to the level of contact (supervision) they are required to receive. For example, an *intensive case* might require the p/p officer to make a "positive" visit to the offender's residence each month—positive meaning an unannounced visit during which the client is actually seen by the officer. Such visits increase the likelihood that a violation of the conditions of probation or parole will be detected. Discretion over rule-enforcement can be limited by making certain actions mandatory. For example, a client found in possession of a firearm or other dangerous weapon, or resorting to the use of narcotics, *must* be the subject of a violation of p/p proceeding. In New York, certain offenders were prohibited from imbibing in *any* alcoholic beverages. Parole officers were *required* to take such persons into custody immediately if evidence of drinking was discovered—no discretion.

REVIEW QUESTIONS FOR CHAPTER 5

1. Jails are usually administered on what level of government?
2. How do jail conditions contribute to plea bargaining?
3. Why are jails so difficult to administer?
4. What were the characteristics of the earliest American correctional institutions?

5. What is meant by the Auburn-type prison?
6. What caused the building of Auburn-type prisons to be discontinued in the United States?
7. What is the connection between rehabilitation and the indeterminate sentence?
8. What is the connection between the determinate sentence and the concept of "just deserts?"
9. How have prison officials traditionally dealt with the problem of being vastly outnumbered by inmates?
10. Why have the courts been reluctant to render decisions in favor of prison inmates?
11. What led to a change in the "hands off" approach to prisons traditionally taken by the judiciary?
12. In what ways has the judicial branch limited the discretion of prison officials?
13. What is meant by prisoner "good time?"
14. What are the basic similarities and differences between the police officer and the correction officer?
15. Parole is an outgrowth of what two concerns?
16. Why have liberals and conservatives criticized parole boards?
17. What are the two basic factors in the "guidelines" (or "salient factor score") approach to parole release consideration?
18. What are the two basic functions of a parole officer?
19. What are the discretionary powers of probation/parole officers?
20. What are the procedures for a violation of parole?
21. What does executive clemency mean?
22. What is the priority concern of jail and prison officials? Why?
23. What is the major purpose of the exercise of discretion in a jail or prison?
24. How is the exercise of discretion in jails/prisons subjected to control?
25. How can a parole board act as a sentence review panel?
26. Why can the discretion exercised by probation and parole officers be even more difficult to control than that exercised by police officers and correction officers?
27. How is probation/parole officer discretion subjected to control?

CHAPTER 6

DISCRETION AND JUVENILE JUSTICE

The juvenile justice system is so distinctly different from that used to respond to adult criminal offenders that it requires a separate chapter.

ORIGINS

A separate system of justice for juveniles was the result of increasing urbanization and depressed social and economic conditions at the end of the 19th century. Overworked and underpaid adults were often unable to exert proper guidance and control over their offspring, who were often left to fend for themselves. On April 21, 1899 "An Act to Regulate Treatment and Control of Dependent, Neglected, and Delinquent Children" was passed in Illinois as the result of the efforts of feminist reformers— "child savers." Other states soon followed and by 1928 all but two states had adopted juvenile court statutes similar to the Illinois Act. The unique aspect of this law, which created the juvenile court, is that it is based on the concept of *parens patriae:* a doctrine deeply rooted in English common law "that the power to protect and act in behalf of helpless people of all types was lodged in the king as parens patriae (the ultimate parent) and, through royal delegation of this power, in the court" (Pettibone, et al., 1981: 12).

The juvenile court was given effective control over youngsters (usually persons under 16–18, varies by jurisdiction) who were:

1. *Delinquent:* persons accused of acts that would be crimes if committed by an adult;
2. *Status Offenders:* persons whose behavior would not constitute a crime if committed by an adult (e.g., chronic truancy, running away from home, disobeying parents); often referred to as PINS (Persons-in-Need-of-Supervision) or CHINS (Children-in-Need-of-Supervision) or MINS (Minors-in-Need-of-Supervision);
3. *Neglected/Dependent:* persons whose parents fail to or are unable to provide care.

155

THE JUVENILE COURT PROCESS

The process used in the juvenile court evolved from legislative and judicial battles between those who stressed the need to *help* children and those who argued for the *legal rights* of children. Throughout most of the twentieth century the "helpers" determined the process which stressed the non-criminal nature of the juvenile court (Lou, 1927: 36–37):

> The distinction between the criminal and chancery [civil] proceedings is important, because the proper attitude of the court toward the child must depend in large measure on an appreciation of this fact. Under criminal procedure, which is assumed to be just and impersonal — with apprehension by warrant and arrest, indictment by grand jury, trial by jury on specific charges, pleading of "guilty" or "not guilty," strict application of the rules of evidence, criminal records and sentences, and penalties — the punitive aspects of the process are emphasized. . . . The purpose [of civil/juvenile court] is not to determine whether or not a child has committed a specific offense, but to discover whether he is in a condition requiring the special care of the state and to understand the child in order that the court may be able to deal with him wisely.

Thus, the juvenile court was successful in avoiding the legal restraints — due process — of the adult criminal court (Lou, 1927: 2):

> In place of magistrates, limited by the outgrown custom and compelled to walk in the paths fixed by the law of the realm, we have now socially-minded judges, who hear and adjust cases according not to rigid rules of law but to what the interests of society and the interests of the child or good conscience demand. In place of juries, prosecutors, and lawyers, trained in the old conception of law and staging dramatically, but often amusingly, legal battles, as the necessary paraphernalia of a criminal court, we have now probation officers, physicians, psychologists, and psychiatrists, who search for the social, psychological, and mental backgrounds of the child in order to arrive at reasonable and just solutions of individual cases.

A clear affirmation of the spirit of (scientific) positivism.

New terminology developed to reflect the non-criminal nature of the juvenile court:

Adult System	*Juvenile System*
arrest	taking into custody
defendant	respondent
information/indictment	petition
arraignment	hearing
trial	adjudication
verdict	finding
guilty (of a crime)	delinquent/in need of supervision/neglected
sentence	disposition

The due process deficiencies of the juvenile court finally came to the official attention of the Supreme Court in the 1967 case of *In Re Gault* (378 U.S. 1). Fifteen year-old Gerald Gault, while on juvenile court probation, was arrested for making an obscene phone call on the complaint of a neighbor. If Gault was an adult the maximum sentence would have been a $50 fine and imprisonment for not more than 60 days. Instead, Gault was committed to a juvenile institution for a term not to exceed 6 years. During the court action that accomplished this, Gault was not advised of his right to remain silent, his right to counsel, was not given an opportunity to cross-examine the complainant (who was not in court) and, based on Arizona law, was denied the right to appeal. Gault was not given a copy of the charges (petition) and no transcript of the proceedings was made.

The Supreme Court ordered the following due process rights for juvenile court proceedings:

1. Written notice of the charges in advance of the hearing.
2. Respondent must be informed of the right to counsel and advised that if he/she cannot afford counsel, one will be appointed by the state.
3. Respondent must be informed of the right to remain silent.
4. Adverse witnesses must be made available for cross-examination.
5. The right to appellate review must be maintained.

In 1970 the Supreme Court (*In Re Winship* 397 U.S. 358) determined that the level of evidence necessary for a positive finding in the juvenile court exceeded that of the civil process in which the "preponderance of evidence" is sufficient (more convincing to the judge than the opposing evidence). The Supreme Court established that level as "beyond a reasonable doubt," the same as in the adult criminal court:

> ... the constitutional safeguard of proof beyond a reasonable doubt is as much required during the adjudicatory stage of a delinquency proceeding as are those constitutional safeguards applied in Gault.... " [W]here a 12-year-old child is charged with an act of stealing which renders him liable to confinement for as long as six years, than as a matter of due process ... the case against him [Winship] must be proved beyond a reasonable doubt."

In 1971 (*McKeiver v. Pennsylvania* 403 U.S. 441) the Supreme Court drew a line between due process in the adult criminal court and that required in the juvenile court by refusing to grant juvenile respondents the right to a jury trial (Sixth Amendment). The court reasoned:

> If the formalities of the criminal adjudicative process are to be superimposed upon the juvenile court system, there is little need for its separate existence.

Perhaps that ultimate disillusionment will come one day, but for the moment we are disinclined to give impetus to it.

In 1975 the Supreme Court (*Breed v. Jones* 421 U.S. 519) ruled that the prosecution of a respondent in criminal court after an adjudicatory proceeding in juvenile court "violated the Double Jeopardy Clause of the Fifth Amendment, as applied to the States through the Fourteenth Amendment." However, many states have provisions allowing the prosecution of a juvenile in the criminal court (as long as no adjudicatory hearing has occured in juvenile court). The State of Illinois, for example, provides (Chapter 37:2–7):

> (3) If a petition alleges commission by a minor 13 years of age or over of an act which constitutes a crime under the laws of this State, and, on motion of the State's Attorney, a Juvenile Judge, delegated by the Chief Judge of the Circuit to hear and determine such motions, after investigation and hearing but *before commencement of the adjudicatory hearing,* finds that it is not in the best interests of the minor or of the public to proceed under this [Juvenile Court] Act, the court may enter an order permitting prosecution under the criminal laws (emphasis added).

INTAKE

Cases enter the juvenile justice system in a variety of ways. The police, as we have noted in Chapter 2, enjoy a great deal of discretion in the way they handle juveniles: a simple reprimand or warning; bring him/her home to parents; refer to a social welfare agency (sometimes as part of a police diversion program); issue a summons or take into custody for a juvenile court referral. Other sources of referral include the youngster's parents or guardians, school officials, private and public agencies.

The police are the most frequent source of referrals to juvenile court, although most police-juvenile contacts are the result of citizen complaints (Smith, et al., 1980: 7). What are the factors that determine the exercise of police discretion when dealing with juveniles? Charles P. Smith and his colleagues (1980) reviewed the research literature for the variables that can influence the police officer's decision about a referral to juvenile court. Note that these variables often overlap and interact.

1. *Seriousness of the Offense.* This is particularly important when the crime is violent or involved sophisticated acts of theft, cases which are likely to result in court referrals.

2. *Prior Record of Offenses.* Some youngsters become known to the police, become labeled as "trouble-makers" or "bad" increasing the likelihood of a formal court referral.

3. *Victim Preference.* Police officers are unlikely to refer youngsters when the victim requests that no action be taken; police are likely to comply with

victim requests, particularly when it is to release a youngster.

4. *Codefendants.* Research indicates that some police officers operate according to an "all or nothing" attitude: arrest the entire group of youngsters or let them all go.

5. *Evidence.* In the absence of sufficient evidence, police are unlikely to make a referral.

6. *Demeanor.* The attitude of the juvenile is likely to affect the police decision in less serious offenses.

7. *Race.* A disputed issue with no clear research findings.

8. *Socioeconomic Status.* Appears to play a weak role in determining police referral decisions.

9. *Sex.* No evidence to support the belief that the sex of the youngster plays a role in police referral decisions.

10. *Age.* While the research findings are not clear, it appears that, all other variables being equal, there is a tendency by the police not to refer younger juveniles to court.

11. *Family Status.* The research findings conflict with respect to such items as the youngster coming from an intact family, one-parent home, or having parents who are alcoholics, etc.

12. *Characteristics of the Police Officer.* A relatively unexplored area of research about which no significant conclusions can be drawn.

Smith (et al., 1980: 245) conclude:

> Overall, decisions depend not only on who the police officer is, but also on who the juvenile is, what his prior contact with the juvenile justice system has been, what the offense is, who the victim or complainant is, and where (in the community) the decision is made.

When a referral is made, by the police, parents or other source (school, social agency), the case is received by an *intake worker* who is usually a probation officer. In accord with the parens patriae concept of the juvenile court, the intake worker has traditionally enjoyed an extraordinary amount of discretion. The worker could dismiss the case, request that a petition be filed, or handle the case informally. Dismissal would end the case; a petition would bring the youngster before a judge; informal handling could involve a number of options such as having the youngster report to the worker on a regular basis ("unofficial probation"). These discretionary powers are those of a prosecutor in the adult system.

The intake function includes a review of legal (as well as social) factors: age of youngster, county of residence, place of offense, elements of the offense, prior record and legal status of respondent. H. Ted Rubin (1980: 304) notes: "The contention has grown that the legal evaluation is one for the prosecutor," and many jurisdictions include the prosecutor (or city corporation counsel) in the intake process, thus affecting the exercise of discretion by the intake worker. The request for a petition is often subjected to prosecutorial review. In some jurisdictions the prosecutor may take certain juvenile offenders directly into the adult criminal system. In any event, because of the *Breed* (double jeopardy) decision, prosecutors must review cases which state law permits to be transferred to the adult criminal court early in the process or lose jurisdiction to the juvenile court.

Typically, the intake worker interviews the child, the parents, and the complainant(s) in order to reach a decision whether or not to have a petition filed. Rubin (1980: 304) points out:

> Statutes, rules, or procedural manuals frequently provide that the intake officer shall advise the child and parents of the child's right to counsel and silence during the intake conference, and that information obtained during the conference is not admissible in evidence at an adjudicatory hearing. But defense attorney participation at a conference is rare, waivers of rights tend to be finessed, and the norm is for the parents to encourage the child to discuss his or her participation in the alleged offense with the intake officer.

In their review of the research literature, Smith and his colleagues (1980: 152) conclude that "Intake screening patterns appear to vary considerably from jurisdiction to jurisdiction," and "there appear to be variations between jurisdictions in what factors enter into the intake screening decision." Generally, "the legal variables of offense and prior record, particularly the latter, are probably the most consistently utilized factors in the decision-making process" (1980: 154).

The intake worker may also have to make a *detention* decision. The State of Illinois (37: 703–4), for example, requires that when a juvenile is delivered to the court:

> The minor shall be immediately released to the custody of his parent . . . unless the probation officer . . . finds that further detention or shelter care is a matter of immediate and urgent necessity for the protection of the minor or of the person or property of another, that he is likely to flee the jurisdiction of the court or that the minor was taken into custody under a warrant.

The decision by an intake worker to have a youngster detained pending a petition and further court action is subjected to an early judicial review.

DETENTION HEARING

Facilities for detaining juveniles are often inadequate and juveniles do not have a constitutional right to bail in the juvenile system. In New York City, for example, the Spofford Youth House has been plagued with scandal and violence. Thousands of juveniles, however, are held (not in juvenile institutions, but) in jails housing adult offenders. Charles Silberman (1978: 320) notes that "juveniles frequently are locked up in adult jails, often in clear violation of state laws requiring minors to be kept in separate facilities." The *New York Times* (December 28, 1983: 11) reports that about 20,000 juveniles jailed with adults each year have not been accused of any crime: are mentally retarded, disturbed, or abused. "Twenty percent are runaways or juveniles who have been caught drinking or who have been found to be sexually promiscuous [invariably girls]. The majority, 65 percent, have been charged with property or misdemeanor offenses." Assault, rape, murder and suicide claim a number of juvenile victims being detained every year. Thus, the decision to detain a juvenile can have very serious implications.*

At the detention hearing witnesses are examined by the state and defense counsel. "If the court finds that it is a matter of immediate and urgent necessity for the protection of the minor or the person or property of another ... or that he is likely to flee the jurisdiction of the court" it may order "the minor be kept or detained in a detention home or county or municipal jail" (Illinois Juvenile Court Act, 37: 703–6). Smith and his colleagues (1980: 124–25) reveal that

> detention rates vary widely from jurisdiction to jurisdiction ... [and] the criteria used in determining whether or not to detain a juvenile pending adjudication also vary widely from jurisdiction to jurisdiction. Perhaps the most consistent factor would be the juvenile's prior record. All the detention decision-making studies indicate that prior record, measured in a variety of ways, is very much a consideration.

Other variables that impact on the detention decision include:

— seriousness of the offense
— family willingness or availability to assume custody
— being a runaway or from out-of-state
— school and employment status

ADJUDICATION HEARING

"Court procedures are sufficiently varied to complicate description. A juvenile may be physically located at intake or a detention facility in either a secure or non-secure environment, depending on the petition that is filed.

*An Idaho case that received national attention highlights the problem. During the summer of 1982, 17-year-old Christopher Peterman was arrested by the police for failing to pay a $73 traffic fine. The young man was placed in the juvenile cell of the county jail where, for 14 hours, he was beaten and tortured by other inmates; he survived for less than 72 hours in custody. The Idaho Attorney General said that the personnel at the jail failed to follow security procedures and the jail was understaffed due to budgetary constraints. There were enough police officers to enforce traffic warrants, but not enough correction officers to protect those arrested (Schmidt, 1982: E4).

At the same time the case may actually pass through several hearings where decisions are made by the court relative to the status of the juvenile:

— detention hearing
— preliminary hearing
— fitness hearing (to certify as adult or juvenile)
— motions-filed hearing
— adjudication hearing
— disposition hearing

"Many juveniles will proceed directly to disposition from the preliminary hearing, while others will have multiple hearings, motions filed and heard, and special fitness hearings prior to the actual disposition. Despite the large number of different possible court procedures, not all of these court procedures need be in every system" (edited from Smith, Black and Campbell, 1979: 30).

The adjudication process in juvenile court resembles that of a bench trial in the adult criminal system. Witnesses are called, examined and cross-examined. In the juvenile court, however, the judge usually does not wear the traditional black robe, nor does he/she sit at a high bench, symbols of the adult system. In most jurisdictions the hearings are closed to those not directly involved in the case (as opposed to the constitutional requirement of a public trial in the adult system). The role of the defense counsel can be described as *ambivalent.*

In the adult system defense counsel has a singular role: *advocate.* As an advocate, counsel must expend all manner of legal effort to gain the best possible outcome for his/her client. The best possible outcome in a criminal trial would be acquittal (although often not realistically attainable). It is not as clear in the juvenile system. Many youngsters, regardless of whether or not their legal "guilt" can be proved beyond a reasonable doubt, are in need of help. Defense counsel success in securing a finding of "petition not sustained" may often seem to be a dubious achievement to defense counsel. Despite the juvenile court retreat from pure positivism toward a more due process-oriented approach, the concept of parens patriae is difficult to discard in practice. The result often resembles the plea bargaining that occurs in the adult system as prosecutor and defense counsel go beyond the evidence and issues of law to focus on the offender and his/her needs. Thus, a finding of "status offender" may actually be based on a petition alleging delinquency and a negotiated settlement that insures help without the label of "delinquent."

The juvenile court's jurisdiction over youngsters whose behavior does not constitute a violation of the criminal law, is a matter of some controversy. Some observers (e.g., Abadinsky, 1976) and organizations (American Society of Criminology, National Council on Crime and Delinquency) have called for the removal of *status offenders* from the jurisdiction of the juvenile court. Critics argue that the court labels youngsters who, despite the non-criminal nomenclature, are often viewed by society and themselves as "bad," if not altogether criminal, as a result of having been subjected to the juvenile court process. In addition, they question the ethical aspects of using official state coercion against persons who have not committed any criminal offense. The juvenile courts often lack the necessary resources for helping all of the youngsters subjected to its jurisdiction. Critics argue that these resources should be allocated for the delinquent youngsters most in need of court help. Those who support the status offense concept maintain that, in reality, there is very little, if any, difference between the status offender and the delinquent youngster. Often it is a matter of degree or simple chance that causes one youngster to be legally viewed as delinquent while another is treated as a status offender. We have already noted that plea negotiations may convert a delinquent into a status offender. Furthermore, supporters argue that without the court and its coercive powers, many of these youngsters would never receive any kind of help.

At the completion of the adjudication stage, the judge makes a *finding*. If the petition is not supported, the case against the youngster is dismissed. Otherwise, s/he is found to be:

(a) delinquent;
(b) neglected; or
(c) in need of supervision,

and the judge orders a pre-disposition investigation (pdi) for the disposition hearing.

DISPOSITION HEARING

As we have noted, the juvenile court is based on the notion of positivism; the court tries to understand and treat "misbehavior." This contrasts with the adult criminal court which is based on a classical (legalistic) approach right through to adjudication (trial). However, in a sentencing stage utilizing a presentence investigation (psi), positivism is brought into the adult system (particularly in states with a system of indeterminte sentences).

Both the psi and the pdi move the focus away from the offense/behavior to the offender/respondent. The pdi will include:

1. a review of court records
2. a review of school records
3. a review of police records
4. interviews with family members

5. interview(s) with respondent
6. Interviews with teachers and school officials
7. interviews with employers and/or youth workers
8. interviews with clergy when appropriate
9. interviews with victim and/or complainant and witnesses
10. results of any psychological or psychiatric exams
11. a recommendation which includes the alternatives available for the
    youngster

As in the adult sentencing stage, the juvenile is entitled to be represented by counsel at the disposition hearing. However, once again, there is an ambivalence built into the role of defense counsel. Is he/she simply an advocate for what the client (youngster) wants, or should the concerns of parents/guardians be allowed to influence the situation? To what extent should the legitimate concerns of society in getting appropriate services for the youngster influence defense counsel?

The role of the judge at this stage is often less important than that of the probation officer (po). While most judicial positions require only a knowledge of relevant law and legal procedure, the real service provided by the juvenile court begins *after* adjudication, after the fine points of law and legal procedure are complete. The focus is on helping the youngster (as opposed to retribution, incapacitation, deterrence—none of which, in theory, should play a role in juvenile court). The education and training of a judge does not necessarily include such relevant disciplines as psychology, sociology and social work—the tools for applying the helping role of the juvenile court. Being well-versed in the law does not provide insight into the behavior of youngsters, most of whom come from an environment quite different from that experienced by most judges.

Smith (et al., 1980: 156) reminds us that "when considering the factors which go into making court dispositional decisions that these are decisions made about a relatively small number of juveniles, and the group which is evaluated for various dispositional outcomes at this level is a group which has already been 'sifted' through several points and from which many juveniles have already been dropped"—important discretionary decisions have already been made. Despite the positivistic notion of a focus on the youngster, Smith (et al., 1980: 203) found that offense is a major factor in the dispositional decision, although "Prior record is about the only factor which consistently appears to be related to judicial dispositional outcomes, particularly the number of prior court referrals or previous offenses."

As in the adult system, research has consistantly found a high rate of agreement between the recommendation of the probation officer in juvenile court and the dispositional decision. However, it cannot be determined to what degree the judge is actually influenced by the po, or whether the influence is in the opposite direction—the judge affecting the recommendation.

The dispositional alternatives available to a judge depend on the services provided in a particular jurisdiction. These include one or any combination of the following:

- probation supervision
- foster care and adoption
- community-based day treatment program
- halfway house or group home (facility which allows extensive contact with the community)
- private school or residential treatment center with varying degrees of security
- mental hospital
- ranch, forestry camp, or farm (facility for those youngsters not in need of the strict confinement of a training school)
- training school (secure facility for long-term care; usually the "bottom line" for juvenile court judges)

Juvenile offenders may also be released to the custody of their parents for placement in a private boarding school or private military academy—dispositions most often limited to youngsters of at least middle-income status. Many juveniles are simply put on probation because there is no other viable alternative, not because it is the best response to the youngster's needs.

Probation in the juvenile system closely resembles that of the adult system. The youngster is required to abide by a set of standard conditions (e.g., obey parents, attend school) and perhaps some special conditions (e.g., attend a drug rehabilitation clinic). If the youngster is sent to a training school, release decisions are usually made by the institutional staff who serve a function similar to that of a parole board. When a youngster is "paroled," he/she is usually supervised by an after-care agency affiliated with the institution or by a juvenile probation officer.

CONTROL OF DISCRETION

Police. The concept of parens patriae expands the normally wide discretionary powers enjoyed by police officers. Since police officers are the major (direct or indirect) source of juvenile court referrals, control of police discretion in this area should be a critical concern. However, this does not appear to be the case. In general, police chief executives do not consider the exercise of discretion with respect to juveniles as an important item. Instead, it is left to the "common sense" of the individual officer, or relegated to a special juvenile unit whose officers determine what to do with juveniles who come to the attention of the police. When juvenile policy is written, it is often drafted in such generalities as to provide little or no guidance for police officers.

For a police agency to control the exercise of discretion with respect to police-juvenile encounters, rules based on department policy are a necessity. For example: "It is the policy of this department to try to avoid a referral to juvenile court except when the behavior constitutes a felony. The following alternatives are to be considered before any referral to juvenile court . . . " In order for policy-based rules to have the intended affect of controlling discretion and reducing unjustified variation in handling juveniles, supervisory review is required. This is more easily accomplished in a police agency that has close supervision and centralized management.

Probation. The discretion exercised by probation staff is often subjected to control by the involvement of prosecutors in the juvenile justice process. Explicit policy guidelines can reduce or control the broad discretion that probation officers in the juvenile system typically enjoy. However, Smith (et al. 1980, III: 156) found "that adequate guidance in the form of written policy manuals is not available to agency staff at any level of the juvenile justice system." When such policy guidelines do exist, however: "There does not appear to be any relationship between a case disposition and agency policy." Obviously, without adequate supervision, policy guidelines, no matter how explicit, cannot guarantee control over discretion.

REVIEW QUESTIONS FOR CHAPTER 6

1. How is the juvenile justice system distinctly different from the adult criminal system?
2. What does the concept of parens patriae have to do with the juvenile court?
3. What are the three (3) categories of cases (children) handled by the juvenile court?
4. Retribution, incapacitation, deterrence and rehabilitation are the purposes of the adult criminal system; what is the purpose(s) of the juvenile justice system?
5. What are the due process rights established for juveniles by the Supreme Court in the decision *In Re Gault?*
6. What is the level of legal evidence required for a finding of delinquency in the juvenile court?
7. What right guaranteed to all criminal defendants is denied to juvenile court respondents?

8. At what stage of the juvenile court process can a case be transferred to the adult criminal court (as per the *Breed* decision)?
9. Intake workers in the juvenile court have functions and responsibilities similar to what actors in the adult criminal system?
10. Who are the most frequent source of referrals to the juvenile court?
11. What are the important variables that are considered by the police in making a referral decision to the juvenile court?
12. What are the options available to the juvenile court intake worker?
13. What steps does the intake worker take in order to decide on which option to exercise?
14. What are the important factors considered in making a detention decision?
15. What is the purpose of an adjudication hearing?
16. Why is the role of defense counsel in the juvenile court different from his/her role in the adult court system?
17. What are the arguments for and against juvenile court jurisdiction over status offenders?
18. What is the relationship between the pre-disposition investigation (pdi) and the disposition hearing?
19. Why is the role of the probation officer in the juvenile court more important than his/her role in the adult court?
20. What are the dispositional alternatives available to the juvenile court judge?
21. How can police discretion in dealing with juveniles be subjected to control?
22. How can the discretion of a probation officer in the juvenile court be subjected to control?

BIBLIOGRAPHY

Aaronson, David E., Nicholas N. Kittrie, David J. Saari and Caroline S. Cooper
  1977   *Alternatives to Conventional Criminal Adjudication: Guidebook for Planners and Practitioners.*
         Washington, D.C.: U.S. Government Printing Office.
Abadinsky, Howard
  1976   "The Status Offense Dilemma: Coercion and Treatment." *Crime and Delinquency* 22
         (October): 456–60.
  1982   *Probation and Parole: Theory and Practice, 2nd Edition.* Englewood Cliffs, N.J.:
         Prentice-Hall.
  1983   *The Criminal Elite: Professional and Organized Crime.* Wesport, CT: Greenwood Press.
Abrams, Norman
  1971   "Internal Policy: Guiding the Exercise of Prosecutorial Discretion." *UCLA Law
         Review* 19 (October): 1–58.
Alschular, Albert
  1968   "The Prosecutor's Role in Plea Bargaining." *University of Chicago Law Review* 36:
         50–112.
  1975   "The Defense Attorney's Role in Plea Bargaining." *Yale Law Review* 84: 1179–1314.
American Bar Association
  1971   *Standards Relating to the Prosecution Function and the Defense Function.* New York:
         Institute of Judicial Administration.
American Bar Association Advisory Committee on the Police Function
  1973   *Standards Relating to the Urban Police Function.* New York: American Bar Association.
American Correctional Association
  1975   *Correction Officers Training Guide.* College Park, MD: American Correctional
         Association.
American Friends Service Committee
  1971   *Struggle for Justice.* New York: Hill and Wang.
Anderson, David C.
  1983   "Attica's Green Guards." *New York Times* (December 22): 22.
Andrews, Lori B.
  1982   "Mind Control in the Courtroom." *Chicago Tribune* (March 28): Section II;
         1, 2.
Bard, Morton and Joseph Zacher
  1976   *The Police and Interpersonal Conflict: Third Party Intervention Approaches.* Washington,
         D.C.: Police Foundation.
Bernstein, Ilene Nagel, Edward Kick, Jan T. Leung and Barbara Schulz
  1977   "Charge Reduction: An Intermediate Stage in the Process of Labelling Criminal
         Defendants." *Social Forces* 56 (December): 362–84.
Bittner, Egon
  1967   "Police Discretion in the Emergency Apprehension of the Mentally Ill." *Social
         Problems* 14. Reprinted in An *Introduction to Deviance.* Edited by William J. Filstead.
         Chicago: Markham.

Black, Donald
  1980   *The Manners and Customs of the Police*. New York: Academic Press.
Blumberg, Abraham S.
  1967   "The Practice of Law As Confidence Game: Organizational Cooptation of a Pro-
          fession." *Law and Society Review* 1: 15–39.
Bloch, Peter and Donald Weidman
  1975   *Managing Criminal Investigations*. Washington, D.C.: U.S. Government Printing Office.
          Breitel, Charles D.
  1960   "Controls in Criminal Law Enforcement." *University of Chicago Law Review* 27
          (Spring): 427–35.
Brown, Michael K.
  1981   *Working the Street: Police Discretion and the Dilemmas of Reform*. New York: Russell
          Sage Foundation.
Buckle, Suzann R. and Leonard G. Buckle
  1977   *Bargaining for Justice: Case Disposition in the Criminal Courts*. New York: Praeger.
Carlton, J. Phil
  1978   *A Crime Agenda for North Carolina*. Raleigh: State of North Carolina.
Carter, Lief H.
  1974   *The Limits of Order*. Lexington, MA: D.C. Heath.
Casper, Jonathan
  1972   *American Criminal Justice: The Defendant's Perspective*. Englewood Cliffs, NJ: Prentice-
          Hall.
  1972   *Criminal Justice: The Consumer's Perspective*. Washington, D.C.: U.S. Government
          Printing Office.
  1978   *Criminal Courts: The Defendant's Perspective. Executive Summary*. Washington, D.C.:
          U.S. Government Printing Office.
Castberg, Anthony D.
  1968   "Prosecutorial Discretion: A Case Study." Ph.D. dissertation, Northwestern University.
Cates, Aubrey M., Jr.
  1961   "Can We Ignore Laws? Discretion Not to Prosecute." *Alabama Law Review* 14 (Fall):
          1–10.
Cawley, Donald F., H. Jerome Miron, William J. Aranjo, Robert Wasserman, Timothy A.
  Manuello and Yale Huffman
  1977   *Managing Investigations: Manual*. Washington, D.C.: University Research Corporation.
Chaiken, Jan M.
  1975   *The Criminal Investigation Process. Vol. II: Survey of Municipal and County Police
          Departments*. Santa Monica, CA: Rand Corporation.
Chaiken, Jan M., Joan Petersilia and Linda Prusoff
  1975   *The Criminal Investigation Process. Vol. III: Observations and Analysis*. Santa Monica,
          CA: Rand Corporation.
Church, Thomas
  1976   "Plea Bargains, Concessions and the Courts: Analysis of a Quasi-Experiment." *Law
          and Society Review* 10: 377–401.
Cicourel, Aaron V.
  1976   *The Social Organization of Juvenile Justice*. London, England: Heinemann.
Cockrell, Tom, ed.
  1983   *Rand Checklist* 300 (July). Rand Institute Newsletter.
Cole, George F.
  1970   "Politics of Prosecution: The Decision to Prosecute." Ph.D. dissertation, University
          of Washington.

Cox, Michael P.
1975   "Discretion: A Twentieth Century Mutation." *Oklahoma Law Review* 28: 311–32.
Curran, Barbara
1983   "The Legal Profession in the 1980's: The Changing Profile of the Legal Profession."
        Paper presented at a Research Seminar of the Fellows of the American Bar
        Association, Atlanta, Georgia, July 30.
Davis, Kenneth Culp
1969   *Discretionary Justice: A Preliminary Inquiry.* Baton Rouge: Louisiana State University
        Press.
1974   "An Approach to Legal Control of the Police." *Texas Law Review* 52. Reprinted in
        The Invisible Justice System. Edited by Burton Atkins and Mark Pogrebin. Cincinnati:
        Anderson.
Dershowitz, Alan M.
1983   *The Best Defense.* New York: Vintage Books.
Donavan, Leslie
1981   "Comments: Justice Department's Prosecution Guidelines of Little Value to
        State and Local Prosecution." *Journal of Criminal Law and Criminology* 72 (Fall):
        955–92.
Dow, Paul E.
1981   *Discretionary Justice: A Critical Inquiry.* Cambridge, MA: Ballinger.
Feeley, Malcolm M.
1979   *The Process is Punishment: Handling Cases in a Lower Court.* New York: Russell Sage
        Foundation.
Fogel, David
1975   *We Are The Living Proof: The Justice Model for Corrections.* Cincinnati: Anderson.
Frantz, Douglas and Charles Mount
1983   "Lawyers Make Off with Court Records." *Chicago Tribune* (December 25): 1, 20.
Fried, Joseph P.
1983   "New York Inmates to Court More Quickly." *New York Times* (November 25): 31.
Gaffney, Christopher
1981   *Small Town Police: An Occupational Ethnography.* Ann Arbor, MI: University Microfilms.
Garmire, Bernard L.
1977   *Local Government Police Management.* Washington, D.C.: International City Manage-
        ment Association.
Gay, William, Theodore H. Schell and Stephen Schack
1977   *Improving Patrol Production: Vol. I.* Washington, D.C.: U.S. Government Printing Office.
Gaylin, Willard
1974   *Partial Justice: A Study in Bias in Sentencing.* New York: Knopf.
Glick, Henry R.
1983   *Courts, Politics and Justice.* New York: McGraw-Hill.
Goldstein, Herman
1963   "Police Discretion: The Ideal Versus the Real." *Public Administration Review* 23:
        148–56.
1977   *Policing a Free Society.* Cambridge, MA: Ballinger.
1979   "Improving Policing: A Problem-Oriented Approach." *Crime and Delinquency* 25
        (April): 236–58.
Goldstein, Joseph
1960   "Police Discretion Not to Invoke the Criminal Justice Process: Low Visibility
        Decisions in the Administration of Justice." *Yale Law Journal* 69 (March): 543–94.

172 *Discretionary Justice*

Greenberg, Bernard, Carola V. Elliot, Lois P. Kraft and H. Steven Procter
  1977 *Felony Investigation Decision Model: An Analysis of Investigative Elements of Information.* Washington, D.C.: U.S. Government Printing Office.

Greenberg, Ilene and Robert Wasserman
  1979 *Managing Criminal Investigations.* Washington, D.C.: U.S. Government Printing Office.

Greenwood, Peter, Jan Chaiken, and Joan Petersilia
  1975 *The Criminal Investigation Process. Vol. I: Summary and Policy Implications.* Santa Monica, CA: Rand Corporation.

Grunson, Lindsey
  1983 "Second Opinions on Medical Examiners." *New York Times* (May 15): E6.

Halberstam, Malvina
  1982 "Towards Neutral Principles in the Administration of Criminal Justice: A Critique of Supreme Court Decisions Sanctioning the Plea Bargaining Process." *Journal of Criminal Law and Criminology* 72: 1–49.

Hanewicz, Wayne B., Christine Cassidy-Riske, Lynn M. Fransway, and Michael W. O'Neill
  1982 "Improving the Linkages Between Domestic Violence Referral Agencies and the Police: A Research Note." *Journal of Criminal Justice* 10: 493–503.

Heumann, Milton
  1978 *Plea Bargaining.* Chicago: University of Chicago Press.

Hunt, Morton
  1982 "Putting Juries on the Couch." *New York Times Magazine* (November 28): 70–72, 78, 82, 85, 86, 88.

Ianni, Elizabeth Reuss
  1983 *Two Cultures of Policing.* New Brunswick, N.J.: Transaction Books.

Jacob, Herbert and James Eisenstein
  1977 *Felony Justice.* Boston: Little, Brown.

Jacoby, Joan E.
  1979 "The Charging Policies of Prosecutors." Pages 75–97 in *The Prosecutor.* Edited by William F. McDonald. Beverly Hills, CA: Sage.
  1982 *Basic Issues in Prosecutor and Public Defender Performance.* Washington, D.C.: U.S. Government Printing Office.

Joint Committee on New York Drug Law Evaluation
  1977 *The Nation's Toughest Drug Law: Evaluation of the New York Experience.* New York: Association of the Bar of the City of New York.

Kadish, Sanford H.
  1962 "Legal Norms and Discretion in the Police and Sentencing Process." *Harvard Law Review* 75: 904–31.

Kaplan, John
  1965 "The Prosecutorial Discretion—A Comment." *Northwestern Law Review* 60: 174–93.

Katz, Lewis, Lawrence B. Litwin and Richard H. Bamberger
  1972 *Justice is the Problem.* Cleveland, Ohio: Press of Case Western Reserve.

Kerstetter, Wayne A. and Anne M. Heinz
  1979 *Pretrial Settlement Conference:* An Evaluation. Washington, D.C.: U.S. Government Printing Office.

Kress, Jack M.
  1976 "Progress and Prosecution." *Annals* 423 (January): 99–116.

Kunen, James S.
  1983 *"How Can You Defend Those People.?"* New York: Random House.

LaFave, Wayne R.
  1965 *Arrest: The Decision to Take a Suspect Into Custody.* Boston: Little, Brown.

1970 "The Prosecutor's Discretion in the United States." *American Journal of Comparative Law* 18: 532–48.

Lagoy, Stephen P., Frederick A. Hussey and John H. Kramer
1978 "A Comparative Assessment of Determinate Sentencing in Four Pioneer States." *Crime and Delinquency* 24 (October): 385–400.
1979 "The Prosecutorial Function and Its Relation to Determinate Sentencing Structures." Pages 209–38 in *The Prosecutor.* Edited by William F. McDonald. Beverly Hills, CA: Sage.

Levens, Bruce R. and Donald G. Dutton
1980 *The Social Service Role of Police: Domestic Crisis Intervention.* Ottawa, Canada: Communication Division of the Solicitor General.

Levin, Martin A.
1977 *Urban Politics and the Criminal Courts.* Chicago: University of Chicago Press.

Lewis, Melvin, Warren Bundy and James L. Hague
1978 *An Introduction to the Courts and Judicial Process.* Englewood Cliffs, N.J.: Prentice-Hall.

Lewis, Peter W. and Kenneth D. Peoples
1978 *The Supreme Court and the Criminal Process: Cases and Comments.* Philadelphia: Saunders.

Littrell, W. Boyd
1979 *Bureaucratic Justice: Police, Prosecutors and Plea Bargaining.* Beverly Hills, CA: Sage.

Lou, Herbert H.
1927 *Juvenile Courts in the United States.* Chapel Hill, N.C.: University of North Carolina Press.

Lundman, Richard J.
1974 "Domestic Police-Citizen Encounters." *Journal of Police Science and Administration* 2: 22–27.
1979 "Organizational Norms and Police Discretion: An Observational Study of Police Work With Traffic Law Violators." *Criminology* 17 (August): 159–71.

Lundquist, John A.
1971 "Prosecutorial Discretion: A Re-Evaluation of the Prosecutor's Unbridled Discretion and Its Potential for Abuse." *DePaul Law Review* 21: 485–518.

Manning, Peter K.
1977 *Police Work: The Social Organization of Policing.* Cambridge, MA: MIT Press.

Margolick, David
1983 "Drunken Driving Case Divides Town." *New York Times* (March 13): 18.
1983 "The Trouble With Law Schools." *New York Times Magazine* (May 22): 20–25, 30, 32, 36, 38.

Mayer, Martin
1969 *The Lawyers.* New York: Dell.

McDonald, William F., Henry H. Rossman and James A. Cramer
1979 "The Prosecutor's Plea Bargaining Decisions." Pages 151–208 in *The Prosecutor.* Edited by William F. McDonald. Beverly Hills, CA: Sage.
1982 *Police-Prosecutor Relations in the United States: Executive Summery.* Washington, D.C.: U.S. Government Printing Office.

McIntyre, Donald M., Jr.
1967 *Law Enforcement in the Metropolis.* Chicago: American Bar Association.

McLeod, Maureen
1983 "Victim Noncooperation in the Prosecution of Domestic Assault." *Criminology* 21 (August): 395–416.

Martinson, Robert
  1974 "What Works?—Questions and Answers About Prison Reform." *The Public Interest* 35 (Spring): 22–54.
Mellon, Leonard R., Joan E. Jacoby and Marion A. Brewer
  1981 "The Prosecutor Constrained By His Environment: A New Look At Discretionary Justice in the United States." *Journal of Criminal Law and Criminology* 72 (Spring): 52–81.
Miller, Frank
  1969 *Prosecution: The Decision to Charge a Suspect With a Crime.* Boston: Little, Brown.
Mills, James
  1969 *The Prosecutor.* New York: Farrar, Straus and Giroux.
  1975 *On the Edge.* Garden City, N.Y.: Doubleday.
Misner, Robert L. and John H. Clough
  1977 "Arrestees As Informants: A Thirteenth Amendment Analysis." *Stanford Law Review* 29 (April): 713–46.
Mount, Charles and Marianne Taylor
  1983 "82% in County Ignore Call to Jury Duty." *Chicago Tribune* (April 17): Section II, 1.
Muir, William Ker, Jr.
  1977 *Police: Street Corner Politicians.* Chicago: University of Chicago Press.
Murphy, Patrick V. and Thomas Plate
  1977 *Commissioner: A View From the Top of American Law Enforcement.* New York: Simon and Schuster.
Neubauer, David W.
  1974 *Criminal Justice in Middle America.* Morristown, N.J.: General Learning Press.
New York Times
  1983 "Thousands of Youths Jailed With Adults Each Year Despite Reform Efforts." (December 28): 11.
Niederhoffer, Arthur
  1967 *Behind the Shield: The Police in Urban Society.* Garden City, N.Y.: Anchor.
Packer, Herbert
  1968 *The Limits of the Criminal Sanction.* Stanford, CA: Stanford University Press.
Pettibone, John M., Robert G. Swisher, Kurt H. Weiland, Christine E. Wolf and Joseph L. White
  1981 *Major Issues in Juvenile Justice Information and Training; Services to Children in Juvenile Courts: The Judicial-Executive Controversy.* Washington, D.C.: U.S. Government Printing Office.
Pilavin, Irvine and Scott Briar
  1964 "Police Encounters With Juveniles." *American Journal of Sociology* 70: 206–14.
Police Chief Executive Committee
  1976 *The Police Chief Executive Report.* Washington, D.C.: U.S. Government Printing Office.
Pound, Roscoe
  1960 "Discretion, Dispensation and Mitigation: The Problem of the Individual Special Case." *New York University Law Review* 35: 925–51.
Powell, Craig, Bruce Hoberg and Lyle Knowles
  1980 "Managing Criminal Investigations: An Analysis of Effectiveness." *Police Chief* (June): 54–55, 76.
"Prosecutorial Discretion: A Re-Evaluation of the Prosecutor's Unbridled Discretion and Its Potential for Abuse."
  1971 *DePaul Law Review* 21 (Winter): 485–518.
Reiss, Albert J.
  1971 *The Police and the Public.* New Haven, CT: Yale University Press.

Rojek, Dean G.
    1979   "Private Justice Systems and Crime Reporting." *Criminology* 17 (May): 100–111.
Rosett, Arthur and Donald R. Cressey
    1976   *Justice By Consent: Plea Bargains in the American Courthouse.* Philadelphia: Lippincott.
Rousseau, Jean Jacques
    1954   *The Social Contract.* Chicago: Henry Regnery.
Rubin, H. Ted
    1980   "The Emerging Prosecutor Dominance of the Juvenile Court Intake Process." *Crime and Delinquency* 26 (July): 299–318.
Rubinstein, Jonathan
    1973   *City Police:* New York: Farrar, Straus and Giroux.
Rubinstein, Michael L., Stevens H. Clarke and Teresa J. White
    1980   *Alasks Bans Plea Bargaining.* Washington, D.C.: U.S. Government Printing Office.
Sanders, William B.
    1977   *Detective Work: A Study of Criminal Investigations.* New York: The Free Press.
Schmidt, William E.
    1982   "When 'Legal Inconsistency' Led to Tragedy." *New York Times* (August 1): E4.
Schur, Edwin M.
    1973   *Radical Non-Intervention: A Re-Thinking of the Delinquency Problem.* Englewood Cliffs, N.J.: Prentice-Hall.
Schuster, Richard L.
    1979   "Prosecutor-Police Relations: An Overview and Case Study From an Organizational Perspective." Paper presented at the Annual Meeting of the American Society of Criminology, Philadelphia, November.
Scott, Eric J. and Stephen L. Percy
    1983   "Gatekeeping Police Services: Police Operators and Dispatchers." Pages 127–44 in *Police at Work.* Edited by Richard R. Bennett. Beverly Hills, CA: Sage.
Shenon, Philip
    1983   "Manhattan Fights Jury Duty Evasion." *New York Times* (November 29): 1, 26.
Sherman, Lawrence W. and Richard A. Berk
    n.d.   "Police Response to Domestic Assault: Preliminary Findings. (An Executive Summary)." Washington, D.C.: Police Foundation photocopy.
    1979   *Sociology of American Corrections.* Homewood, IL: Dorsey.
Shover, Neal
    1979   *Sociology of American Corrections.* Homewood, IL: Dorsey.
Silberman, Charles E.
    1978   *Criminal Violence, Criminal Justice.* New York: Random House.
Singer, Richard
    1978   "In Favor of 'Presumptive Sentences' Set by a Sentencing Commission." *Crime and Delinquency* 24 (October): 401–27.
Skolnick, Jerome H.
    1966   *Justice Without Trial.* New York: John Wiley.
Smigel, Erwin O.
    1973   *The Wall Street Lawyer.* Bloomington, IN: Indiana University Press.
Smith, Charles P., T. Edwin Black and Fred R. Campbell
    1979   *A National Assessment of Case Disposition and Classification in the Juvenile Justice System: Inconsistent Labeling.* Washington, D.C.: U.S. Government Printing Office.
    1980   *A National Assessment of Case Disposition and Classifcation in the Juvenile Justice System: Inconsistent Labeling. III.* Washington, D.C.: U.S. Government Printing Office.

Smith, Charles P., T. Edwin Black and Adrianne W. Weir

1980   *A National Assessment of Case Disposition and Classifcation in the Juvenile Justice System: Inconsistent Labeling.* Washington, D.C.: U.S. Government Printing Office.

Stanley, David T.

1976   *Prisoners Among Us: The Problem of Parole.* Washington, D.C.: Brookings Institution.

Steffins, Lincoln

1958   *The Shame of the Cities.* New York: Hill and Wang. Originally published in 1902.

1958   *The Autobiography of Lincoln Steffins.* New York: Harcourt, Brace, Jovanovich. Originally published in 1931.

Stewert, James K.

1982   *The Effects of the Exclusionary Rule: A Study in California.* Washington, D.C.: U.S. Government Printing Office.

Sudnow, David

1965   "Normal Crimes: Sociologcial Features of the Penal Code." *Social Problems* 12 (Winter): 255–76.

Taft, Philip B., Jr.

1980   "Dealing With Mental Patients." *Police Magazine* (January): 20–25.

Task Force on the Police

1967   *Task Force Report: The Police.* Washington, D.C.: U.S. Government Printing Office.

Task Force on Policing in Ontario

1967   *The Police Are the Public and the Public Are the Police.* Ontario, Canada: Solicitor General.

Texas Criminal Justice Council

1974   *Model Rules for Law Enforcement Officers: A Manual on Police Discretion.* Gaithersburg, MD: International Association of Chiefs of Police.

Twentieth Century Fund Task on Criminal Sentencing

1976   *Fair and Certain Punishment.* New York: McGraw-Hill.

Uhlman, Thomas M. and N. Darlene Walker

1980   "'He Takes Some of My Time; I Take Some of His': An Analysis in Judicial Sentencing Patterns in Jury Cases." *Law and Society Review* 14 (Winter): 323–41.

United States Bureau of Justice Statistics

1980   *Justice Agencies in the United States.* Washington, D.C.: U.S. Government Printing Office.

Vance, Carol S.

1974   "The Prosecutor's Discretion: A Statement of Policy By the District Attorney of Harris County (Houston), Texas." Houston: Harris County District Attorney photocopy.

van den Haag, Ernest

1975   *Punishing Criminals.* New York: Basic Books.

Vera Institute of Justice

1977   *Felony Arrests: Their Prosecution and Disposition in New York City's Courts.* New York: Vera Institute.

Visher, Christy A.

1983   "Gender, Police Arrest Decisions and Notions of Chivalry." *Criminology* 21 (February): 5–29.

von Hirsch, Andrew

1976   *Doing Justice: The Choice of Punishments.* New York: Hills and Wang.

Vorenberg, James

1976   "Narrowing the Discretion of Criminal Justice Officials." *Duke Law Review Journal* 4 (September): 651–97.

Wachtel, David
    1983   "The Effects of Traditionalism on the Navajo Police Officer." *Police Studies* (Fall): 57–62.

Waldstein, Frederic A.
    1983   "Administering the Prosecutor's Office: The Environmental Factor." Paper delivered at the Annual Meeting of the Academy of Criminal Justice Sciences, San Antonio, Texas, March.

Walsh, William F.
    1983   "Leadership: A Police Perspective." *Police Chief* (November): 26–29.

Weimer, David
    1980   "Vertical Prosecution and Career Criminal Bureaus: How Many and Who?" *Journal of Criminal Justice* 8: 369–78.

Westley, William A.
    1972   *Violence and the Police: A Sociological Study of Law, Custom and Morality.* Cambridge, MA: MIT Press.

Whisenhand, Paul M.
    1977   *Crime Prevention: A Practical Look at Deterrence of Crime.* Boston: Holbrook.

Wice, Paul B.
    1978   *Criminal Lawyers: An Endangered Species.* Beverly Hills, CA: Sage.

Wileman, Fred A.
    1976   *Policy Development in Police Agencies.* Madison, WI: Board of Regents of the University of Wisconsin System.

Wilkins, Leslie, Jack M. Kress, Don M. Gottfredson, Joseph C. Caplin and Arthur M. Gelman
    1978   *Sentencing Guidelines: Structuring Judicial Discretion.* Washington, D.C.: U.S. Government Printing Office.

Wilson, James Q.
    1975   *Thinking About Crime.* New York: Basic Books.
    1976   *Varieties of Police Behavior.* New York: Atheneum.
    1978   *The Investigators.* New York: Basic Books.

Wilson, Jerry
    1975   *Police Report: A View of Law Enforcement.* Boston: Little, Brown.

Zawitz, Marianne W., Editor
    1983   *Report to the Nation on Crime and Criminal Justice: The Data.* Washington, D.C.: U.S. Government Printing Office.

AUTHOR INDEX

179

SUBJECT INDEX